of this evolution and challenge the reader to question if this could also be occurring in our own country."

    —MARY ANN STACHOW, Xavier University of Louisiana

Praise for the first edition:

"New Testament scholar Michael Cosby has written a uniquely wonderful book, a combination of an academic biography of the biblical Barnabas, a surgical dissection of the modern legend of the saint, and a sympathetic and personal account of how and why Cypriots have turned their bridge-building apostle into a bridge-burning nationalist. In destroying the myth of the warrior Barnabas, Professor Cosby seeks to restore to all Cypriots something greater: the Barnabas of peace and understanding."

    —CHRISTOPHER SCHABEL, University of Cyprus

"Topics touching on religiously based national beliefs require great care in both research and presentation. Cosby has done his due diligence in searching out the New Testament roots and later historical elaborations of the life and ministry of the early Christian known as Joseph Barnabas. His meticulous examination of data regarding this saint is presented in a very readable fashion, but he also demonstrates great sensitivity to the religious sentiments of modern Orthodox Cypriots."

    —MARY ANN STACHOW, SBS, Xavier University of Louisiana

Creation of History

Second Edition

Creation of History

THE TRANSFORMATION OF BARNABAS
FROM PEACEMAKER TO WARRIOR SAINT

Second Edition

Michael R. Cosby

CASCADE *Books* · Eugene, Oregon

CREATION OF HISTORY
The Transformation of Barnabas from Peacemaker to Warrior Saint.
Second Edition

Cascade Books
An Imprint of Wipf and Stock Publishers
199 W. 8th Ave., Suite 3
Eugene, OR 97401

www.wipfandstock.com

PAPERBACK ISBN: 978-1-7252-6902-6
HARDCOVER ISBN: 978-1-7252-6903-3
EBOOK ISBN: 978-1-7252-6904-0

Cataloguing-in-Publication data:

Names: Cosby, Michael R., author.

Title: Creation of history : the transformation of Barnabas from peacemaker to warrior saint. second edition / by Michael R. Cosby.

Description: Eugene, OR: Cascade Books, 2021 | Includes bibliographical references and indexes.

Identifiers: ISBN 978-1-7252-6902-6 (paperback) | ISBN 978-1-7252-6903-3 (hardcover) | ISBN 978-1-7252-6904-0 (ebook)

Subjects: LCSH: Barnabas, Apostle, Saint. | History—Philosophy. | Historiography. | History, Ancient—Historiography. | Cyprus—Religious life and customs.

Classification: LCC BS2452.B28 C58 2021 (print) | LCC BS2452.B28 (ebook)

To all of our beloved friends in Cyprus,
especially the family of Dafnis Panagides

"Myths are born easily, become established as facts with the passing of time, and die with difficulty. Often this is because they serve a purpose or fit in with the preconceptions of those who believe them."

(CHRISTOPHER SCHABEL, "THE MYTH OF QUEEN ALICE")

Contents

Illustrations

Color versions of all photos in this book may be seen at
www.michaelrcosby.com/barnabas.

Unless otherwise noted, all photographs
and illustrations are by Michael Cosby

Preface

What if you found out that some of your core convictions were based on fabricated stories? How would you respond? This book addresses that sobering scenario in the converging realms of religion, politics, and history on the eastern Mediterranean island of Cyprus. Reality is not always what we believe it to be. Some of our beliefs are based on created history.

Years ago, while writing a textbook on the Apostle Paul, I became fascinated with his mentor, Joseph, called Barnabas. As I searched the literature to see what was written about this early Christian leader, I was shocked at the dearth of published material. But what really caught my attention was realizing that Barnabas, a leader known for his conflict resolution skills in the New Testament, today is viewed as a warrior saint in Cyprus where he was born.

How did such a radical conversion happen? I needed to know. Thus began the journey that finally took me to Cyprus as a Fulbright Fellow in 2011 to track down what was written through the centuries about Barnabas to discover when and why a peacemaker came to represent Greek Cypriot nationalism. I translated hundreds of Greek texts written over many centuries and slowly pinpointed the circumstances that brought about the transformation.

However, I did not spend all my time in a research library. I wanted to hear oral history, to listen to what Cypriots said about Barnabas, whom they revere as their founding apostle. My many conversations with Greek Cypriots helped me understand how beliefs about a first century saint changed through the centuries in ways that fundamentally altered his persona.

As the reasons for the transformation of Barnabas slowly emerged from the dark recesses of the past, contemporary connections began to appear. The developing narrative of how Barnabas evolved to address later historical situations became a cautionary tale that transcends conditions in Cyprus. Greek Orthodox Cypriots today believe in a Barnabas who was created over centuries, but most are completely unaware of the evolution of beliefs about their founding saint. He is a creation of convenience—a peacemaker coopted to become a combatant in the long-standing conflict between Greeks and Turks.

Modern historians are uncovering many such examples of created history—of narratives that developed over time—often to justify certain people's actions and to vilify behaviors of others. The more we dig into the origin of accounts about people and events, the more we realize how often beliefs are based on incidents that never happened but were invented and told enough times that they became accepted as historical reality. Facing the facts of such created histories can be extremely unsettling.

Following the publication of the first edition of this book, I continued to probe into the overarching Barnabas narrative, and I found that I needed to face the fact that I got several things wrong. Although the overall thesis of the first edition remains entirely intact, I needed to correct some material, especially regarding the overstated significance of a text by Florio Bustron written in 1560. I am embarrassed to admit that I allowed myself to be misled regarding Bustron's description of Cypriot archbishops.

In 2017, I returned to Cyprus and conducted more sophisticated, on-site studies of frescos and icons of Barnabas from the twelfth through the seventeenth centuries, which refined my research. In the second edition, I provide additional photos of the frescos and icons that are particularly significant for my study of Barnabas. Also, after reading additional articles by two Cypriot scholars, Paul (Benedict) Englezakis and Michalis Michael, I gained a more nuanced understanding of key events in Cyprus during the sixteenth, seventeenth, and eighteenth centuries.

For the first edition, I decided not to write a technical monograph. I chose instead to use a narrative approach—to take readers on the journey of discovery with me, tracking down clues for how the peace-loving Barnabas of the New Testament became a warrior saint in Cyprus. Consequently, I incorporated my personal interactions with Greek Cypriots with my historical investigation. In the second edition, I maintain this narrative approach but add historical details in specific places in order to buttress my thesis on the origin of the Cyprus archbishop's unique privileges—which connect directly to Barnabas. To provide a book that is not pedantic and boring, I relegated the technical aspects of my research to footnotes.

My decision to use a narrative approach largely results from contemplating modern investigations of brain function. These studies indicate human beings are essentially hard wired to listen to stories. We enjoy reading narratives much more than plodding through technical analyses of data. We also more readily remember details from stories. The history of how Barnabas became a symbol of Cypriot nationalism is fascinating. But to see how this transformation of Barnabas facilitated the violent division of the Republic of Cyprus adds an eerie, contemporary dimension to this study of the interface of religion, politics, and history. I love my friends in Cyprus, and I apologize for revealing that many of their beliefs about Barnabas are creative fictions that over time became historical facts through repetition of the stories. But I encourage all my readers to view the transformation of Barnabas in Cyprus as a caution when contemplating your own core beliefs.

Michael R. Cosby

January 2021

Acknowledgments

I deeply appreciate the funding provided by the Fulbright Scholar Program that made possible my initial research in Cyprus. I want to thank the staff members at the Fulbright Office in Nicosia for their cheerful assistance in orienting us to the country in 2011. Daniel Hadjittofi and Ioli Kythreotou were wonderful. Thanks also to Stelios and Anthoula Savvides, our Fulbright sponsors who served us lavish meals in their lovely home and went out of their way to make us feel welcome. The untimely death of Stelios has been a source of grief to us.

Thanks to Thomas Davis, former director of the Cyprus American Archaeological Research Institute (CAARI), for convincing us to live at the institute, where we met many fascinating scholars. Thanks to Andrew McCarthy, Evi Karyda, and Vathoula Moustakki at CAARI, for being helpful in so many ways during our stay at CAARI in 2011.

Thanks to His Beatitude Chrysostomos II, Archbishop of Nova Justiniana and all Cyprus, who made available the splendid resources of the archbishopric. Thanks also to the archbishopric scholars who gave their time generously to advise me and allowed me to photograph the fresco in the Cathedral of St. John that depicts Barnabas, Anthemios, and Zeno.

Thanks to Christos Koukliotis, Director General of the Archbishop Makarios III Foundation, for taking the time to show us icons of Barnabas in the Byzantine Museum next to the Archbishopric in Nicosia. He generously sent official photos of these icons and granted permission for me to use them in my book on Barnabas. Thanks also to Ourania Perdiki for granting permission to publish her photo of the Barnabas fresco in *Panagia Asinou*. Because of my research on Barnabas, I was also granted special permission to photograph frescos of Barnabas in several of the mountain churches in Cyprus—without using a flash, of course.

The Most Reverend Neophytos, Metropolitan of Morphou, was particularly insightful when discussing traditions about Barnabas. The venerable Archimandrite Gavriel, Abbot of the Holy Monastery of Apostle Barnabas, included us among his spiritual children and shepherded us. One of his closest followers was a wonderful lady who lovingly assisted us. Cyprus lost a national treasure when Father Gavriel died in 2013.

I owe much to Prof. Christopher Schabel, a medievalist at the University of Cyprus and a former member of the Cyprus Fulbright Commission, for his helpfulness and wise counsel. I am also grateful to Cypriot scholars such as Andreas Foulias, Nicholas Coureas, Fr. Savaas, Faidon Papadopoulos, Andreas Kakoullis, George Christodoulou, Christodoulos Hadjichristodoulou, and Michalis Michael. I sought their advice and they kindly responded. Of course, my appreciation for their counsel does not imply that they agree with everything in this book.

Thanks to Dafnis Panagides for the many hours he spent in 2017 sharing his wealth of knowledge about the history and geography of Cyprus. Because of Dafnis, we met many Greek and Turkish Cypriots who recounted their personal experiences with the ongoing conflict between those of Greek and Turkish ancestry. These thoughtful and generous people opened our eyes to the complexities of the longstanding division between ethnic groups on the island. Thanks also to Kyriacos Markides for his books about Orthodox spirituality and for introducing us to Dafnis. To our great sadness, Dafnis died shortly before his ninetieth birthday, just days before we arrived in Cyprus on a covert mission to help celebrate his birthday.

Thanks to Rita Finger and Nancy Heisey for their feedback on my translation of the sixth-century speech, *Laudatio Barnabae apostoli*.

Thanks most of all to my wife, Lynne, for her involvement in many aspects of my research into the Barnabas of history and legend. Her keen editorial advice is invaluable. We have spent many hours dialoguing about Cyprus and Barnabas and now are collaborating on yet another project focusing on Cyprus.

Finally, unless otherwise noted, all my quotations of the Bible come from the New Revised Standard Version, produced by the Division of Christian Education of the National Council of the Churches of Christ in the United States of America, 1989.

Abbreviations

AD	*anno Domini*
AT	author's translation
BC	before Christ
BCE	before the Common Era
c.	*circa,* approximately
CE	Common Era
cf.	*confer,* compare
ed(s).	editor(s), edited by
e.g.	*exempli gratia,* for example
esp.	especially
et al.	*et alii,* and others
etc.	*et cetera,* and the rest
Gk.	Greek
Heb.	Hebrew
i.e.	*id est,* that is
ibid.	*ibidem,* in the same place
MS(S)	manuscript(s)
n.	note
n.d.	no date
n.p.	no place; no publisher; no page
no(s).	number(s)

NS	new series
NT	New Testament
orig.	original
OT	Old Testament
p(p).	page(s)
pap.	Papyrus
repr.	Reprinted
sec.	section
ser.	Series
trans.	translator, translated by
v(v).	verse(s)
vol(s).	volume(s)

Abbreviations of Resources

ABD

The Anchor Bible Dictionary, 6 vols. Ed. David N. Freedman. New York: Doubleday, 1992.

ANF

Ante-Nicene Fathers: The Writings of the Fathers Down to A.D. 325, 10 vols. Eds. Alexander Roberts and James Donaldson. Edinburgh: T. & T. Clark, 1867–73.

BDAG

Greek-English Lexicon of the New Testament and Other Early Christian Literature, 3rd edition. Eds. Walter Bauer, Frederick W. Danker, W. F. Arndt, and F. W. Gingrich. Chicago: University of Chicago Press, 2000.

BHG

Bibliotheca hagiographica graeca, 3rd edition, 3 vols. Ed. François Halkin. Subsidia Hagiographica 8a. Bruxelles: Société des Bollandistes, 1957 (reprinted 1986).

CCCM

Corpus Christianorum: Continuatio mediaevalis. Currently 336 vols. Leuven: Turnhout,1966–

CCSG

Corpus Christianorum: Series graeca. Currently 85 vols. Institute for Early Christian and Byzantine Studies. Leuven: Turnhout, 1977–

CCSL

Corpus Christianorum: Series latina. Currently 206 vols. Leuven: Turnhout, 1953–

CSEL	*Corpus scriptorum ecclesiasticorum latinorum.* Currently 100 vols. Berlin: DeGruyter, 1866–
CSHB	*Corpus scriptorum historiae byzantinae,* 50 vols. Bonn: 1828–1897. https://archive.org/details/corpusscriptoruo1theogoog.
DNP	*Der neue Pauly: Enzyklopadie der Antike.* Eds. Hubert Cancik and Helmuth Schneider. Leiden: Brill, 1969–
DOP	*Dumbarton Oaks Papers.* Washington, DC: Dumbarton Oaks Center for Byzantine Studies, 1941–
IDB	*The Interpreter's Dictionary of the Bible,* 4 vols. Ed. George Arthur Buttrick. Nashville: Abingdon, 1962.
LCL	Loeb Classical Library. Harvard: Harvard University Press, 1913–
LSJ	Henry George Liddell, Robert Scott, and Henry Stuart Jones. *A Greek-English Lexicon,* 9th ed. Oxford: Clarendon, 1996.
NPNF[1]	*Nicene and Post-Nicene Fathers, Series 1.* 14 vols. Ed. Philip Schaff. Edinburgh: T. & T. Clark, 1886–1900.
NPNF[2]	*Nicene and Post-Nicene Fathers, Series 2.* 14 vols. Ed. Philip Schaff. Edinburgh: T. & T. Clark, 1886–1900.
NRSV	New Revised Standard Version of the Bible. National Council of the Churches of Christ, 1989.
OGIS	*Orientis graeci inscriptiones selectae.* Ed. W. Dittenberger. 2 vols. Leipzig, 1903–1905.
PG	*Patrologia graeca* [= *Patrologiae cursus completus: Series graeca*]. 162 vols. Ed. J.-P. Migne. Paris, 1857–1886
PGL	*Patristic Greek Lexicon.* Ed. G. W. H. Lampe. Oxford: Oxford University Press, 1968.
PL	*Patrologia latina* [= *Patrologiae cursus completus: Series latina*]. 217 vols. Ed. J.-P. Migne. Paris, 1844–1864.
TDNT	*Theological Dictionary of the New Testament.* 10 vols. Eds. Gerhard Kittel and Gerhard Friedrich. Trans. Geoffrey W. Bromiley. Grand Rapids: Eerdmans, 1964–1976.
TLG	*Thesaurus Linguae Graecae* (database of Greek texts).

Scripture Abbreviations

Hebrew Bible/Old Testament:

Gen	Genesis	Song	Song of Songs
Exod	Exodus	Isa	Isaiah
Lev	Leviticus	Jer	Jeremiah
Num	Numbers	Lam	Lamentations
Deut	Deuteronomy	Ezek	Ezekiel
Josh	Joshua	Dan	Daniel
Judg	Judges	Hos	Hosea
1–2 Sam	1–2 Samuel	Obad	Obadiah
1–2 Kgs	1–2 Kings	Mic	Micah
1–2 Chr	1–2 Chronicles	Nah	Nahum
Neh	Nehemiah	Hab	Habakkuk
Esth	Esther	Zeph	Zephaniah
Ps (pl. Pss)	Psalm(s)	Hag	Haggai
Prov	Proverbs	Zech	Zechariah
Eccl	Ecclesiastes	Mal	Malachi

New Testament:

Matt	Matthew	1–2 Thess	1–2 Thessalonians
Rom	Romans	1–2 Tim	1–2 Timothy
1–2 Cor	1–2 Corinthians	Phlm	Philemon
Gal	Galatians	Heb	Hebrews
Eph	Ephesians	Jas	James
Phil	Philippians	1–2 Pet	1–2 Peter
Col	Colossians	Rev	Revelation

CHAPTER ONE

Discovering Created History

I did not mean to cause trouble. I really didn't. But digging up the past can uncover upsetting information. What if the past is not as we were taught? What if historical investigation brings to light details that challenge our beliefs about events in our cultural heritage? Such discoveries can be particularly painful when they reveal legendary elements in our national, ethnic, or religious beliefs. I confess I am guilty of contributing to such truth-induced turmoil.

Trouble arose because of my intense curiosity about Joseph, an early church leader from Cyprus whom Jesus' Twelve apostles called Barnabas. The New Testament portrays Barnabas as a peacemaker, as a leader adept at facilitating compromise solutions to ethnic conflict in the early Christian movement. However, Greek Cypriots today revere him as a warrior saint, asking him in prayer to expel the Turks from their island. How did such a radical transformation occur? How, many centuries after his death, did Barnabas the negotiator become a symbol of Greek Cypriot nationalism and a combatant in the intractable conflict between ethnic Greeks and Turks in Cyprus? I simply had to know.

So in 2011, I journeyed to Cyprus as a Senior Fulbright Fellow to conduct research on how, through the centuries, legends about Barnabas changed the image of the apostle. I wanted to learn as much as I could about Barnabas from those who reverence him most. Orthodox Cypriots consider him to be their apostle, the one who ensured the independence of their church.

As I plodded through the historical evidence, the story of Barnabas and the role he came to play in the political divide in Cyprus slowly unfolded like a cold case mystery. Details long buried slowly came to light, connections between events became clear, and finally the entire set of circumstances began to emerge from the shadows. Unfortunately, my research into the development of beliefs about Barnabas exposed serious flaws with what modern Cypriots affirm about him. The implications for their faith and politics are immense.

When, toward the end of my time on the island, I explained the results of my research on Barnabas to members of the Cyprus Fulbright Commission, one member told me, "I am a secular man. I only go to church to attend weddings and funerals. But somehow I always thought I could trust Barnabas. I feel like I have been kicked in the stomach."

The implications of my research, however, extend beyond Cyprus. All of us believe stories that have little or no basis in fact—we are simply unaware of the origins of our beliefs. Facing our collective past can be troubling. What if historical investigation demonstrates that some of our dearest religious or cultural beliefs resulted from a chain of suspicious events we knew nothing about? Do we believe the truth will set us free, or would we rather just leave things buried?

I know from personal experience that this question is not merely rhetorical. Some of what I learned as a child about my cultural and religious heritage turns out to be fabricated—created history. Graduate school proved to be disconcerting as I learned to look for evidence and not just accept as true the stories I heard from authority figures. My worldview was shaken when I began to realize that some of what I thought was history is actually based on legendary events that were accepted as fact after people told and retold these stories.

Modern scholars probing into American history routinely discover new examples of the fabrication of events to bolster particular narratives told to make a group of people look better or worse. I regularly hear interviews where historians recount finding that yet another *historical* event never actually happened. Of course, we need to be cautious and realize that historians are not exempt from inventing their own narratives to bolster whatever ideology they promote. I used to share the following wisdom with my students: "You need to be open minded. But do not be so open minded that your brains fall out." I don't even remember where I first heard this maxim, but I adopted it as my own.

The point is that, when I recount what I discovered about how Orthodox Christians in Cyprus came to believe what they do about Barnabas, I do not stand aloof from the implications. They affect me. They affect you. Reading about the created history of others might pose no personal challenge if we keep a certain distance; but when we connect with their story, life gets more complicated. We might groan and ask, "When does it stop?"

The Difference between History and Legend

When I arrived in the eastern Mediterranean island of Cyprus in August 2011, I knew I had much to learn. I went to solve a puzzling mystery, and I did not know what I would find. My wife and I set out on an adventure that would involve not just examining ancient documents but also inter-acting with modern Cypriots to learn about their beliefs—and how their viewpoints are connected with the history of the island.

Every culture has its heroes, and sorting fact from fiction is a delicate task. Many people in the United States know more about the legendary George Washington than they do about the historical George Wash-ington. Unfortunately, beliefs based on legends sometimes exert more influence on society than beliefs based on careful analysis of primary sources. Scholars studying George Washington analyze documents from Washington's time, sort through the discrepancies they discover, and seek to reconstruct what probably happened. They also try to pinpoint when legends about Washington appeared and worked their way into America's national heritage.

Research in this area abounds and is readily available in books and on the web.[1] The story of Washington chopping down the cherry tree is a long-lasting legend created as a means of glorifying Washington and making him an example of virtuous living. Mason L. Weems, who published *The Life of Washington* in 1800, invented the story, and it first appeared in 1806 in the fifth edition of his biography of Washington. William H. McGuffey adopted the story and further embellished it in 1836 for his series of children's books, called McGuffey Readers—which "remained in print for nearly a hundred years and sold over 120 mil-lion copies."[2] Because of Weems and McGuffey, the cherry tree legend became part of America's cultural heritage, accepted as true by millions until pesky historians tracked down the origins of the story.

1. See, for example, Lengel, *Inventing George Washington*.

2. Jay Richardson, "Cherry Tree Myth" on the Mt. Vernon website: http://www.mount vernon.org/research-collections/digital-encyclopedia/article/cherry-tree-myth/.

Writing history involves a complicated dance, with the past and the present as awkward partners. We all perceive the past through the lens of our own experience, so there is no such thing as a completely objective history. However, we can clean much of the grime off our cultural-heritage lens if we approach analysis openly and honestly. And sometimes outsiders notice details insiders miss, simply because outsiders do not share all of the same cultural assumptions.

Crossing Cultural Divides

My wife, Lynne, and I tried not to filter what we heard from people in Cyprus through our Western cultural lenses, but we were not completely successful. Neophytos, the Metropolitan of Morphou, told me that, until I quit thinking like a Westerner, I would never understand Eastern Orthodox beliefs.[3]

In part, I had to learn that, when conducting research on Barnabas, I was not just studying a figure from the past. For Cypriots, St. Barnabas is a living and active presence on the island today. I also learned that the more mystically oriented Orthodox leaders cared little about what I sought to find. The influential Metropolitan of Limassol, after listening patiently as I explained my research project, wished me well but added that the results of my study were of little concern to him. He said he was not much interested in history but in the mystical experience of faith—the divine transformation that comes through spiritual disciplines. I asked him if he thought my research was a waste of time. "No," he replied, "but whatever you discover will not affect my faith in the least."

In my October 9 journal entry, I wrote, "Living in Cyprus is for me a bit like standing with one foot in 2011 and the other in the earlier centuries of the church . . . I regularly hear stories from my new Orthodox friends about miraculous events. Today, after church, I heard about a saintly Cypriot woman who, when she was fourteen, was taken by the Virgin Mary to a sacred mountain—as in picked up and physically flown there. I also heard stories about Jesus appearing to people while they sat at table—after they prayed that Jesus would be their guest at table." My perspectives, so dominated by Western, rational thought, constantly kept me in the position of a respectful but skeptical outsider.

3. For those unfamiliar with the hierarchy of bishops in Cyprus, the archbishop occupies the highest rank, the metropolitans rank second, and then the bishops.

An important aspect of Orthodox faith is veneration of the remains of saints. In that same, October 9 journal entry, I wrote, "At the tombs of saints, people report smelling sweet aromas that signal the presence of the saint. Some smell it; some don't. The saint decides which people receive the ability to smell the fragrance. Yesterday, my friend Marios told me that people must not judge the strength of their faith by whether or not Barnabas allows them to smell the fragrance. Barnabas decides who receives the sensation."

I do not pretend to understand all that happens in the world, but I have difficulty believing such stories. I have not experienced anything resembling the accounts I heard about holy men and women physically seeing Jesus or talking all night with a long-dead saint in a hermitage, or teleporting their bodies to appear to someone in another country. But as I listened to my gracious hosts describe such events, I noticed no hesitance or insincerity in their voices. Listening to these descriptions was part of my education as a scholar conducting research in a culture where people's assumptions are foreign to me.

Early in our time in Cyprus, we met a young priest who hails from Texas, is a convert to Orthodoxy, spent six months on Mt. Athos, and married a Cypriot woman. He conducted the only English-based liturgy on the island—which we attended with some frequency. He took us to the nearby *Agios Iraklidios* Monastery (Monastery of St. Iraklidios), where Orthodox nuns live and work together.

Having a priest as our guide opened doors. A delightfully hospitable nun led us into their chapel. She also unlocked the door at the entrance of a cave purported to have contained the remains of Iraklidios—a saint with a reputation for healing peoples' backs. As a matter of fact, one of the parishioners at the Church of St. Nicholas told Lynne and me about how he lay down in front of the tomb of St. Iraklidios and had an out-of-body experience. He explained that, afterward, his back was healed—which got our attention, because I had recently suffered a back injury.

During a kayaking accident in November 2010, I severely herniated a disc in my lower back. So, as the nun was leading us out of the tomb of St. Iraklidios, Lynne whispered to me, "What can it hurt? Go lie down on the rug in front of the tomb and pray for healing." I admit I felt awkward, but my injury plagued me. I lay down on the rug, confessed my situation and tried to quiet my thoughts and be open to supernatural intervention. Nothing happened.

My injured back provided motivation to pray to a saint, something I had never before considered. Pain is a strong motivator. In my defense, however, I honestly tried to grasp Orthodox beliefs regarding veneration of saints. My questions about St. Barnabas often confused those I asked, because their understanding of Christian faith and experience differs fundamentally from mine. Different Orthodox churches are dedicated to different saints, but because members of a congregation feel a special affinity to one saint does not mean they do not venerate others. For example, St. Andrew is known for helping women safely deliver their babies. Consequently, many women pray to this saint while pregnant—and many name their sons Andreas (Andrew) to honor St. Andrew. Of course, we wanted to know why we were not meeting men named Barnabas.

Lynne and I are curious individuals. We listened eagerly, and Cypriots responded warmly, accepting us and telling us their stories. Being genuinely interested in others brings many rewards. The first person we met in Cyprus, the driver who took us from the airport to Nicosia where we were to live, told us about leaving Cyprus as a boy to live in Great Britain and then returning to Cyprus years later to raise his children. He talked non-stop about his family, about politics in Cyprus and about his cultural heritage. All we did was listen and ask questions. It was the first of many such conversations.

To maintain the privacy of individuals in this book, I have not used their actual names, except in the case of Father Gabriel, who is now deceased, and some well-known people on the island.

In addition to these impromptu chats, we arranged formal interviews of monks and priests in order to ask about oral traditions regarding Barnabas. Our goal was to learn from people in all walks of life—to listen to their stories and try to grasp the larger, historical and social context of my investigation. Our experiences exceeded our expectations. At times our encounters with people amazed us.

Barnabas: Founder and Protector of the Church of Cyprus

During the first weeks in Cyprus, I labored in the library, translating ancient Greek texts and making progress on this aspect of my research. But other aspects of our research lagged, because we were not yet part of the social network. We were making little headway in arranging for a visit to the Monastery of Apostle Barnabas in the Turkish-occupied northern part of Cyprus. When the day finally arrived for us to go to the monastery, we had been on the island two months. Chrystalla, a devoted follower of a prominent monk named Father Gabriel, picked us up at 3:30 pm, drove us across the island, through the Turkish checkpoint into occupied territory, and to the monastery that held a growing fascination for us. She escorted us around the site, and we took photos of the monastery in silhouette as the sun sank low in the sky. On the trip back into the city, Chrystalla gazed at me and said, "Father Gabriel believes the Apostle Barnabas called you here from America." The pronouncement totally took me off guard. I am seldom so shocked that I am completely speechless, but on this occasion I sat in stunned silence.

Chrystalla continued with total sincerity. "Barnabas brought you to Cyprus to learn about him. He will equip you to complete your work. Then he will send you back home to teach Christians in the West to venerate him properly."

Barnabas, missionary coworker with the apostle Paul, died nearly 2,000 years ago. The idea that Barnabas journeyed to America to recruit me was a foreign concept. From my perspective, I had come to Cyprus to conduct research on an important, early Christian leader. I made no supernatural connection with my historical investigation, and my belief system did not include venerating saints and praying to them as intermediaries.

"Sorry," I finally replied, "but I simply do not have the skills necessary to accomplish all you expect." With complete conviction she responded, "Barnabas would not have brought you here unless he knew you could complete this task."

Just then Chrystalla's cell phone rang, and she spoke briefly in Greek with the caller. When finished, she turned to me and announced, "That was Father Anastasios. He said Father Gabriel wishes you to join them for dinner tonight. They await our arrival. They want to hear all about our trip."

While gliding through rural Cyprus in her comfortable Mercedes, I chafed at my newly discovered identity as ambassador of a first-century saint. In less than one hour, we would arrive at *Metochi tou Kykkou*, a monastery in Nicosia. In this monastic complex lived the Very Reverend Archimandrite Gabriel, the Abbot of the Holy Monastery of Apostle Barnabas. What would I say while having dinner with one of the most famous monks on the island?

I glanced over my shoulder at my wife in the back seat of the car. She smiled. We had expected adventures during our four months in Cyprus, but how does one prepare for situations like this one? "Barnabas called me here from America?" I thought. "What have I gotten myself into? How do I respond to such expectations?"

Our trip to the monastery and dinner with the abbot culminated an uncanny series of events. A few weeks earlier, in September, a scholar at the Archbishopric had told me over the phone about Father Gabriel: "He knows more about Barnabas than anyone else on the island. He is a national treasure. You must see him." I wondered how I could possibly arrange such an audience. I soon learned. And it all began when the battery in my wife's MacBook died.

As fortune (or was it Providence?) would have it, only a few blocks from the archaeological center where we lived was a store that sold and repaired Macintosh computers. As we waited in the lobby for the technician to replace the battery, we conversed with the owner, who asked why we were in Cyprus. I explained I had come on a Fulbright grant to conduct research on the island's patron saint, Barnabas. The man beamed. "You must meet my friend at the Chevy dealership two blocks down the street. He is a spiritual child of Father Gabriel, the abbot of the Monastery of Apostle Barnabas. My friend can get for you a copy of a book on Barnabas written by Cypriot scholars. It is in Greek, of course, but you can translate it." He wrote the man's name and phone number on a business card.

A few days later, we met the owner of the Chevy dealership, a busy man who took a few minutes to talk about the island's beloved Barnabas. Then he handed me a 2009 publication on Barnabas: *Η ΙΕΡΑ ΒΑΣΙΛΙΚΗ ΚΑΙ ΣΤΟΥΡΟΠΗΓΙΑΚΗ ΜΟΝΗ ΑΠΟΣΤΟΛΟΥ ΒΑΡΝΑΒΑ: Ο ΒΙΟΣ ΤΟΥ ΑΠΟΣΤΟΛΟΥ ΒΑΡΝΑΒΑ—ΟΙ ΠΗΤΕΣ Η ΙΣΤΟΡΙΑ— ΤΗΣ ΜΟΝΗΣ—Η ΑΡΧΙΤΕΚΤΟΝΙΚΗ.* For decades, I had taught Koine Greek, the language of the New Testament, but modern Greek differs substantially from ancient Greek. I inwardly cringed as I thumbed through this collection of essays, and I thought, "How will I find the time to translate all these pages?"

Meeting a National Treasure

A month after purchasing the book on Barnabas, Lynne and I attended a concert of traditional, eastern Mediterranean music in Peristerona, a village west of Nicosia. We had met one of the musicians on a daytrip to the Troodos Mountains, when we stopped in Peristerona to see the Church of Saints Barnabas and Hilarion (to our chagrin, we discovered this saint was a different Barnabas). The musician had been very helpful in getting us into the locked church and had invited us to the concert. At the open-air venue, we were obviously outsiders; and a friendly man came up and asked if we were from the American Embassy. When he learned the nature of my research, he said that during the intermission he would introduce me to Neophytos, Metropolitan of the Morphou region, who was attending the concert. The man also told me that he would have a lawyer friend named Andreas call me. Andreas was a spiritual child of Father Gabriel, and he could arrange to introduce me to the Father. In Cyprus, personal connections make things happen.

We had a great time at the concert, and we did indeed meet Neophytos. People were welcoming; and during the intermission, one very jolly man insisted that I drink some *Zivania*. It was my first experience with the clear, potent, Cypriot alcoholic drink. And the young lawyer, Andreas, did call us and give us directions on where and when to meet Father Gabriel. "No need to come early," he explained. "Just come right before the liturgy is over."

So it happened that, on a Sunday morning in late October, we drove to the monastery in Nicosia called *Metochi tou Kykkou* and waited in the courtyard. When liturgy concluded, Orthodox Christians streamed from the church building and began engaging each other in cordial conversations. My wife and I were obviously outsiders, seated on a bench at the edge of the activities. A young man, who turned out to be Andreas, approached and said, "You must be Dr. Cosby."

"Yes," I replied, and introduced him to Lynne. I felt hot in my sport coat—and apprehensive.

"Father Gabriel is still in the sanctuary," he explained. "He will soon go to his apartment. Please wait outside his door." He pointed to our left and said, "There, where the people are standing. I will tell you when he is ready to receive you."

Watching the man walk away, I wondered how one should behave in the presence of a national treasure. Time moved slowly as Lynne and

I stood near the designated door, trying not to look too uncomfortable. Soon the lawyer ushered us into the sitting room of the monk's modest apartment, which swarmed with activity.

After we were introduced, Father Gabriel indicated I was to sit in a chair placed beside him on his right—which I took to be a place of honor. The room resonated with animated chatter. Of course, people were speaking Greek, so I only understood snatches of sentences. Lynne was seated on a sofa nearby, surrounded by women; and she had an advantage: these ladies were speaking to her in English. An elderly woman who had spent much of her adult life in Canada soon sat by Lynne and began telling her life story. Little did we know at this time that she and her husband would become some of our best friends in Cyprus.

Father Gabriel surveyed the happy interaction of his followers. Everything revolved around this frail, nearly ninety-year-old patriarch. Because of where I was seated, people had to lean over me to kiss his hand and receive his blessing. I felt conspicuous and out of place. People were friendly, but they kept looking at me quizzically. Finally, activities began to subside, and the room became progressively less populated.

"You may sit by your wife now," said the lawyer. So I joined Lynne on the couch, where we listened to the waning conversation. A woman across the room scrutinized us and asked, "Why are you here?" The room grew quiet. I gave her the brief version. She nodded approvingly. The low buzz of conversation resumed.

Father Gabriel gestured for one of his followers, Chrystalla, to translate for us, and the old monk studied my face with penetrating but kind eyes. I explained that, as a New Testament scholar, I had great respect for Barnabas and I had come from the United States to learn all I could about this important leader of the early church. Father Gabriel glowed with pleasure and pointed to the icon of Barnabas on the wall behind him—an icon he personally had painted.[4] When he discovered I had not yet been to the Monastery of Apostle Barnabas, he told Chrystalla, one of his closest disciples, to take me. With no hesitation she nodded "Yes." One does not question Father Gabriel.

---

4. In the West, some insist that artists "write" icons. The confusion evidently arose due to misunderstandings of the Greek *eiconographia*. For brief explanations, see sites such as https://orthodoxhistory.org/2010/06/08/icons-are-not-written/ or https://russianicons.wordpress.com/2011/08/31/is-an-icon-painted-or-written/.

FIGURE 1

Icon of Barnabas painted by Father Gabriel.
Color versions of all photos in this book may be seen at
www.michaelrcosby.com/barnabas.

At the end of our meeting, Father Gabriel got out a copy of *Apostle Varnavas: the Founder and Protector of the Church of Cyprus,* by Marios T. Stylianou. Modern Greeks pronounce *beta* (β) with a "v" sound, so they say Varnávas instead of Barnabas (accenting the second syllable) and Gavriel instead of Gabriel. So, when I quote snatches of conversations with Cypriots in this book, I am taking a bit of liberty and modifying the way they actually pronounce certain words in order to avoid confusion for readers in the West. Also, because I did not record most of these conversations, I have used what I wrote soon afterward in my journal as the basis of my quotations of what people said. Memory is not infallible, so I do not claim tape-recorder accuracy; but I provide a close approximation of the actual words spoken. I have not intentionally misrepresented anyone.

Marios Stylianou dedicated *Apostle Varnavas: the Founder and Protector of the Church of Cyprus* to "my spiritual father, Reverend father Gavriel Siokouros." The venerable Father Gabriel now took the copy of this book he was giving to me and wrote in Greek on the title page "With love and warm wishes" and signed his name. As I received the gift and read the title, I thought, "Founder and Protector. Interesting! I wonder what they mean by *Protector*?" I soon learned.

Into Turkish Occupied Northern Cyprus

Three days after we met Father Gabriel at his monastery apartment in Nicosia, Chrystalla picked us up after she got off work and drove us into Turkish-occupied northern Cyprus to visit the tomb of St. Barnabas. We were well aware of the hostilities between the Greek Cypriots in the South and Turk Cypriots in the North. So were not surprised when Chrystalla took the longer, southern route to the tomb, so she could drive the fewest kilometers possible through the Turkish controlled north. She became visibly agitated when she stopped at the checkpoint and showed our passports to the serious looking Turkish guards. Her animosity lessened as we drove through the countryside and approached our destination. But she remained tense and alert.

Chrystalla explained that Greek Orthodox Christians cannot celebrate sacred liturgy in the Monastery of Apostle Barnabas, a situation that weighs heavily on them. Decades ago Turkish thieves stole most of the icons originally adorning this monastery church and sold them on the black market. Turkish authorities later converted the church into a museum and tourist destination, and they brought icons from other plundered Orthodox churches and crudely attached these works of art to the walls of the monastery church.

Father Gabriel worked for years to get approval to take his followers to the burial site of his beloved Barnabas. Turkish officials finally granted permission for him to come once a month to celebrate the liturgy, but only at the tiny chapel built over the tomb of the saint. The monastery church remains off limits for them to gather as a place for worship. Understandably, Father Gabriel and his followers deeply resent being denied the right to assemble in what they consider their church and spiritual home. They hate the fact that their cherished church is merely a museum, and they despise the way Turkish tourists walk around the sanctuary showing disdain instead of reverence. But they are politically powerless to change the situation.

When we arrived at the monastery grounds, Chrystalla first took us to the underground tomb of St. Barnabas, over which stands a small chapel. Descending the stone steps to the cave below, we stood reverently at the tomb of the saint. Then we heard the voices. Looking up the steps, I saw five Muslim men descending toward us. I sensed a disastrous confrontation looming—but more about that later.

FIGURE 2

Traditional tomb of Apostle Barnabas.

The Muslim men turned out to be Sufis, members of a mystical sect of Islam; and we indeed had a very memorable encounter with them. Afterward, Chrystalla led us the short walk from the chapel to the monastery complex. Because we were there in the late afternoon, the monastery grounds were largely deserted. The scene seemed peaceful, and a friendly dog escorted us as we walked around the outside of the monastery. But we felt the tension in Chrystalla. At the main entry gate, she spoke to the Turkish guards, asking them to let us go inside the monastery complex.

They told her we would have to pay the admission fee. I was willing to do so, but she refused. "Children do not pay to enter their own home! Father Gabriel forbids it." That ended the matter. We did not go into the monastery.

FIGURE 3

Monastery Church of the Apostle Barnabas.

We returned to the car and started the drive back toward the border crossing. Only after Chrystalla had reentered the Republic of Cyprus did she relax. She soon parked on the roadside and called Father Anastasios to report that we were out of the Turkish-occupied North and our mission had been a success. She clicked off her phone and then made the pronouncement that Barnabas had specifically chosen me to come to Cyprus. A few minutes later, her phone rang, and after a short exchange, she told us that we would join Father Gabriel for a late supper. On the return drive to Nicosia, I wondered what a meal with Father Gabriel would involve. What would be served at the table of this famous monk? *I did not expect the pigeon.*

Pigeon Meat, Miracles, and Research Woes

Seven of us sat around the table in his modest kitchen. Burly Father Anastasios, Father Gabriel's understudy, skillfully and artistically spread the table with traditional Cypriot foods. As I watched the refined way he handled the food, I wondered if he had once been a chef.

As we passed the food around the table, I stared suspiciously at the plate with pigeon. The scrawny pieces of gray, scalded-looking meat did not inspire confidence in me. I gazed hesitantly at the dark meat on the platter, selected a small piece and put it on my plate—just to be polite. Father Gabriel objected. He spoke no English, but with gestures he communicated that my choice was inadequate. Jovially, he fingered through the pigeon pieces on the platter, selected a larger one and put it on my plate. I smiled and said Ευχαριστώ ("Thank you"). To my surprise, the taste was pleasant.

The meal was delicious and the conversation lively. Father Gabriel turned out to be a witty man with an endearing personality. He mostly smiled and listened, enjoying the banter of his followers. Lynne and I felt welcome and accepted. I told Chrystalla how much we appreciated their hospitality—they made us feel like family. She translated my comment for Father Gabriel. He smiled and responded to our gratitude. Chrystalla said to us, "Father says he considers you to be among his spiritual children. You *are* part of our family."

After a while, he wanted to hear all about our trip to the monastery. He was especially interested in Chrystalla's account of our remarkable conversation with Sufi Muslims at the tomb of Barnabas. Once satisfied with her report, he asked me what I wanted to know from him.

Of course, I had many questions in my mind about how Orthodox Christians view saints, but I decided to focus my questions on Barnabas's sphere of influence. He explained that Barnabas is active on the island today, healing people at his tomb and working to restore the island to Greek Cypriots—the rightful owners. I asked if saints are territorial, operating primarily in the area around where they are buried. "Yes," he said, and then he explained more about how saints work for the good of their people. He recounted a miracle story as an example, telling about the healing of a paraplegic named Marios Stylianou.

FIGURE 4

Father Gabriel (left) after a special liturgy
at the Monastery of Apostle Barnabas. Photo by Lynne Cosby.

Father Gabriel explained that Barnabas had appeared to Marios
in a vision and told him to write a book to honor the saint. Barnabas
promised Marios that after he finished the book he would be healed. So,
when the book was published, Father Gabriel took Marios to the tomb of
Barnabas. Some men carried him in his wheelchair down the stone steps
to the casket in the small cave. Following the prayers of Father Gabriel,
Marios stood up and walked.[5]

To be honest, such stories create cognitive dissonance for me. The
belief that saints heal people still seems strange. As a biblical scholar, I
am accustomed to studying the New Testament to learn what leaders like

5. For a brief description of this event, see the end of the following site: http://www.
johnsanidopoulos.com/2009/06/apostle-barnabas-and-church-of-cyprus.html.

Barnabas accomplished while alive on earth. I am not used to concentrating on what saints have done following their physical deaths. Soon, however, I began to understand the importance of such beliefs for my research on Barnabas.

Greek Cypriots do not focus on what the New Testament says about Barnabas. They focus on what they claim the saint has done since his death—especially events that happened in the late fifth century when Barnabas miraculously preserved the independence of the Church of Cyprus. Tracking down historical clues to those events and assessing their historicity occupied my attention for many months. No one had previously traced the development of traditions about Barnabas from the first century until today, so I had a massive amount of work to do, searching through ancient Greek documents.

Curiosity inspired me, and I happily launched into the project. I did not know what I would discover, nor did I anticipate the controversy I might create—or the turmoil I would experience.[6] Translating ancient texts about Barnabas is one thing; analyzing them in light of warm relationships with people whose lives I might upset by my research is another matter entirely. I was not prepared for the emotional aspects of my research—or of my desire not to distress anyone. However, my commitment to intellectual integrity would not let me fudge on my discoveries. I had to report what I found, regardless of the personal cost.

6. My wife and I found the Greek Cypriots to be wonderfully friendly and hospitable. When they discovered I was conducting research on Barnabas, they were genuinely pleased and went out of their way to put me in contact with monks and priests who told me about their beloved founder. His Beatitude Chrysostomos II, Archbishop of Nova Justiniana and all Cyprus, pronounced his blessing on my work and made available the splendid resources of the Archbishopric. I deeply appreciate the generosity of the people at the Archbishopric. Outside the Archbishopric, the Most Reverend Neophytos, Metropolitan of Morphou, was particularly helpful in discussing traditions about Barnabas. The venerable Archimandrite Gavriel (Gabriel) treated us like family and blessed us not only with an icon of Barnabas but also included us among his spiritual children on a trip to the tomb of Barnabas for a special liturgy. His followers were quite accommodating, especially one wonderful lady who lovingly shepherded us. We developed great affection for the Orthodox disciples of Barnabas.

I also owe much to scholars on the island who helped me to refine my research: Christopher Schabel, Nicholas Coureas, Fr. Savaas, Faidon Papadopoulos, George Christodoulou, Christodoulos Hadjichristodoulou, et al. The list is long, including the staff at the Cyprus American Archaeological Research Institute (CAARI) where we lived (Andrew McCarthy, Evi Karyda, and Vathoula Moustakki) and the scholars from various countries whom we met at CAARI (including Michael Metcalf, Gregory Horsley, and numerous others). Mine was truly a collaborative project.

In my September 25 journal entry, I wrote the following:

> My historical and cultural research is blended with the personal stories I hear from Cypriots. How will I sort out all of the stories I hear and do justice to the Cypriots, who are going out of their way to help me? I do not know.
>
> Father Gabriel told me he is mostly concerned with personal faith (esoteric, spiritual experience), not scholarship. How do I maintain my integrity as a scholar, dealing with the many nuances of history and the sometimes awkward disconnects between what people tell me and what I read in ancient texts? I must be honest in my analysis of data. I must not offend my new friends who so unselfishly give of themselves to help my research. I honestly seek to bring honor to Barnabas, because I believe his leadership example provides a much-needed approach to problem solving. [I will try] to assemble the data in a way that honors both the sincere, Orthodox faith of my friends, as well as my own rigorous analysis of historical events.

Becoming beloved outsiders who were graciously included into the spiritual family of Father Gabriel brought expectations that my research would, of course, validate their beliefs. The model of a detached historian did not apply in my situation. I began to feel uneasy with my role, because of the deep affection I felt toward my new friends. What if I discovered things that would undermine their faith? What if they felt like I betrayed them? I plunged forward, not knowing what I would find.

Theosis, not History

My first experience interviewing a monk occurred prior to our initial meeting with Father Gabriel, and this conversation proved to be quite enlightening. In the hills north of Limassol, in the small village of Monagri, stands the Monastery of Archangel Michael (Μοναστήρι Αρχαγγέλου Μιχαήλ), where Father Gennadios (pronounced Yen-ná-the-ōs), a monk sent from Mt. Athos, was directing the work of rebuilding this ancient monastery. Mt. Athos, the secluded center of Orthodox mysticism, provides an important setting for the pursuit of *theosis* through asceticism and meditation. Orthodox Christians use the term *theosis* to describe the transformation that causes a person to become more like God (*Theos*). They believe true theology comes from mystical union with God, not from rational thought.

Father Gennadios is popular with youth, especially football (soccer) players. He has a lively sense of humor and multitasked during the entire time I spoke with him. Following liturgy, Father Gennadios entertained a few of my questions, excused himself to go counsel someone, returned to continue the interview, stopped to receive the local mayor who simply walked into the monk's office and began speaking to him, etc. While our host was away, Lynne and I continued the dialog with Dafnis, another national treasure who functioned as our translator. During this protracted interview time, I began to realize that the nature of my research was changing as I learned more about Eastern Orthodoxy.

When Father Gennadios returned, he explained that when St. Thomas Aquinas (1225–1274), the famous Catholic theologian, attempted to explain Christian beliefs in philosophical terms, the Catholic Church took a drastic turn in the wrong direction. "It is blasphemous," he said, "to think you can figure out God with your mind." He called the Western Christian approach of using human reason to formulate theology "seriously misguided." He asserted that one does not *understand* God; one *experiences* God through following the directions of saintly people whose experience of God is deep.

Although many monks are well educated in various disciplines, they do not believe education is the way to enlightenment. Formal education is not important for a village priest, for example; but a pious life is essential for anyone who gives spiritual guidance to others. Father Gennadios added that the Bible is just another book if it does not deeply affect the way a person lives. *Theosis*, not mere intellectual study, should be the goal of life.

Because of their reverence for elders and guides, the idea of analyzing the historicity of traditions about the saints, including Barnabas, seems odd to them. My quest to uncover the historical developments of beliefs about Barnabas diverged sharply from their acceptance of traditions regarding saints.

However, I did not challenge faith in these stories. I was in Cyprus to learn, and as a student I absorbed all I could. But I sensed a collision course, and the matter weighed heavily on me. Scholars do not work in a vacuum. We are not hermetically sealed packages. We have our biases. In my case, I felt sincere respect for my Orthodox mentors even as I dug up the past in an attempt to trace the origins and evolution of their beliefs about Barnabas.

Scholarly Neglect of Barnabas

Years before going to Cyprus, I became fascinated with Barnabas while writing a book on the apostle Paul.[7] Increasingly, I realized Barnabas was a towering figure in the early Christian movement,[8] an effective leader adept at mediating difficult situations of ethnic strife. But when I began collecting books and articles on the man, I found very few. Honestly, I was shocked to discover the slight attention given to Barnabas in the history of the church.

Barnabas was Paul's mentor—an innovative leader who recruited Paul to be his coworker. Together, they forged a theology of salvation by faith in Christ alone, without keeping the laws of Moses. Paul gets the credit for this effort, because of his letters and his major role in the Acts of the Apostles; but Barnabas deserves much more acclaim than he gets from scholars for his seminal input into what came to be known as Pauline theology. "If anyone influenced Paul theologically, then Barnabas must have done so more than any other person."[9] Yet scholars largely ignore him.

Bernd Kollmann, who wrote one of the few existing books about Barnabas, laments "the remarkable lack of interest scholars have shown in Barnabas."[10] Compared with the thousands of books about the apostle Paul, the number written about Barnabas is miniscule.[11] Only *one* detailed analysis of New Testament passages pertaining to Barnabas exists— written in German by Markus Öhler.[12] And no one had explored how

7. Cosby, *Apostle on the Edge*.

8. Conzelmann, *History of Primitive Christianity*, 158, calls Barnabas "one of the most important personalities of the primitive church." Weiser, *Die Apostelgeschichte*, 1:138, describes Barnabas as one of the main figures of the early Christian movement.

9. Hengel and Schwemer, *Paul Between Damascus and Antioch*, 205.

10. Kollmann, *Joseph Barnabas: His Life and Legacy*, 2.

11. In 1876, Braunsberger published *Der Apostel Barnabas*. Representing a bygone era, the author assumes an almost completely uncritical approach to church traditions. In 1998, 122 years later, Kollmann published *Joseph Barnabas*, a helpful but brief book. The sixty-eight page English translation followed in 2003: *Joseph Barnabas: His Life and Legacy*. For additional material on Barnabas, see Radl, "Das 'Apostelkonzil' und seine Nachgeschichte, dargestellt am Weg des Barnabas," 45–61; and Hengel and Schwemer, *Paul Between Damascus and Antioch*, 205–24.

12. In 2003, Öhler published his *Habilitationsschrift*, entitled *Barnabas: Die historische Person und ihre Rezeption in der Apostelgeschichte*. This 566-page tome investigates the literary and historical context of all relevant NT material about Barnabas. Öhler's book is the standard work on Barnabas in the NT. In fact, it is the only exhaustive study of Barnabas in existence.

traditions about Barnabas developed over the centuries. Such neglect is tragic. In our era of polarized politics, ethnic division, and religious wars, we need more models of bridge builders—leaders like Barnabas—who bravely pursue peaceful solutions to conflicts.

Christians in the West often associate Barnabas primarily with his generous contribution of money to care for the poor in Jerusalem (Acts 4:36–37). They seldom realize that his act of benevolence pales in significance to his leadership accomplishments. Barnabas encouraged people and saw potential when others did not. For example, he courageously brought Saul (Paul) of Tarsus to the Jerusalem apostles, believing Saul's conversion was genuine when the other Christians thought it was a ploy to trap them (Acts 9:26–27). "He took a chance, gambled on Paul's integrity, believed the best and sponsored him when everybody else suspected the worst. Barnabas built a bridge when everyone else erected barriers."[13]

According to Acts, even during the early days of the church, cultural divisions among the followers of Jesus necessitated resolution. Acts 6:1 says, "the Hellenists complained against the Hebrews because their widows were being neglected in the daily distribution of food."[14] Palestinian Jewish Christians evidently distanced themselves somewhat from Hellenistic Jewish Christians (who primarily spoke Greek and often came from regions outside of Palestine), and the unequal treatment of widows created tension. This controversy, however, existed among Jewish Christians, who mostly assumed Jesus came only to save Jews. Gentiles were excluded. Comprehending the universal implications of the gospel message took years.

Not surprisingly, Hellenistic Jewish followers of Jesus were the first to diverge from the norm of preaching only to Jews. A few began preaching the gospel also to gentiles in Antioch—with much success (Acts 11:19–21). The Jerusalem apostles so trusted Barnabas that they sent him to investigate this situation at Antioch and to provide leadership for the ethnically diverse, new congregation. Meanwhile, Paul dwelt in his native Tarsus, lost from view to the emerging church for perhaps as much as a decade. Barnabas journeyed to Tarsus and recruited him to come to Antioch and help minister to the multi-ethnic congregation. He mentored Paul, who blossomed and became one of the most significant

13. Evans, "Barnabas the Bridge-Builder," 249.

14. Unless otherwise noted, all biblical quotations come from the New Revised Standard Version of the Bible (National Council of the Churches of Christ, 1989).

figures in the history of Christianity. Were it not for Barnabas, church history might have been quite different.

When Barnabas and Paul left Antioch on their first missionary journey, Barnabas was still the main leader. They went first to Cyprus, the homeland of Barnabas. After traversing the island from east to west, they traveled north into what today is south central Turkey. According to Acts, however, their success preaching to gentiles provoked protest from Jewish Christians in Judea and resulted in a major debate regarding gentiles and Jesus (Acts 15:1–6). Consequently, Barnabas and Paul traveled to Jerusalem to argue their position. Together, they helped to build a bridge between Jewish Christians and gentile Christians. But the initiative probably came mostly from Barnabas.

Building Bridges Versus Burning Bridges

Paul was a firebrand who at times was more prone to burn bridges than to build them. He frequently found himself in conflict with Jewish Christians who insisted gentile converts must keep the laws of Moses. Paul would not back down. He even publically confronted the apostle Peter when this major church leader came from Jerusalem to Antioch. Paul took offense at the way Peter was handling a complex situation involving table fellowship with gentile Christians. He would not even listen to Barnabas, who sided with Peter in the disagreement. In Paul's mind they were hypocrites, pure and simple (Gal 2:11–14). His inflexibility contributed to a major rift with Barnabas.

On their first missionary journey (c. 47–48 CE), they took with them the young John Mark, a cousin of Barnabas. Unfortunately, Mark abandoned Paul and Barnabas midway through the journey and returned home to his mother in Jerusalem (Acts 13:13). Paul was annoyed and not inclined to give Mark a second chance. Barnabas, however, insisted they bring Mark with them on the second journey (c. 49 CE). The ensuing argument between apostles became so intense that Paul and Barnabas parted company (Acts 15:36–41). Over time, however, Paul cooled off and was reconciled with Mark. He also sought better relations with Jerusalem.

About six years after his split with Barnabas (c. 55 CE), Paul collected money from gentile Christians and took it to struggling Christians in Jerusalem (1 Cor 16:1–4; 2 Cor 8–9; Rom 15:25–27). He even asked the Christians in Rome to pray that the Jerusalem Christians would take the money (Rom 15:30–31). By the time Paul wrote his epistle to Philemon (c. 60–62 CE), he mentioned Mark in the letter as one of his fellow workers (Phlm 24). Most likely, the mediating influence of Barnabas had an effect on Paul.

Barnabas, the benevolent bridge-builder, labored at developing compromise solutions that brought people together—although the incident with Paul regarding Mark shows the Cypriot apostle could be pretty persistent also. We owe this man a huge debt, but we rarely recognize his importance. Ironically, many Christians view Barnabas as Paul's assistant and primarily admire him only as an example of generosity.

One of my research goals when I went to Cyprus was to see how his stature in the New Testament as a mediator had influenced the faith and practice of Greek Cypriots. Unexpectedly, I discovered that Barnabas has, over the centuries, assumed a much different function in Cyprus. I had to sort through what was history and what was legend.

Research often leads scholars down paths they do not expect, but my findings put me in the painful position of uncovering historical problems with the foundational beliefs that Cypriots have about Barnabas. The tumultuous history of Cyprus has played a significant role in shaping what the Orthodox Christians there believe about Barnabas. Furthermore, turmoil continues to boil on the island. Greek Cypriots face constant conflict with Turks, who occupy the northern third of the island. To my surprise, I found out how Barnabas became part of this struggle.

CHAPTER TWO

The Apostle Barnabas
in his Homeland of Cyprus

Cyprus is a popular tourist destination with lovely mountains and pic-
turesque beaches. It is also the site of an ugly, long-lasting conflict
between Greek Cypriots and Turks. In 1571, the Ottoman Turks conquered Cyprus and settled some of their soldiers on this island where
the native population was predominantly Greek Orthodox Christians.
Cyprus remained under Turkish domination until 1878, when Great
Britain gained control. In 1960, after a tumultuous time of Greek Cypriot
nationalists fighting against British occupation, the UK granted Cyprus
its independence. The Republic of Cyprus was conceived in violence and
born in ethnic turmoil.

The Turkish minority of Cyprus found itself threatened by Greek
nationalists, and bloody clashes sporadically erupted. In 1974, the Turkish army invaded Cyprus in a quick and brutal war, expelling about
180,000 Greek Cypriots from their homes in the northern third of the
island. About 50,000 Turkish Cypriots fled to the north. Over 1,500
Greek Cypriots and about 500 Turkish Cypriots are still listed "missing"
as a result of the warfare. Cyprus remains a divided land, with embittered
Greek Cypriots in the south and defiant Turkish Cypriots in the north.
United Nations troops enforce a ceasefire in the Green Line, a buffer zone
between north and south that zigzags across the island. And, ironically,
Barnabas has become a combatant.

FIGURE 5

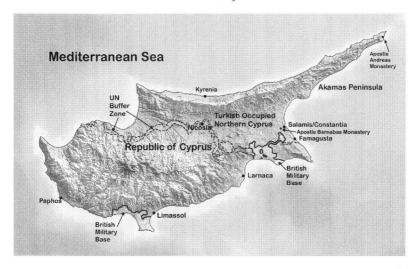

Modern Cypriot Beliefs about Barnabas

Modern Cypriot beliefs about Barnabas diverge significantly from the New Testament depiction of the man, morphing him from a leader involved in creative solutions to conflicts in the early church to a warrior saint for Orthodox Christians. Today he is a symbol of Greek Cypriot national independence and one who passes on his power to the archbishop in Nicosia. A complicated blend of politics and religion has produced a modern Barnabas who bears little resemblance to the New Testament version of him. He stands at the nexus of religious, ethnic, and political turmoil, a consensus builder made complicit in the ongoing strife.

While in Cyprus, my wife and I asked numerous Cypriots—from a postal worker to shop owners to waiters to academics—what they knew about Barnabas. To our surprise, virtually no one responded with information from the New Testament. With obvious pride in their apostle, they explained what they had learned in school: how Barnabas intervened in the late fifth century to save the Church of Cyprus from being ruled by the Patriarch of Antioch in Syria, just to the east of the island. They all told us about Emperor Zeno siding with Cyprus in the dispute with Antioch and about his granting special, imperial privileges to Cypriot archbishops.

According to the story, when Cypriot ecclesiastical independence tottered, Barnabas, who had been dead hundreds of years, suddenly appeared in a timely vision to Anthemios, the archbishop of Cyprus, and explained where to find his body, buried under a carob tree near the east coast city of Salamis. This supernatural intervention became the foundation for modern beliefs about Barnabas, the saint who rescued the island in a time of great need.

FIGURE 6

Wall painting in the Archbishopric, depicting Emperor Zeno giving imperial privileges to Anthemios, Archbishop of Cyprus, in the late fifth century. Note that Anthemios wears a red cape, and the scepter he receives has a globe with a cross on top—called a *globus cruciger*.

A Wikipedia article on the Church of Cyprus articulates the main points we heard repeatedly around the island. The naïve nature of this article illustrates why scholars seldom trust (without further verification) the details provided by this online encyclopedia.

> In 478, Archbishop Anthemios of Cyprus, following a vision, found the grave of St. Barnabas and his relics. On the saint's chest rested a copy of the Gospel of Matthew. The church was thus able to send a cogent argument on its own behalf to the Emperor: the discovery of the relics of its reputed founder, Barnabas. Zeno confirmed the status of the Church of Cyprus and granted its Archbishop the "three privileges": namely to sign his name in *cinnabar*, an ink made vermillion by the addition of the mineral cinnabar; to wear purple instead of black robes under his vestments; and to hold an imperial sceptre (i.e. a gilt staff of silver, topped by a gold *globus cruciger*) instead of the regular episcopal crosier.

Signing one's name in red ink was a jealously guarded privilege limited to the Byzantine emperor alone during the fifth century. Why would Emperor Zeno grant such a privilege to Anthemios? Furthermore, the *globus cruciger* consists of a globe, symbolizing the earth, with a cross on top, symbolizing the emperor's universal rule over the earth through Christ the heavenly king. These imperial symbols of terrestrial rule, limited to the emperor alone, seem totally out of place when given to an archbishop. Much more appropriate is the religious symbolism of the episcopal crosier—the bishop's ornamental staff topped by a crook resembling a shepherd's staff, symbolizing care for the flock of Christ.

However odd these symbols of earthly, imperial rule might be in the Cyprus archbishop's scepter and in his privilege of signing documents with red ink, both children and adults recounted to us varying versions of these same details.[1] This pervasive Cypriot narrative about Barnabas, Archbishop Anthemios, and Emperor Zeno, with its strong political implications, has been taught so successfully that we never met

---

1. Some gave the tomb-discovery date as 473, others as 475, and still others as 478. Modern historians assign a date of 488. The date of 473 arises from ancient sources such as Étienne de Lusignan, *Chorograffia et breve historia universale dell'isola de Cipro. Excerpta Cypria,* 165, provides an English translation: "A church is shown dedicated to the Apostle S. Barnabas, and the place where he was martyred and buried in a well, together with the Gospel of S. Matthew, written in the Evangelist's own hand, which was found there about the year 473." Victor of Tunis assigns a date of 488 in his *Chronicon continuans ubi prosper desinit* (Patrologia Latina 68: col. 947). Hill provides a good summary of the reasons for assigning a date of 488 in *A History of Cyprus,* 1:276–77.

a single Cypriot who raised any questions about its authenticity.[2] But I, a curious outsider, wondered about the origin of the Cyprus archbishop's unique privileges—privileges shared by no other Orthodox archbishop in the world. At what point in history and for what reasons were Roman symbols of terrestrial rule assigned to the religious leader of Cyprus?

Absence of Barnabas in Cyprus

I presumed that, given the significance of his stature as the one who ensured their independence, Barnabas would be well represented in the iconography of Cyprus. But on the island as a whole, Barnabas does not receive nearly as much attention as I expected. In most churches, icons of other saints predominate. St. George killing the dragon, St. Mamas riding the lion, St. Paul, and many others are much more visible than Barnabas. In 2011, I found only one small icon of Barnabas in the marvelous collection of icons in the Byzantine Museum in Nicosia. Amazed, I asked a curator, and he told me that another icon of Barnabas was being refurbished and would be returned to the collection. In 2019, when I last visited the Byzantine Museum, two icons of Barnabas were on display: a large one painted c. 1550 and a modest-sized icon painted in 1691. However, in light of the total number of icons in the museum collection, two icons of Barnabas is proportionately quite small.

The same absence is also apparent in publications. As I paged through lavishly illustrated books devoted to the icons of Cyprus,

Note on Name Spellings

Deciding which spellings to use for Greek names is problematic, so I adopted a hybrid approach. When describing well-known historical characters, such as Epiphanius, I use the Western (Latinized) spellings in order to avoid confusion for readers in the West. When describing people little known to readers in the West, such as Anthemios, I use the Greek sounding versions of the names commonly heard in Cyprus. This compromise seems to be necessary—almost unavoidable.

---

2. I later became aware that a Cypriot scholar named Paul Englezakis had, in fact, briefly challenged the historicity of the archbishop's imperial privileges years before I started my research. See Englezakis, "Archbishop Kyprianos's Inkstand," 269–72. His observations seem not to have made much of an impact on Greek Cypriot beliefs about the archbishop's privileges. I doubt that many even know what he wrote about the matter. In a later chapter, I will give full recognition to the importance of Englezakis's observations.

I was shocked to find very few images of Barnabas.[3] Few churches and monasteries are named after St. Barnabas. And in this Orthodox culture where people are named after saints, many men are named Andreas; but I rarely met anyone named Barnabas.

However, the Archbishopric, seat of religious power and the main institution to benefit from a powerful Barnabas, is one of the most visible focal points for veneration of Barnabas. In a niche near the main entryway is a mosaic of Barnabas. The archbishop's office displays a large icon of Barnabas. The main assembly room where the archbishop meets with other leaders has a series of four recent paintings on one wall portraying Barnabas appearing in a vision to Anthemios, Anthemios discovering the body of Barnabas, Anthemios giving the copy of Matthew's Gospel to Zeno, and Zeno giving the three imperial privileges to Anthemios. Older versions of these paintings may be found in the eighteenth-century fresco in the National Cathedral of St. John, adjacent to the archbishopric, and in the mid-twentieth-century frescos in the Monastery Church of Apostle Barnabas near ancient Salamis. Recent paintings of the Anthemios cycle also appear in a few of the newer churches in and around Nicosia.

Another interesting political connection to Barnabas may be seen in the Troodos Mountains, above the Kykkos Monastery, at the memorial honoring Archbishop Makarios, the first president of Cyprus. An imposing, bronze statue of Makarios, thirty feet high and weighing twelve tons, stands at the end of the parking lot. His left hand holds the imperial scepter, topped with the *globus cruciger*, clearly representing the imperial privileges from Zeno. Lining the path from the statue up the hill to Makarios's tomb are dozens of mosaics, each depicting an Orthodox saint. The mosaic closest to the tomb of Makarios portrays Barnabas—symbolically linking the apostle with the first president of Cyprus, who was simultaneously archbishop and president. The large statue of Makarios, called Big Mak by many Cypriots, and the mosaic of Barnabas next to the archbishop's mausoleum illustrate the connection between religious and political power on the island. The innovative, problem-solving apostle of the New Testament has been given the mantle of political deliverer.

3. For example, Papageorghiou's *Icons of Cyprus* has 211 large pages of beautiful photographs—not a single one of Barnabas. In the sumptuous photographic collection of Sophocleous, *Icons de Chypre*, pages 299–544 present photographs; but Barnabas is conspicuously absent from this book. Barnabas's image appears only on pages 408–9 as one small part of a double-page spread showing an iconostasis. *Cyprus, the Holy Island: Icons through the Centuries*, edited by Sophocleous, has but one photograph of a 1673 icon of Barnabas on 108.

FIGURE 7

Bronze statue of Archbishop Makarios, first president
of the Republic of Cyprus. Note especially the large scepter,
which is topped by a *globus cruciger*. Photo by Lynne Cosby.

Tracing the transformation of Barnabas from peacemaker to power broker defies oversimplification. Key events in this history only make sense in light of the larger narrative, with its complicated twists and turns. To understand the volatile, ethnic strife in Cyprus today and the role Barnabas plays in it, we must look at the larger, historical context. This story bursts with religious and political intrigue.[4]

Forty-Five-Year-Old Wounds

Painted on a mountainside north of Nicosia, two huge flags glare down on the city: the flags of Turkey and the self-proclaimed Turkish Republic of Northern Cyprus (TRNC). Each is about the size of four football fields.

---

4. I have relegated technical aspects of the investigation to footnotes so specialists may use these to explore specific details in greater depth. Given the sweep of history and the varied disciplines involved in telling this saga, no individual has expertise in all the areas involved.

At night, thousands of lights illuminate the TRNC flag, continuously beaming a political lightshow. The cycle begins with a star, then adds the Islamic crescent, then progressively adds the rest of the flag until it completely shines its defiance down on the Greek Cypriot capital. Nothing is subtle about this message of triumph. "You want it, come and get it. We dare you!"

Each time we walked along the UN buffer zone, we were eerily aware of Turkish soldiers watching us from guard towers as we passed razor wire and sandbags blocking entry into the north. Numerous buildings along the buffer zone are riddled with bullet holes or have larger, gaping holes blown in them. They stand as silent witnesses to the violence of 1974. Signs forbid taking pictures in the area.

At the center of the Greek Cypriot psyche is their forced expulsion from the northern part of the island by the Turkish army in 1974. For them, that year lives in infamy. We heard about it daily in the pained memories of those who told us their stories. And we did not need to ask. The stories bubble out of a never-ending spring of bitterness in the land of Barnabas's birth, as the following examples illustrate.

During coffee one day at the Cyprus American Archaeological Research Institute in Nicosia, a middle-aged Greek Cypriot woman told of hearing explosions in 1974 and seeing Turkish paratroopers coming down from the sky. Tears filled her eyes as she recounted the terror she felt. She looked at Lynne and me and said Americans cannot understand the impact war has on people, because the United States has not been invaded. We have not experienced the nightmare of soldiers advancing on our cities—of having to leave everything we own to escape with our lives. She added that one of her cousins never returned from the north. He died there—his body dumped in a mass grave. She had to leave the room to regain her composure.

A few weeks later, during a meal in a private home, we listened to an elderly woman describe how her family fled the east coast city of Famagusta in 1974. She had no time to gather family photographs or even to wait for her husband, who was out for an early morning swim in the Mediterranean. She grabbed the children and fled south, praying that her husband would escape. He did—barely. For months, they slept in their automobile in an orchard, hoping they could return home when the conflict subsided. That was over 46 years ago. After a few years of mere existence and relying on the kindness of others, they immigrated to Canada, arriving with nothing.

Her husband recounted how he worked long hours to build a business, selling imported goods to Cypriot Canadians—cultural things that reminded them of home. When the couple's sons were grown, these young men immigrated to Cyprus and served their mandatory time in the military. Our friends also returned to their motherland and built a house. The wife told us she felt like she was displaced twice. They missed their Cypriot friends in Canada, but they found a spiritual family in Nicosia and seemed fairly happy. When they spoke of their home in Famagusta, however, their eyes filled with tears and their voices trembled.

One evening in Nicosia, we attended an international conference on preventing illicit trafficking of cultural items from Cyprus. Turkish thieves in the north have long plundered Greek Orthodox artifacts and sold them with complete impunity on the black market. Some of these men are well known but continue to go unpunished for their crimes. The harshest and most politically charged address at the conference came from a bishop who read a statement from the archbishop. We were not accustomed to clergy being so aggressively political. In Cyprus, separation of religion and politics is less apparent than in more religiously diverse democracies. Virtually all Greek Cypriots are Orthodox, whether they attend liturgy or not. It is part of their cultural identity. And most look resentfully north to the invaders—the Turks who stole their land, expelled their people, desecrated their churches, and sold their precious icons to unscrupulous dealers.

In a book chronicling the desecration and destruction of Orthodox churches in the north,[5] we examined nauseating photos of destroyed churches, of churches used as barns for sheep, or turned into warehouses for storing produce, or converted into restaurants or bars or mechanic shops; all looted of their icons and other artwork. We observed pictures showing where Turkish thieves hastily hacked ancient frescos off of church walls to sell on the black market.

Later, on a trip to northern Cyprus, my wife and I witnessed many demolished or vandalized Orthodox churches—and many desecrated Greek graveyards. The crumbling condition of the once thriving Monastery of St. Andreas at the eastern tip of the Karpas Peninsula illustrated the sad situation in which Turkish authorities refused to stop the destruction.[6]

5. Papageorghiou, *Christian Art in the Turkish-Occupied Part of Cyprus.*

6. When we returned to Cyprus in 2017, we learned to our delight that the Monastery of St. Andreas had, in fact, recently been restored in a cooperative venture.

FIGURE 8

**Crumbling remains of the once-thriving Monastery of St. Andreas
in Turkish-occupied northern Cyprus.**

We learned that Greek Cypriot schoolteachers make sure their students learn about such destruction and displacement. Parents rehearse the stories to their children. *Turk* is synonymous with villain—murderous villain. They view Turkey as a bully, flexing its muscles and seeking to dominate the entire region. They point out that Turkey's military force is the second largest of any NATO country, with a highly visible military presence in the northern part of Cyprus they occupy.

The version of history proclaimed north of the Green Line, however, differs dramatically. Turkish Cypriots view the 1974 invasion of Cyprus as a peacekeeping mission by Turkey—a necessary measure to protect the lives of Turkish Cypriots terrorized by Greeks. They post graphic documentaries on the Internet to reveal the atrocities committed against them from 1963 to 1974. Videos on YouTube send a clear message: bloodthirsty Greek Cypriot nationalists were determined to massacre the Turks and eliminate them from the island. A quick Internet search reveals dueling propaganda videos produced by Turkish Cypriots and Greek Cypriots.

Because we lived in the south, we primarily heard stories from Greek Cypriots. But we know there are two sides to the conflict. Each ethnic group both suffered and inflicted suffering. Few on either side will

---

Through Dafnis Panagides, we met the Turkish Cypriot civil engineer who oversaw the reconstruction work. This engineer explained that he is in the process of restoring other Orthodox churches and monasteries in the Turkish north of Cyprus.

admit to the atrocities committed by their own ancestors. Both seek vindication for themselves and condemnation for the other.

One book that tells stories from both perspectives is *Echoes from the Dead Zone: Across the Cyprus Divide* by Yiannis Papadakis. While conducting his research, Papadakis lived in various locations in Turkey, the Republic of Cyprus, and the TRNC. He listened to different perspectives and in his book tells the conflicting accounts. Many Greek Cypriots consider him to be a traitor because he does not completely condemn the Turks—thus, potentially weakening the Greek Cypriot position. But *Echoes from the Dead Zone* is one of the most helpful books on what has come to be called the Cyprus Problem, because Papadakis recounts reports from both sides. More importantly, he gives voice to the common people and chronicles their painful experiences. Many conflict-resolution experts have worked on the island since 1974, but the Cyprus conflict is so complicated that their peacemaking efforts have failed to resolve the situation.

At the archaeological institute in Nicosia where my wife and I lived, one student resident was finishing her degree in conflict archaeology. She was part of a team tasked to oversee excavation of mass graves, identify the dead and then to notify living relatives. To accomplish their work, they needed the cooperation of officials from the TRNC and the Republic of Cyprus. TRNC officials refused to cooperative. Digging up evidence of atrocities meets stiff resistance.

The Growth of Christianity on Cyprus

Orthodox Cypriots trace the beginning of their church to the missionary efforts of Barnabas and Paul, who came to the island around 47 CE (Acts 13:1–12).[7] Information about the development of the church in Cyprus is spotty, but Christianity gradually emerged as a political force. In 300, Cyprus had significant urban centers along its coastline, and the majority of Cypriots worshiped a pantheon of deities (Aphrodite, Zeus, and Apollo were popular). But when Constantine emerged victorious as emperor in 324 and provided protection for Christians, many people began to see his military victory on earth as proof of the ascendance of the Christian God in heaven—dominating the other gods.

---

7. According to Acts 11:20, some unnamed Cypriot Christians seem to have preached in Cyprus prior to the apostles.

Seismic activity enhanced the spread of Christianity among the Cypriot Greeks. Thomas Davis points out that, when earthquakes brought widespread destruction to the island, Christians offered convincing theological explanations for the devastation. Massive quakes in 332, 342, 365, and 370 shook the foundations of polytheistic belief in Cyprus.[8] When earthquakes destroyed the major shrines of pagan religions, Christians proclaimed that the destruction was God's judgment on paganism.[9]

Epiphanius (born ca. 310–20, died ca. 403) became bishop of Salamis, on the eastern coast of Cyprus, in 367. A tireless and fierce opponent of any beliefs he considered heretical, his legacy in the history of Cyprus is far more significant than that of the more conciliatory Barnabas. Following the banning of non-Christian rituals in 382 by Emperor Theodosius, Epiphanius led a campaign that destroyed most pagan temples in Cyprus and killed many non-Christians. Under the leadership of men like Epiphanius, the population of Cyprus became increasingly Christian. When the Roman Empire divided in 395, Cyprus became part of the Byzantine Empire—an extremely important legacy today among Greek Cypriots.

Foreign Powers Subjugated Cyprus

During the following centuries, various invaders both ravaged and subjugated Cyprus. Beginning in 649, Arabs launched devastating raids, destroying cities and churches and pillaging the island for 300 years. The Byzantine emperor Nikephoros II Phokas defeated Arab armies and restored Byzantine rule to Cyprus in 965. But ongoing theological disputes between leaders of what later became Roman Catholicism and Eastern Orthodoxy complicated conditions in the Eastern Mediterranean. Arguments simmered over such issues as whether or not priests should marry, whether to use leavened or unleavened bread for communion, and what was the proper way to conduct liturgy.

During the Third Crusade, in 1191, Richard the Lionheart, king of England, took over Cyprus and used it as a supply base for his campaign to retake the Holy Land. Richard soon sold Cyprus to the Knights Templar, who returned it to Richard in 1192, who then turned it over to Guy

8. Davis, "Earthquakes and the Crises of Faith," 9.
9. Davis, "Earthquakes and the Crises of Faith," 11–15.

de Lusignan, a French crusader. The Lusignan dynasty ruled the island for three centuries. They built beautiful castles, cathedrals, and monasteries, and these structures attracted attention from merchants of Venice.

FIGURE 9

St. Nicholas's Cathedral in Famagusta. This Gothic structure, consecrated in 1328, was converted into a mosque in 1571 after the Ottoman Turks conquered the city.

In 1472, the Lusignan leader James II married Caterina Cornaro, from a Venetian noble family; but he died under suspicious circumstances a few months later—leaving his pregnant wife regent of Cyprus. His son by Caterina, James III, died mysteriously in 1474, prior to his first birthday, making Caterina the queen of Cyprus. The young Caterina was mostly a figurehead, with Venetian merchants controlling the government. They convinced her to abdicate the throne in 1489, and the Republic of Venice formally took control of the island and ruled it until the Ottoman Turks conquered Cyprus in 1571.

Following the Turkish invasion, the Ottomans gave land grants in Cyprus to Turkish soldiers. The Ottomans periodically changed the way they governed Cyprus, in part to deal with the problems of corrupt Turkish overlords exploiting and abusing the Orthodox population. They set up a type of feudal government, made Orthodoxy the official Christian presence on the island, and allowed a degree of self-government among the Greek inhabitants. In 1660, the Ottomans appointed the Cypriot archbishop to be the ruler (*ethnarch*) of the Orthodox inhabitants of the island and gave to him the responsibility of collecting taxes for the Turks—a development that proved to be extremely significant in the emerging beliefs about Barnabas's connection to the civil powers of the archbishop.

Empires Rise and Fall

Over the next few centuries, the Ottoman Empire slowly crumbled. Following the Turkish war with Russia (1877–78), the weakened Ottomans ceded control of Cyprus to the United Kingdom—which established naval bases on Cyprus and used the island's strategic location close to the Suez Canal to enhance its colonial policies. The UK annexed Cyprus in 1914, during World War I, and officially made it a colony in 1925.

During World War I, the British Prime Minister, David Lloyd George, promised the leaders of Greece that, if the Greeks would fight on the side of the Allies against the Central Powers (which included what was left of the Ottoman Empire), Greece would regain much of the territory in Asia Minor that had once been part of the Byzantine Empire and was still home for many ethnic Greeks. Some Greek politicians found the offer attractive, and they argued for the need to protect ethnic Greeks in Asia Minor. In fact, justifications existed for such concern. In 1915 a radical group called the Young Turks had slaughtered hundreds of thousands of ethnic minorities in the Ottoman Empire. Most victims were Armenian, but some were Greek.

After the end of World War I, Greece invaded Turkey in 1919—with disastrous results. Greek forces attacking Asia Minor initially succeeded, and the ethnic Greeks of the area largely viewed the Greek soldiers as liberators. But the soldiers perpetrated atrocities against the local Turkish population: murdering, raping, and plundering. Turkish soldiers committed similar atrocities against ethnic Greeks in the Black Sea region:

murdering, raping, and plundering. Both sides sometimes followed a scorched earth policy. Grim battles raged from 1919 to 1922. Turkish revolutionary forces led by Mustafa Kemal (later known as Atatürk—which means Father of Turkey) finally repelled the Greek army, resulting in massive dislocation of people. A million Turkish citizens of Greece found themselves uprooted and expelled to Turkey, and 1.5 million Greek citizens of Turkey found themselves driven from their homes and having to resettle in Greece or elsewhere. Many of these dislocated Turks and Greeks had to flee lands that their families had inhabited for many generations—in some cases, many centuries.

Thus, the Greek dream of restoring part of the Byzantine Empire failed. The British promise of Greeks regaining control of the land in western Turkey turned out to be false. It only succeeded in rekindling ancient animosity. Cyprus, with its combination of Greek and Turkish citizens, was caught up in the larger conflict.

Birth of the Republic of Cyprus

In the 1950s, Greek Cypriot nationalists conducted an insurrection against British rule. Led by Georgios Grivas, in 1955 they founded *EOKA* (Εθνική Οργάνωσις Κυπρίων Αγωνιστών = National Organiza-tion of Cypriot Fighters) in an effort to overthrow British control. *Enosis*, union with Greece, was their rallying cry. But *enosis* had major implica-tions for the balance of power in the region. Tensions boiled. Periodic fighting erupted between Greek and Turkish Cypriots.

When Britain granted independence to Cyprus in 1960, negotia-tors from Britain, Turkey, and Greece established a government system whereby Turkish Cypriots, who made up only 18 percent of the popu-lation, gained a 30 percent quota of government control and had per-manent veto power. The Greek Cypriot majority deeply resented being forced to concede such significant political power to the minority Turk-ish population of the island. Neither the new constitution nor the new flag represented the will of Greek Cypriots, who fought for independence but ultimately had to settle for outsiders imposing on them a form of gov-ernment they did not want. Meanwhile, the push for *enosis* continued.

FIGURE 10

Freedom Monument in Nicosia depicting Greek Cypriots being released from a British prison in 1959, just before Cyprus gained independence.

During 1963–1964, conflict flared between ethnic Greeks and Turks in Cyprus, resulting in the UN deploying forces to stop the fighting. Many Turks moved into enclaves for safety. Turkey attempted to invade Cyprus in 1964 but backed down after USA president Lyndon Johnson sent a strongly worded warning. Complicating matters, in 1967, a coup d'état in Greece toppled the civilian government and led to further instability in the region. Fighting again erupted in Cyprus, with Greek national- ists attacking Turkish villages in southern Cyprus, killing 27 people. In response, Turkey bombed Greek Cypriot forces and again prepared to invade.

By 1970, many Turkish Cypriots believed that Greek nationalism threatened their existence. Dreams of panhellenism, the recreation of a Greek powerhouse in the eastern Mediterranean, fueled further con- flict. Innocent Turkish Cypriots were terrorized, and Turkish insurgents fought back. Both sides committed atrocities, but Greek Cypriots greatly outnumbered Turkish Cypriots.

Hostilities subsided for a while. Archbishop Makarios, the first elected president of Cyprus, had for years pursued *enosis*—union of Cyprus with Greece. However, he finally began to see that the time was not right for this drastic move. He pragmatically gave up the idea (at least temporarily) and sought to build an independent Cyprus. He wrote to the military ruler of Greece, Taxiarkhos Dimitrios Ioannides, and requested all Greek military personnel be removed from Cyprus. In 1974, Ioannides responded with a military coup d'état that ousted Makarios and briefly established a Greek military government on the island.

Criticism of both President Makarios and General Grivas

Cypriot author Kypros Tofallis describes both Archbishop Makarios, the president, and Georgios Grivas, a Cypriot born general in the Greek army who led the insurrection against British rule in Cyprus, as ambitious megalomaniacs who stubbornly pushed for enosis with Greece (A History of Cyprus, 2nd edition, 169). Tofallis explains that, in spite of the intense animosity between these two leaders, after Grivas died in 1974, Makarios declared an amnesty for Grivas's fighters and also gave a eulogy for Grivas—the man who tried to overthrow him. Tofallis asserts, "If this is not some kind of Political Masochism on the part of Makarios and the right wing dominated House of Representatives, one wonders what is!" (286).

While president, Archbishop Makarios attempted to push through thirteen proposals to amend the Constitution of Cyprus—without first consulting his Turkish vice-president, or the three countries that helped to draft the original constitution of the Cyprus Republic to ensure the rights of the Turkish minority. Makarios got the vice president to agree on most of these proposals, but then the archbishop changed his mind and "wanted to abolish the post of Vice-President!" (347). He refused to compromise, wanting all power in the hands of Greek Cypriots. In the end, however, he became willing to make many compromises he previously rejected. "Had he agreed in 1972 with the Turkish Cypriots on the issue of local government, the course of Cypriot history would have been very different. Both Makarios and Grivas were prisoners of their oaths and nationalism. The Cypriot people have been paying ever since for their leaders' mistakes as well as the barbarous and illegal Turkish invasion and occupation" (348).

Tofallis says the leaders of both sides made many tragic errors and were hostage to their nationalism, viewing themselves first and foremost as "Greeks" and "Turks" and not as "Cypriots" (380). Tofallis adds that Britain and the USA could have prevented the Turkish invasion—but they put their strategic and economic interests ahead of human rights.

Mustafa Bülent Ecevit, prime minister of Turkey, expressed grave concern for the safety of the Turkish Cypriots. But he failed to gain guarantees of direct intervention from the UK, so he ordered an invasion of northern Cyprus. On July 20, 1974, Turkish forces established a corridor linking north Cyprus with Nicosia. On July 23, the Greek military junta collapsed. In August, Turkish forces launched a second offensive, overwhelmed Greek defenders and expanded their control to about thirty-six percent of the island, establishing a separate Turkish state in the north. The US, occupied with other concerns, including the resignation of President Richard Nixon, did not intervene to stop Turkey. Since then, all attempts at working out a viable solution to the problem have been unsuccessful.

In 1983, the north declared itself to be the Turkish Republic of Northern Cyprus (TRNC). Only Turkey recognizes this political entity. No other country in the world acknowledges the TRNC as a legitimate state. In violation of the Geneva Convention and UN resolutions, Turkey opened immigration of Turkish nationals into Cyprus. Today, these immigrant Turks outnumber Turkish Cypriots in northern Cyprus—a situation deeply resented by many Turkish Cypriots. The immigrants are often less educated and more religiously conservative than the Turkish Cypriots, which has changed the culture of the north. Turkey pumps the equivalent of $40 million annually into the faltering economy of the TRNC. They also maintain a large military presence.

Today, 30,000–40,000 Turkish troops occupy northern Cyprus, which has a total population of around 300,000.[10] Another 5,000 Turkish Cypriot Security Forces, backed up by 26,000 reserve forces, result in a heavily militarized north. Tensions remain high.

The United Nations and the European Union recognize the legitimacy only of the Republic of Cyprus. UN resolutions 353, 357, 358, 359, 360, and 365 condemn the occupation of northern Cyprus by the Turkish army. Turkey ignores these resolutions, and the illegal presence of its military in Cyprus impedes Turkey's efforts to join the European Union.

---

10. This figure may be far less than the actual population. The TRNC is not known for truthful reporting of population figures, probably because of the illegal immigration of many from Turkey. On December 4, 2011, my wife and I were stranded in the north, confined to quarters in a rundown hotel in Bogaz. We had not been informed of the census scheduled for that day, and were completely unaware that all people in the TRNC were required to remain in their place of domicile the entire day, until 6:00 p.m. The government shut down the entire state for the day so that poll workers could go door to door and physically count everyone. Tourists beware!

All attempts at reconciliation and reunification of Cyprus have failed. What one side finds acceptable, the other side views as deplorable.

To their credit, the Cyprus Fulbright Commission staff members attempted to foster better relationships between Greek and Turkish Cypriots. Their main office is just south of the UN-controlled Green Line, but when I was there in 2011 they also maintained an office just north of the Green Line. In addition, they had a building inside the buffer zone where people from both north and south could meet together on neutral ground. But their efforts were unusual—and diminishing funding for their programs has forced them to scale back their peace efforts. Animosity oozes from both sides of the Green Line. And, oddly enough, Barnabas has become part of the ongoing conflict.

Barnabas as Greek Cypriot Deliverer

Greek Cypriots view Barnabas not just as a religious figure from the past but as a living presence. They look to him to restore freedom to occupied northern Cyprus and let his spiritual children once again live in their ancestral villages and rebuild their lives and their churches. Unlike me, they do not view Barnabas as an important leader from the past whom they should study. They believe Barnabas intercedes for and works on behalf of his people on the island—the Greek Cypriots. Consequently, many Cypriots were puzzled by my emphasis on digging up the past.

When Neophytos, Metropolitan of Morphou, told me that, until I quit thinking like a Westerner, I would never understand Orthodox spirituality, he exhibited no malice. He was trying to help me see my paradigm is wrong and is therefore keeping me from experiencing the truth. He freely admitted that Eastern Orthodox monks and priests hold differing views on important issues, but he considered these to be intramural squabbles among those belonging to the True Church, which preserves the doctrine and spirituality tracing all the way back to the apostles. This Metropolitan is a visionary leader who calls Orthodox Christians to repent of their own sinful behaviors and to reject the nationalism that has brought so much misery to the island. Other leaders on the island do not share his viewpoint.

The director of theological education in Cyprus, whose office is at the archbishopric, took time to serve as translator when I met with the archbishop. During a later conversation, he expressed frustration with the way some Protestants accuse Orthodox Christians of idol worship because of the prominence of icons in Orthodox churches. He used the analogy of American government to explain the hierarchy recognized by Orthodox Christians: Americans do not go directly to our president if we have a request. We go to local, elected officials whose job it is to listen to our concerns and act on our behalf. Those officials take our concerns to higher authorities if necessary.

He explained that Orthodox Christians pray to the saints, who have achieved a high degree of spiritual enlightenment and work on behalf of their people. The saints function as intermediaries, taking requests to higher authorities. The *Theotokos* (Virgin Mary) has ready access to Jesus and intercedes on behalf of those who pray to her. He concluded by saying Orthodox Christians acknowledge the proper chain of command and operate respectfully within it. They do not presume to go directly to God with every little issue. And when they show reverence for icons, they are expressing proper respect for the ones whom the icons represent.

When talking with most Cypriots, I was surprised to learn that they are barely aware of Protestantism. It is, for the most part, irrelevant to them. They did, however, express strong reservations about any theology that does not understand the active role of saints. To view saints as important leaders who died long ago but have no ongoing function for God's people seems disrespectful to Orthodox Christians. Several told me Protestants are quite young in their faith and hopefully will mature and grow into the truth of Orthodoxy.

Greek Cypriots are much more aware of their differences with Catholicism, and they say especially harsh things about the Latins who for centuries subjected the island. But, of course, since 1571 their main conflict has been with the Turks; and some Cypriots today pray to Barnabas for deliverance.

The Very Reverend Archimandrite Gabriel, who died in 2013, was for many years the Abbot of the Monastery of Apostle Barnabas. This wonderful old man wrote the following about the role of Barnabas in remedying the injustices initiated by the 1974 invasion (which the Turks code-named *Operation Attila*).

> The Turkish Attila expelled the Greeks from the occupied areas and everything was deserted . . . The monastery of Apostle Varnavas remained silent for 30 or so years abandoned in the hands of the occupation forces as a Museum. Now, after the opening of communication points with the occupied areas there is nostalgia for a mass to be held at his Tomb, where his grace made us worthy of celebrating mass in his honor and receive at this

location the bright light of his blessed presence . . . His presence is live and He is responding to the claims of the faithful . . . Our saints live throughout time and are on our side helping us . . . I am glad that even now he [Barnabas] appeared to our dear Marios Stylianou, in difficult times of a struggle against foreign occupation, urging him to protect his historic personality to all of us who have forgotten him . . . I wish the grace of the Trinity of God, by the intercession of the wishes of the most glorious Apostle Varnavas the Son of Supplication, help us rid our tormented country from the Turkish invasion and occupation and bring freedom to his Monastery allowing the return of those entitled to run it so that mass will be celebrated again and that the light of Orthodoxy will be radiated again from there.[11]

FIGURE 11

Archimandrite Gabriel (left), Abbot of the Monastery of Apostle Barnabas, and some of his spiritual children. Michael Cosby sits next to the monk beside Fr. Gabriel. Photo by Lynne Cosby.

Fr. Gabriel was one of the kindest, most generous men I have ever met. For this saintly man to pray that Barnabas would rid Cyprus of the Turkish invaders reveals the depth of the feelings toward Turkey felt by even the most devout Greek Cypriots.

11. Stylianou, *Apostle Varnavas*, 25. The book was published in Greek with English translations in parallel columns. At times the English translation is a bit awkward.

The Archimandrite Photios S. Constantinou expresses more overt nationalism when he says the following regarding Barnabas. Most of his words are a quotation of what the Archimandrite Kyprianos wrote in his *History of Cyprus* in 1788.

> I do not know of any other Apostle to have honoured to such an extent his own country or to have appeared so loving for his country as our compatriot Varnavas. During his life he rid his compatriots of the detestable religion of pagans, teaching them the true religion of our Lord Jesus Christ. Dead he freed his country from the exploitation of the power loving and jealous Clergy of Antioch. Truly and without any doubt the Son of Supplication Varnavas fulfilled fully the motto: "Fight for Church and Country."
>
> Thus, as Cypriots we have a great duty and owe a lot to the saviour of our souls to the benefactor and giver of our Ecclesiastical Glory! . . . Concluding, let us wish that Apostle Varnavas, the founder and protector of our Church performs a miracle and Cyprus gets rid of the Turks from his own country that he loved so much and for the sake of which he became a martyr having suffered such a tragic death.[12]

His statement about the "jealous Clergy of Antioch" refers to Peter, Patriarch of Antioch in the late fifth century; and the account of Barnabas's martyrdom comes from the fifth-century Acts of Barnabas. Such blending of religious and political concerns seems quite normal in Cyprus. The Orthodox Church is *the* church of Cyprus. Although many Greek Cypriots are quite secular and rarely attend sacred liturgy, they are Orthodox. It is their national identity. To fight for the country is to fight for the church.

Greek Cypriot nationalists would like to restore the glories of the Byzantine Empire. To change the name Istanbul back to Constantinople would be a grand prize. Conversely, Turkish nationalists would like to restore the glories of the Ottoman Empire. But most Greek and Turkish Cypriots just try to earn a living and raise their families. Leaders make drastic decisions. The common people suffer as a result. The wounds inflicted before and after 1974 still fester.

Both sides have legitimate complaints against the other. But participants in a conflict rarely admit to their own faults, preferring instead to

---

12. Stylianou, *Apostle Varnavas*, 103–4, 106. For an English translation of the passage in Kyprianos, see Hackett, *History of the Orthodox Church of Cyprus,* 25.

place all the blame on the other. Blaming is easier than admitting one's own contributions to a conflict—even though it detracts from reconciliation and resolution. Of course, making such an observation is much simpler for an outsider like me. I did not have to flee to the north or south to save my life. I did not lose everything because political radicals stirred conflict conditions to the point that everyone got involved, like it or not.

Freedom Fighter Turned Pacifist

Dafnis, one of our dearest friends in Cyprus, joined the Cypriot resistance against the British in the 1950s. At one point, Georgios Grivas, the leader of EOKA, hid for about three months from the British military in a room dug under Dafnis's garage. Dafnis spent three years in a British prison for his involvement in the resistance. The British released him just before they granted independence to the island.

Dafnis's father, Solomon, loved birds and kept an aviary on the porch of their house. When he saw his liberated son step off the bus in front of their home, he opened the aviary door and released all the birds. As Dafnis told this story, he got tears in his eyes. So did we. Hearing him recount this deeply symbolic gesture was an emotional experience. For me it became a sort of metaphor for Cyprus as a nation.

Greek Cypriots considered Dafnis a heroic freedom fighter and elected him to their first parliament in 1960. But over time he became very disillusioned with the divisive leadership of both Archbishop Makarios and General Grivas. He went to the United States on a Fulbright program, and he ended up at Iowa State University, where he earned a bachelor's degree, a Master's degree, and was working on his PhD in horticulture. But the 1974 Turkish invasion of Cyprus interrupted his graduate work. Before he finished his dissertation, he returned to Cyprus to help with the humanitarian crisis. He became a pacifist, environmentalist, and social activist. He was the most fascinating person we met in Cyprus.

Until his death in Feburary 2019, Dafnis lived in his family's ancestral home in Limassol. Once a secluded farmhouse, now it is scrunched amidst buildings that have grown up all around—a tiny green island with a yard full of exotic plants from around the world. Dafnis maintained a much larger version of his father's aviary and loved to watch the birds inside it. My wife and I have spent many hours listening to Dafnis tell stories. He was also our tour guide, showing us out-of-the-way places in the mountains, including secluded churches with their wonderful frescos.

Through encounters with such colorful characters, we gained a perspective on the interface of faith, spirituality and politics that few people experience who do not actually live in Cyprus.

Amidst the continual tension with the Turks in the north, many Greek Cypriots look to Barnabas as the saint who ensured their ecclesiastical independence in the fifth century and who now works to liberate their island. They do not see Barnabas as a skilled negotiator who listened to both sides of conflicts in the early church and helped to formulate compromise solutions. If they did, they might find that following his example could make a lasting difference in Cyprus today.

My task, therefore, was straightforward, yet enormously intimidating. I needed to mine nearly 2,000 years of history in the eastern Mediterranean area to uncover clues that illuminated how Barnabas the mediating peacemaker in the New Testament became Barnabas the political liberator in later centuries. Were it not for a massive, electronic database that allowed me to search thousands of Greek documents for the name Barnabas, my research would have been insurmountable. [13]

Computer technology provided the tools necessary to locate relevant passages, most of which I had to translate in order to decipher. But as I followed the trail of evidence, I located the historical settings during which new beliefs about Barnabas took root and grew into the present view of him as protector of Cypriot Orthodox Christians. I discovered

13. I used the database provided by *Thesaurus Linguae Graecae* (*TLG*) to locate all uses of ΒΑΡΝΑΒΑΣ in Greek texts from the first through the fifteenth century (by using BAPNABA in the search engine, I identified all the inflected forms of the name). The *TLG* team, based at the University of California, Irvine, has digitized most Greek texts from the eighth century BCE to beyond the fall of Byzantium in 1453 (http://www.tlg.uci.edu/about/).

that Barnabas, although largely relegated to a secondary status as a saint for most of the past 2,000 years, periodically emerged as a savior figure during times of national need. I did not anticipate the degree to which political connections have determined the development of traditions about Barnabas. In fact, I was shocked by what I found. My research involved a large amount of tedious analysis, but when clues began to surface and a coherent chronicle began to take shape, the eyestrain and headaches gave way to the excitement of discovery. I learned much about how Barnabas the peacemaker became Barnabas the warrior saint—a remarkable example of the creation of history and the development of a cultural heritage.

CHAPTER THREE

Barnabas the Negotiator of the New Testament

> Barnabas is perhaps the most attractive character in the New
> Testament. All the evidence indicates he was a warm-hearted
> generous personality who had a splendid gift of discerning
> merit in others, of inspiring confidence where suspicion pre-
> vailed, and of reconciling opposing factions. In a word, he was
> a bridge-builder—the type of man for whom there is desperate
> need today.[1]

My investigation began with the portrayal of Barnabas in the New Testament. What do the earliest documents reveal about the man? Although limited in scope, the New Testament texts paint a fairly consistent picture of this significant leader.

Barnabas led in developing a theological perspective that moved the church from a messianic offshoot of Judaism to a universal religion that welcomed gentiles. He facilitated the transition toward Jewish and gentile Christians working together as equals in proclaiming the good news about Jesus, the Christ. Of course, some Jewish Christians fought this transition, demanding the gentiles become proselyte Jews, submitting to circumcision and keeping kosher food laws. Barnabas represented a more progressive wing of the church; but he functioned as a mediator between the conservative Jewish Christians, who insisted on the laws of Moses as a prerequisite for inclusion in the church, and the radical gentile Christians, who rejected Mosaic laws outright.

---

1. Evans, "Barnabas the Bridge-Builder," 248–49.

In spite of his importance in the early church, however, Barnabas is a secondary character in the New Testament. In Acts, he emerges as a leader in the development of a multi-ethnic movement—but only until Paul becomes the central figure in the narrative. Afterward, Barnabas virtually dissapears. Except for references to Barnabas in Acts and Paul mentioning him in 1 Cor 9:6 and Gal 2:1, 9, 13, the rest of the New Testament says nothing about him. Paul became such a dominant force that he overshadowed his mentor. Polarizing personalities often gain more attention than mediating ones.

Most of the information about Barnabas in the New Testament comes from Acts, written sometime during the 80s, several decades after Barnabas and Paul died.[2] Acts addresses a different social situation than the one Paul faced when writing his letters decades earlier.[3] During Paul's life, Jerusalem was the geographical center of the Christian faith; and significant numbers of Jewish Christians opposed the evangelization work spearheaded by Barnabas and Paul. But the Jewish war against the Romans in 66–70 CE changed all that. According to the fourth-century historian Eusebius, Christians largely abandoned Jerusalem prior to the Jewish rebellion against Rome, which ended disastrously for the Jews in 70.[4] By the time Acts was written, the church in Jerusalem was no longer the focus of power. As C. K. Barrett says, "The anti-Pauline missions that had emanated from Jerusalem had lost their base of operations" and the church as a whole accepted the mission to the gentiles. Consequently,

---

2. Although New Testament scholars debate the historicity of Acts, as well as the identity of its author, most believe Acts was written after 80 CE. Lively discussions continue over the identity of the author of the Gospel of Luke and the Acts of the Apostles, and many scholars question the second-century tradition that Paul's friend, Luke, penned the scrolls. However, commentators do agree the same author wrote both works. For a detailed study, see Tannehill, *Narrative Unity of Luke–Acts*. Because identifying the author of Luke-Acts is not essential for the present study on Barnabas, I leave aside these matters and for convenience simply use the traditional designation of the author as Luke.

3. Barrett, *Acts*, 2:xxxvii–xxxix, provides a good summary of the differences.

4. "On the other hand, the people of the church in Jerusalem were commanded by an oracle given by revelation before the war to those in the city who were worthy of it to depart and dwell in one of the cities of Perea which they called Pella. To it those who believed on Christ migrated from Jerusalem, that when holy men had altogether deserted the royal capital of the Jews and the whole land of Judaea, the judgement of God might at last overtake them for all their crimes against the Christ and his apostles" (*Hist. eccl.* 3.5.3, K. Lake, LCL). Epiphanius also mentions Christians fleeing to Pella (*De pond. et mens.* 15).

when Acts describes contentious events in the early church, it does so during a time of increasing consensus—not while the struggles still raged.[5]

By this time the incendiary theological debate over inclusion of gentiles was largely settled, although certainly not to everyone's satisfaction. Acts looks back on earlier decades and shows the miraculous expansion of the church from its beginning in Jerusalem, the center of Judaism, to its establishment in the capital city, Rome. Although Acts does recount some of the struggles and problems in the church, overall it gives a positive depiction of Christians multiplying steadily under the leading of the Holy Spirit.

Conversely, Paul's letters, mostly written during the tumultuous 50s, reveal firsthand some painful aspects of the struggle for the soul of the emerging church. Galatians in particular expresses raw emotions as Paul defends himself against Jewish-Christian detractors. Because issues pertaining to gentile inclusion in the church still boiled, Paul sometimes dictated letters in the heat of conflict, using sarcasm and hyperbole to argue his position.[6]

Although Acts was written from a later perspective, its narrative provides our most significant source for details about Barnabas. Luke was selective regarding which stories he included in his history of the early Christian movement. He focused on the actions of his central characters and left untold many other events. Scholars debate how much of Acts consists of created history, but it remains the most complete resource we have for information about the life of Barnabas. And because Barnabas is not one of the main heroes in Acts, Luke would be less likely to invent material about him as a means of glorifying him. For example, Acts contains no speeches attributed to Barnabas, whereas Paul frequently delivers speeches in the narrative. Some of what Acts reports about Barnabas

---

5. Barrett, *Acts*, 2:xli.

6. Paul's letters reveal a man who at times feels intense emotional turmoil (see especially 2 Cor 1–9), in contrast with the heroic figure depicted in Acts, in which he exhibits brilliant rhetorical ability. In 2 Cor 10:9–11, Paul admits his opponents consider him to be a weakling and a poor public speaker: "I do not want to seem as though I am trying to frighten you with my letters. For they say, 'His letters are weighty and strong, but his bodily presence is weak, and his speech contemptible.' Let such people understand that what we say by letter when absent, we will also do when present." Defensively and sarcastically, he adds, "I think that I am not in the least inferior to these super-apostles. I may be untrained in speech, but not in knowledge; certainly in every way and in all things we have made this evident to you" (2 Cor 11:5–6).

might not be historical, but the overall depiction of Barnabas in Acts is probably accurate.

Model of Benevolence

According to Acts, Barnabas emerged as a leader of the nascent Christian movement in the 30s and 40s. Acts initially presents him as a model of charity—a specific example of the generosity characterizing the early followers of Jesus in Jerusalem.

> There was not a needy person among them, for as many as owned lands or houses sold them and brought the proceeds of what was sold. They laid it at the apostles' feet, and it was distributed to each as any had need. There was a Levite, a native of Cyprus, Joseph, to whom the apostles gave the name Barnabas (which means 'son of encouragement') [more likely 'son of exhortation,' i.e., 'preacher'[7]]. He sold a field that belonged to him, then brought the money, and laid it at the apostles' feet. (Acts 4:34–37)

Barnabas, a wealthy Cypriot from the tribe of Levi, voluntarily brings money to the apostles for distribution to the poor. Acts 4:37 does not specify whether he sold land located in Cyprus or near Jerusalem. Generosity, not location, is the focus. Authors of later traditions added details

---

7. Scholars promote different theories for the origin of the name Barnabas. See, for example, Brock, "ΒΑΡΝΑΒΑΣ ΥΙΟΣ ΠΑΡΑΚΛΗΣΙΣ," 93–98. The *bar* prefix is Aramaic for *son*, but *nabas* does not mean *encouragement*. Rather, the word indicates the god Nebo, resulting in a puzzling "Son of Nebo"—not a name the Jewish apostles would concoct. Perhaps the apostles used the Hebrew *nabi*, which means prophet, resulting in "Son of a prophet" (or "Son of a preacher," pointing to his ability to proclaim the gospel). Luke interprets the name with παράκλησις, which can mean either encouragement (Acts 13:15; 1 Cor 14:3; 2 Cor 8:17; 1 Thess 2:3; 1 Tim 4:13; Heb 6:18; 12:5; 13:22) or exhortation (Luke 2:25; 6:24; Acts 9:31; 15:31; Rom 15:4; 2 Cor 1:3–7; 7:4, 7, 13; 2 Thess 2:16; Phlm 7). In Rom 12:8 and Phil 2:1, παράκλησις could mean either encouragement or exhortation in context. Therefore, one could translate υἱὸς παρακλήσεως in Acts 4:36 either as "Son of Encouragement" or "Son of Exhortation." Acts 11:23 uses the imperfect form παρεκάλει of the verb παρακαλέω to say Barnabas exhorted the new believers in Antioch to remain faithful, and Acts 13:15 uses παράκλησις when speaking of a word of exhortation (λόγος παρακλήσεως). In the Acts narrative, Barnabas is both an effective preacher and an encouraging individual. In Acts 4:36, however, evidence favors the translation "son of exhortation" = "preacher." See Barrett, *Acts*, 1:258–59.

about his land holdings in their efforts to lengthen the story of Barnabas, but Acts remains brief and vague on the matter.

Barnabas was not unusual in being a land-owning Levite. Other ancient authors claim numerous Jewish landowners lived in Cyprus.[8] Philo of Alexandria, a Jewish scholar writing in the first century, says Cyprus had many Jewish colonies (*De legatione ad Gaium* 282), and the Jewish historian Josephus mentions wealthy Jews dwelling in Cyprus (*Ant.* 13.284). Although Num 18:20; Deut 10:9; 12:12, 18–19; and 14:27–29 say Levites were not to own property, later texts indicate Levites were landowners. In Jer 32:6–7, God actually commands the priest Jeremiah to buy a plot of land. The fact is, during the first century, not all Levites served in the temple,[9] and many of them were affluent. Generosity, not wealth, was Barnabas's noteworthy characteristic.

Barnabas next appears in Acts 9:26–27 as an advocate for Saul of Tarsus, the former persecutor of Christians. After Saul's dramatic conversion on the road to Damascus and his adventures preaching about Jesus in Damascus, he had returned to Jerusalem and sought to join Christians there. Understandably, they feared his motives and remained reluctant to welcome this young zealot into their midst. Barnabas convinced them otherwise.

> When he [Saul] had come to Jerusalem, he attempted to join the disciples; and they were all afraid of him, for they did not believe that he was a disciple. But Barnabas took him, brought him to the apostles, and described for them how on the road he had seen the Lord, who had spoken to him, and how in Damascus he had spoken boldly in the name of Jesus. (Acts 9:26–27)

Luke does not explain why Barnabas trusted Saul, but subsequently in Acts the two men minister together. Centuries later, Christian authors began to speculate that Saul and Barnabas were classmates who studied

8. 1 Macc 15:15–24 describes a second-century-BCE letter sent by the Roman senate to a number of regions, including Cyprus (15:23), promising protection for Jews. Dio Cassius (writing c. 230 CE) briefly mentions in his *Roman History* an insurrection in Cyprus (c. 117 CE), "under the leadership of a certain Artemion. There . . . two hundred and forty thousand perished, and for this reason no Jew may set foot on that island, but even if one of them is driven upon its shores by a storm he is put to death" (*Hist. Rom.* 68. 32.2–3; E. Cary, LCL). See Schürer, *History of the Jewish People*, 1:531–32.

9. Ezek 44:10–17 limits to Zadokite priests the honor of offering sacrifices to the LORD in the inner sanctuary. The Levites are relegated to the lower status of helpers of the Zadokites. See the detailed article by Rehm, "Levites and Priests," 4:297–310.

under Gamaliel. Acts, however, contains no such information. We simply do not know whether they knew each other prior to the event described in Acts 9:26–27. What we do know is that their personalities differed substantially.

Barnabas was a mediator; Saul was a firebrand. Luke first mentions Saul in Acts 7:58—8:3, where he describes Saul's participation in the murder of Stephen and his subsequent persecution of Christians. His radical conversion on the road to Damascus did not change his personality or his zeal. Saul's proclamation of Jesus in Jerusalem stirred strife in the city and resulted in a Jewish plot to kill him—much as he had experienced earlier in Damascus (Acts 9:23–25, 29–30). When the other followers of Jesus learned of the conspiracy to kill Saul, they sent him back to his hometown of Tarsus (Acts 9:29–30). Interestingly, after he left, "the church throughout Judea, Galilee, and Samaria had peace and was built up" (9:31).

Luke briefly dangles this detail of Saul as troublemaker in his narrative and then proceeds to tell the story in Acts 10 of Peter's vision of unclean animals in a sheet and his subsequent journey to Caesarea to preach the gospel to gentiles at the house of Cornelius. So important is this transition in the narrative of Acts that Luke not only tells the story of Peter preaching to God-fearing gentiles in Caesarea, but he also recounts Peter describing the entire event to Jewish Christians in Jerusalem who objected to his actions (Acts 11). Their stunned amazement reveals a great deal about the resistance they felt toward gentiles joining the Jesus movement: "When they heard this, they were silenced. And they praised God, saying, 'Then God has given even to the Gentiles the repentance that leads to life'" (11:18).

Innovative Leader in Antioch

Increasingly, Acts focuses on the gospel going to non-Jews outside of Judea. Acts 11:19 says some of the Christians who fled Jerusalem preached the gospel to Jews in Phoenicia, Cyprus, and Antioch—but not to gentiles. Acts 11:20–21, however, adds that a few Christians from Cyprus and Cyrene also began to evangelize gentiles in Antioch, a city where such activity was more likely to happen than in Jerusalem.

Syrian Antioch, commonly called Antioch on the Orontes (or Antioch the Beautiful or Antioch the Great), was the third largest city in the

Roman Empire. Only Rome and Alexandria exceeded its population.[10] Antioch was a wealthy city known for its architectural beauty and cultural achievements. From the time Seleucus I founded it in 300 BCE, Jews made up a significant percent of the population. According to Josephus, many Jews congregated in the city, because they enjoyed citizens' rights and could practice their religion without interference (*J.W.* 7.43–44). He adds, "they were constantly attracting to their religious ceremonies multitudes of Greeks, and these they had in some measure incorporated with themselves" (*J.W.* 7.45; Thackeray, LCL).[11] Jews in Antioch had more social interaction with gentiles than did most Jews in Judea, and the fledgling Christian movement in Antioch experienced less tension over Jewish food laws and the practice of circumcision.[12] But the apostles resided in Jerusalem, where such tensions remained high.

When word of the gentile conversions in Antioch reached Jerusalem, the news caused consternation for some—in spite of Peter's visit to the household of Cornelius in Acts 10. Jewish Christians from Cyprus and Cyrene had taken independent initiative in preaching to gentiles. This initiative held the potential for considerable tension, and at this important point in the story, Barnabas returns to the narrative of Acts.

> News of this came to the ears of the church in Jerusalem, and they sent Barnabas to Antioch. When he came and saw the grace of God, he rejoiced, and he exhorted them all to remain faithful to the Lord with steadfast devotion; for he was a good man, full of the Holy Spirit and of faith. And a great many people were brought to the Lord. Then Barnabas went to Tarsus to look for Saul, and when he had found him, he brought him to Antioch. So it was that for an entire year they met with the church and taught a great many people, and it was in Antioch that the disciples were first called "Christians." (Acts 11:22–26)

10. For a good description of Antioch and characteristics of its Jewish population, see Longenecker, "Antioch of Syria," 8–21. For a book on the city, see Downey, *History of Antioch in Syria.*

11. Josephus says of the Jews, "it was in Antioch that they specially congregated, partly owing to the greatness of that city, but mainly because the successors of King Antiochus had enabled them to live there in security" and "granted them citizen rights on an equality with the Greeks" (*J.W.* 7.44; Thackeray, LCL). See also Kraling, "Jewish Community at Antioch," 130–60; and Meeks and Wilken, *Jews and Christians in Antioch.*

12. Cohen, "Crossing the Boundary and Becoming a Jew," 13–33; Hill, *Hellenists and Hebrews,* 118–21; Sanders, "Jewish Association with Gentiles and Galatians ii. 11–14," 170–88; and Dunn, "Incident at Antioch (Gal. ii. 11–18)," 129–82.

The Jerusalem apostles so respected this Jew from Cyprus that they commissioned him to oversee the first mixed-race church. Barnabas journeyed to Antioch, investigated the situation, and experienced joy over gentiles joining the church. This passage focuses on Barnabas's skills as a preacher and his effectiveness as a leader, not on his benevolence. Now he was not merely giving money to the Jerusalem apostles but was himself the main leader of a thriving, diverse congregation with all its potential and problems.

After an unspecified amount of time working in Antioch, Barnabas traveled north to Tarsus to recruit the fiery, former rabbi Saul to assist him. In the multi-ethnic congregation at Antioch, followers of Jesus began to see themselves not as an offshoot of the synagogue but as a separate entity. Consequently, people started calling them Christians.[13] At this stage, Barnabas was clearly the main leader. Acts 11:27–30 specifies that, during a time of famine, the Christians in Antioch took a collection for believers in Judea, "sending it to the elders by Barnabas and Saul" (not "Saul and Barnabas").[14]

When they returned to Antioch, they brought with them from Jerusalem a cousin of Barnabas: "John, whose other name was Mark" (12:25).[15] Like Barnabas, Mark belonged to a wealthy family, which is

13. See Tacitus, *Ann.* 15.44.2; Suetonius, *Nero* 16.2; Pliny, *Ep.* 10.96.1–13 for gentile use of the term Christian.

14. Josephus reports a famine during the reign of Tiberius Alexander (c. 46–48 CE). Alexander's mother, Helena, provided aid for people in Jerusalem: "Now her coming was very advantageous for the people of Jerusalem; for at that time the city was hard pressed by famine and many were perishing from want of money to purchase what they needed. Queen Helena sent some of her attendants to Alexandria to buy grain for large sums and others to Cyprus to bring a cargo of dried figs. Her attendants speedily returned with these provisions, which she thereupon distributed among the needy. She has thus left a very great name that will be famous forever among our whole people for her benefaction. When her son Izates learned of the famine, he likewise sent a great sum of money to the leaders of the Jerusalemites" (*Ant.* 20.51–53, L. H. Feldman, LCL).

15. Col 4:10 calls Mark the ἀνεψιός of Barnabas, which could mean cousin or perhaps nephew. Paul later mentions Mark in his list of associates: "Epaphras, my fellow prisoner in Christ Jesus, sends greetings to you, and so do Mark, Aristarchus, Demas, and Luke, my fellow workers" (Phlm 23–24). Tradition indicates a close relationship between Mark and Peter. 1 Pet 5:13 mentions Mark as being Peter's son. Eusebius quotes Papias as saying Mark was a disciple of Peter: "And the presbyter used to say this, 'Mark became Peter's interpreter and wrote accurately all that he remembered, not, indeed, in order, of the things said or done by the Lord. For he had not heard the Lord, nor had he followed him, but later on, as I said, followed Peter, who used to give

evident from the description of his mother's house in Acts 12:12–13. This passage reports Peter going "to the house of Mary, the mother of John whose other name was Mark, where many had gathered and were praying. When he knocked at the outer gate, a maid named Rhoda came to answer." Mary had servants and owned a home large enough to host the prayer meeting; she was an honorable woman. Unfortunately, her son abandoned Barnabas and Saul during their first missionary journey (13:13), which ultimately caused the dissolution of this dynamic team (15:37–39).

Eclipsed by Paul

After Barnabas and Saul returned to Antioch, they led the first planned missionary journey recorded in Acts (c. 47 CE).

> Now in the church at Antioch there were prophets and teach-
> ers: Barnabas, Simeon who was called Niger, Lucius of Cyrene,
> Manaen a member of the court of Herod the ruler, and Saul.
> While they were worshiping the Lord and fasting, the Holy
> Spirit said, "Set apart for me Barnabas and Saul for the work to
> which I have called them." Then after fasting and praying they
> laid their hands on them and sent them off. (Acts 13:1–3)

As the group's main leader, Barnabas's name appears first in the list; Saul's name is last. Luke's description of the other leaders illustrates the diversity of the Christians in Antioch. Simeon is called *Niger* (Νίγερ), a latinized term meaning dark complexioned (in the New Testament it occurs only in this passage). Perhaps Simeon came from northern Africa, as did Lucius of Cyrene. The northern Africa connection is interesting in light of Acts 11:20, which identifies Jewish followers of Jesus from Cyprus and Cyrene as the first to proclaim the gospel to gentiles in Antioch.

Manaen represents wealthier members of the church who enjoyed higher status in Antioch. As a member of Herod's court, he was political-ly well connected. That Barnabas—and not the more socially significant Manaen—has pride of place in this list of church leaders also provides a hint of the dignity given to this Cypriot.

---

teaching as necessity demanded but not making, as it were, an arrangement of the Lord's oracles, so that Mark did nothing wrong in thus writing down single points as he remembered them. For to one thing he gave attention, to leave out nothing of what he had heard and to make no false statements in them'" (*Hist. eccl.* 3.39.15, K. Lake, LCL).

Not surprisingly, Barnabas begins the first missionary journey by taking Saul and John Mark to his homeland of Cyprus. His social and religious connections there provided opportunities to meet with local Jews in synagogues and to proclaim the message of Jesus.

> So, being sent out by the Holy Spirit, they went down to Seleucia; and from there they sailed to Cyprus. When they arrived at Salamis, they proclaimed the word of God in the synagogues of the Jews. And they had John also to assist them. (Acts 13:4–5)

The port city of Seleucia, fifteen miles southwest of Antioch near the mouth of the Orontes River, provided a transit point to Salamis on the east coast of Cyprus. Although later Christian authors claim Salamis was the hometown of Barnabas, Acts mentions nothing about such matters. Salamis was one of the two major cities of Cyprus, and in former times it had been the capital. But the Romans had taken over the island in 58 BCE. In 22 BCE, Cyprus became a senatorial province, with the proconsul living in New Paphos on the southwest side of the island, a location closer to Rome than the eastern port of Salamis.

Luke quickly advances the narrative to get the three missionaries from Salamis to Paphos. He does not divulge how long the trip took, or whether they conducted evangelistic efforts across the southern part of the island. Instead, he focuses on events at Paphos, where they gain access to an influential man, the proconsul.

> When they had gone through the whole island as far as Paphos, they met a certain magician, a Jewish false prophet, named Bar-Jesus. He was with the proconsul, Sergius Paulus, an intelligent man, who summoned Barnabas and Saul and wanted to hear the word of God. But the magician Elymas[16] (for that is the translation of his name) opposed them and tried to turn the proconsul away from the faith. (Acts 13:6–8)

---

16. Jesus, the Greek form of the Hebrew name Joshua, was fairly common among Jewish people. Ironically, in this story, a magician named Bar-Jesus ("Son of Jesus") seeks to prevent Sergius Paulus from believing the message Barnabas and Saul proclaim about Jesus of Nazareth. Luke's explanation of the meaning of *Elymas* is problematic. *Elymas* is not a Greek word and is not a translation of Bar-Jesus. Luke seems to indicate the name means μάγος = magician. Some commentators speculate *Elymas* comes from the Arabic *'Alim*, which means wise man. The *Magi* from the east in Matthew 2 were astrologers who predicted the coming Messiah. But why a Roman ruler would use an obscure Semitic nickname to describe Bar-Jesus is unclear.

That Sergius Paulus would value advice from a magician is not surprising. Magic was widely practiced and highly respected in the first century.[17] Educated leaders often consulted priests, who predicted the future by interpreting dreams, the movements of stars, the entrails of sacrificial animals, the way flocks of birds flew, and how smoke rose from incense. Saul, however, challenges the resistance of Bar-Jesus[18] and pronounces judgment on the magician.

> But Saul, also known as Paul, filled with the Holy Spirit, looked intently at him and said, "You son of the devil, you enemy of all righteousness, full of all deceit and villainy, will you not stop making crooked the straight paths of the Lord? And now listen—the hand of the Lord is against you, and you will be blind for a while, unable to see the sun." Immediately mist and darkness came over him, and he went about groping for someone to lead him by the hand. When the proconsul saw what had happened, he believed, for he was astonished at the teaching about the Lord. (Acts 13:9–12)

Sergius Paulus, much impressed by this display of supernatural power, believes the message about Jesus.

At this point in the Acts narrative, Saul begins to emerge as the dominant force in gentile evangelization. Moreover, for the first time, Luke indicates Saul was also known as Paul, which could have been his *cognomen*—last name.[19] For Paul, who identifies himself proudly as a member of the tribe of Benjamin (Phil 3:5), Saul was an honorable name; because Saul, the first king of Israel, was from the tribe of Benjamin. However,

---

17. Philo of Alexandria, a faithful Jew, says the following about magic. "Now the true magic, the scientific vision by which the facts of nature are presented in a clearer light, is felt to be a fit object for reverence and ambition and is carefully studied not only by ordinary persons but by kings and the greatest kings, and particularly those of the Persians, so much so that it is said that no one in that country is promoted to the throne unless he has first been admitted into the caste of the Magi" (*Spec. Laws* 3.100; Colson, LCL). For gentile writers mentioning Jewish magic, see Strabo, *Geog.* 16.2.39; Pliny, *Nat. Hist.* 30.11.

18. The fifth-century Acts of Barnabas 23 claims Bar-Jesus incited a Jewish mob to murder Barnabas during a subsequent missionary trip to Cyprus. Later Christians loved to connect people and events, filling in details and inventing backstory.

19. Romans typically had three names (e.g., Lucius Valerius Flaccus). The *praenomen* was a name chosen by one's parents, the *nomen* was a family or clan name, and the *cognomen*, which began as a nickname (often based on some physical characteristic), was initially used to differentiate between men having the same name, but later became a family name. Luke does not specify Paul's *praenomen* or *nomen*.

the apostle always uses the name Paul in his letters—which address predominantly gentile audiences. Apparently, Saul was his Jewish name, and Paul was perhaps his Roman name. Or, perhaps Sergius Paulus became a benefactor of Paul and Barnabas, and Paul adopted a new name out of respect for his patron. We simply do not know.

What does become apparent is that, beginning in Acts 13:9, Paul plays the dominant role in the narrative; and Barnabas starts to fade into the background. They journey north to the mainland of what today is south central Turkey until they reach Pamphylia, and at this point, Paul emerges as the main preacher. Also at this time in the story, John Mark abandons them and returns to his mother in Jerusalem: "Then Paul and his companions set sail from Paphos and came to Perga in Pamphylia. John, however, left them and returned to Jerusalem" (Acts 13:13). His desertion later causes a major split between Barnabas and Paul, which leads to the complete disappearance of Barnabas from the narrative. Luke's shift in leadership emphasis is clear in Acts 13:13: instead of "Barnabas and Saul," now it is "Paul and his companions."

Most likely, the three missionaries did not have a developed itinerary when they left Antioch but figured things out as they went along. Acts does not specify why they journeyed from Paphos to Pamphylia. Perhaps their interaction with Sergius Paulus led to their decision to take a ship to Pamphylia.[20] Luke does not say. But Paul now overshadows his mentor. Paul, not Barnabas, delivers the sermon in the synagogue in Antioch of Pisidia (Acts 13:14–41).[21] Beginning in 13:42 Luke uses "Paul and Barnabas," reversing the prior order of their names (13:42, 43, 46, 50; 14:1, 15:2, 22, 35, 36). However, in three succeeding verses, Luke again places Barnabas's name first (14:14; 15:12, 25).

In the city of Lystra, Paul heals a lame man, which incites residents in the area to identify the duo as deities: "Barnabas they called Zeus, and Paul they called Hermes, because he was the chief speaker" (14:12). In this context, where the people of Lystra believe Barnabas

20. Mitchell, "Population and land in Roman Galatia," 1053–81; see n134 on 1074.

21. On their missionary journey, Paul and Barnabas speak to both Jews and God-fearers (13:16, 26). God-fearers were apparently gentiles who were attracted to the higher moral and ethical teaching proclaimed at the synagogues but balked at being circumcised and following kosher food laws in order to become proselyte Jews. Many of the converts on the missionary journey appear to have been God-fearers. See Levinskaya, "God-fearers: Epigraphic Evidence," 51–82; "God-fearers and the Cult of the Most High God," 83–103; "God-fearers: The Bosporan Kingdom," 105–16; and "God-fearers: The Literary Evidence," 117–26.

to be Zeus,[22] the main deity of the Greek *pantheon* (their entire set of gods and goddesses),[23] and the more talkative Paul to be his messenger, Hermes, the narration returns briefly to the previous pattern: "When the apostles Barnabas and Paul heard of it . . ." (14:14).[24] A similar reversal occurs during the Jerusalem Council in Acts 15: "The whole assembly kept silence, and listened to Barnabas and Paul as they told of all the signs and wonders that God had done through them among the Gentiles" (15:12). Barnabas's position as the main leader returns here, as it does in the letter written to gentile Christians by the apostles: "we have decided unanimously to choose representatives and send them to you, along with our beloved Barnabas and Paul . . ." (15:25). However, Paul's eclipse of Barnabas is well under way in Acts 14.

Paul and Barnabas returned to Antioch and remained there for some time (Acts 14:26–28). But as stories of their success among the gentiles spread through the churches, conservative Jewish Christians from Jerusalem journeyed to Antioch to insist that gentiles must follow the laws of Moses: "Unless you are circumcised according to the custom of Moses, you cannot be saved" (Acts 15:1). According to Acts, the ensuing debate over the legitimacy of the preaching of Barnabas and Paul on the first missionary journey resulted in the convening of a meeting in Jerusalem to consider gentile salvation.

Paul and Barnabas went from Antioch to Jerusalem to argue their case that gentiles did not need to obey the laws of Moses. They successfully defended their version of the gospel during a protracted debate, primarily by recounting stories of God doing miracles among the gentiles. Vindicated, they returned to Antioch with an official letter from the Jerusalem apostles.

> The brothers, both the apostles and the elders, to the believers of Gentile origin in Antioch and Syria and Cilicia, greetings. Since we have heard that certain persons who have gone out from us, though with no instructions from us, have said things to disturb you and have unsettled your minds, we have decided unanimously to choose representatives and send them to you, along

22. Centuries later, Chrysostom claimed Barnabas was the more stately of the pair, so the people of Lystra called him Zeus (*Catena* 235).

23. In Greek, πᾶν means *all* and θεός means *god*. Pantheon designates all of their gods—not to be confused with the Pantheon, a famous building in Rome.

24. For details on Lystra and the identification of Barnabas and Paul with Zeus and Hermes, see Witherington, *Grace in Galatia*, 420–23.

> with our beloved Barnabas and Paul, who have risked their lives
> for the sake of our Lord Jesus Christ. We have therefore sent
> Judas and Silas, who themselves will tell you the same things
> by word of mouth. For it has seemed good to the Holy Spirit
> and to us to impose on you no further burden than these essen-
> tials: that you abstain from what has been sacrificed to idols and
> from blood and from what is strangled and from fornication. If
> you keep yourselves from these, you will do well. Farewell. (Acts
> 15:23–29)

This compromise solution eliminated circumcision and kosher food
laws as requirements, while insisting on certain, basic behaviors from
gentiles.[25]

According to Acts 15:36–41, however, their victory soon gave way
to bitter argument over John Mark. Paul wanted to return to the places
they visited on their first journey to see how their converts were doing,
but he was emphatic about not taking John Mark.

> Barnabas wanted to take with them John called Mark. But Paul
> decided not to take with them one who had deserted them in
> Pamphylia and had not accompanied them in the work. The
> disagreement became so sharp that they parted company; Barn-
> abas took Mark with him and sailed away to Cyprus. But Paul
> chose Silas and set out, the believers commending him to the
> grace of the Lord. He went through Syria and Cilicia, strength-
> ening the churches. (Acts 15:37–41)[26]

Two strong personalities collided over Barnabas's cousin, and they went
separate ways. To describe their division, Luke employs the verb *apocho-
rizo* (ἀποχωρίζω), which Matt 19:39 uses to describe divorce ("what God
has joined together, let no one *separate*").

---

25. According to 1 Cor 8:1–13, Paul tolerated eating food sacrificed to idols under some circumstances. NT scholars have long explored such tensions between Acts
and Paul's letters. I have chosen to keep such explorations to a minimum in order to
prevent my study of Barnabas from becoming too lengthy and diminishing reader
interest.

26. Luke's use of imperfect verb tenses in verses 37–38 indicates an ongoing argument: Barnabas was wanting (ἐβούλετο) to take Mark; Paul was insisting (ἠξίου) they
not take one who abandoned them previously. The translation "deserted" of ἀφίστημι
in v. 38 accurately reflects the meaning of the word. Mark abandoned or deserted
them. The noun form of this word (ἀποστασία [*apostasia*]) often means apostasy in
the NT.

After Paul and Barnabas parted ways, Barnabas disappears entirely from Acts. From this point forward, Luke focuses on Paul's missionary journeys. We read nothing about the experiences of Barnabas and Mark in Cyprus. Their story remained untold until the late fifth century, when an anonymous Cypriot wrote the Acts of Barnabas (creating a history to address a current political situation). Paul became one of the most significant figures in the history of the church. Barnabas sailed into obscurity, emerging only sporadically in Christian writings.

Paul versus Barnabas

Two Pauline letters contain brief comments regarding Barnabas. In 1 Cor 9:6, Paul mentions Barnabas as a single, self-supporting missionary.

> This is my defense to those who would examine me. Do we not have the right to our food and drink? Do we not have the right to be accompanied by a believing wife, as do the other apostles and the brothers of the Lord and Cephas? Or is it only Barnabas and I who have no right to refrain from working for a living? (1 Cor 9:3–6)

Typically in his letters, Paul refers to the apostle Peter by using his Aramaic name, Cephas. In Greek, *Peter* means rock (or rocky), and in Aramaic, *Cephas* means rock (or rocky)—same name, different languages. In this passage, Paul expresses no rancor with regard to Barnabas. He merely uses his friend as an example while defending himself.

His references to Barnabas in Gal 2:1, 9, 13, however, contain mixed emotions toward his former mentor. Paul mentions Barnabas in 2:1–10 as a trusted colleague who accompanied him to Jerusalem to argue for the validity of their theological position that gentile Christians did not need to be circumcised. However, he accuses Barnabas of hypocrisy in 2:13. Unfortunately, most commentators merely assume Paul's accusation is entirely justified and do not consider the possibility Barnabas had good reasons for not supporting Paul in his controversy with Peter over not eating with gentile Christians in Antioch.

Paul's authority and integrity were under attack, and his fiery letter to the Galatians exhibits considerable frustration and anger. In this epistle, Paul lashes out at Jewish-Christian opponents who call his theology deficient. In addition to the annoyance steming from his opponents' accusations, Paul felt the sting of having his friend and coworker

Barnabas side with Peter and the other Jewish Christians in Antioch in the controversy over table fellowship with gentiles. "When Paul dictated Galatians, he erupted like a volcano, spewing forth molten accusations and condemnations. In this letter we see the apostle at his most volatile— even his most vulgar. His anger burns so hot that in a blast against Jewish Christian opponents in Gal. 5:12 he declares, 'I wish those who unsettle you would castrate themselves!'"[27] Galatians boils with overstatement and sarcasm.

Paul's honor as an apostle is at stake, and he aggressively defends himself. In his narration of events in Gal 1:11—2:14, he asserts the divine origin of his call to be an apostle and refutes any claim he was subservient to Peter (*Cephas*), James, and John. But there are subtle indications that he previously sought approval from the Jerusalem apostles for his gospel message to the gentiles. Paul finds himself in the awkward position of having to defend his own position and condemn other major Christian leaders, including Barnabas and Peter. So he overstates his importance as a member of the Antioch delegation.

At first, he refers benignly to Barnabas in Gal 2:1–10, when describing their journey from Antioch to Jerusalem, but he magnifies his leadership role. Although Barnabas probably led this delegation,[28] Paul writes as if he were the leader. Obviously, to say Barnabas led the group from Antioch would work against Paul's rhetorical strategy of emphasizing his own authority. He faces a complex set of issues.[29]

On the one hand, Paul respects the authority of the Jerusalem apostles enough to visit them to obtain an endorsement of the theology he and Barnabas developed.

> Then after fourteen years I went up again to Jerusalem with
> Barnabas, taking Titus along with me. I went up in response to

27. Cosby, *Apostle on the Edge,* 121. For more details on this topic, see Cosby, "Galatians: Red Hot Rhetoric," 296–309.

28. Martyn observes, "Luke portrays Barnabas as one of the giants in the earliest church . . . Would not such a person play in the meeting a much more important role than is given to him in Paul's account?" (*Galatians,* 216–17).

29. Scholars debate whether the event Paul describes in Gal 2 corresponds to the Jerusalem Council (c. 49 CE) described in Acts 15. Some believe the consultation with the Jerusalem apostles Paul describes in Gal 2:1–10 corresponds to the famine relief visit mentioned in Acts 11:27–30. Others believe Gal 2:1–10 recounts events occurring during the debate described in Acts 15, regarding whether or not gentile Christians need to follow the laws of Moses. For a helpful chart comparing material from Acts with what Paul says in Galatians, see Chance, *Acts,* 152–53.

> a revelation. Then I laid before them (though only in a private
> meeting with the acknowledged leaders) the gospel that I pro-
> claim among the Gentiles, *in order to make sure that I was not
> running, or had not run, in vain.* (Gal 2:1–2, emphasis mine)

On the other hand, to increase his own stature, Paul distances himself
from any notion that he does the bidding of Peter, James, and John. Indeed, his description of these men borders on sarcasm: "And from those
who were supposed to be acknowledged leaders (what they actually were
makes no difference to me; God shows no partiality)—those leaders contributed nothing to me" (Gal 2:6).

He insists the Jerusalem apostles recognized that God called him
(and Barnabas) to bring the good news to gentiles—although he primarily keeps the focus on himself.

> On the contrary, when they saw that *I* had been entrusted with
> the gospel for the uncircumcised, just as Peter had been en-
> trusted with the gospel for the circumcised (for he who worked
> through Peter making him an apostle to the circumcised also
> worked through *me* in sending *me* to the Gentiles), and when
> James and Cephas and John, who were acknowledged pillars,
> recognized the grace that had been given to *me*, they gave to
> *Barnabas and me* the right hand of fellowship, agreeing that *we*
> should go to the Gentiles and they to the circumcised. [10] They
> asked only one thing, that *we* remember the poor, which was
> actually what *I* was eager to do. (Gal 2:7–10, emphasis mine)

James and Cephas and John agreed God entrusted Paul (or was it Barnabas
and Paul?) with the gospel message to gentiles,[30] and the Jerusalem
apostles were to take the gospel primarily to Jews. But Paul does not stop
with claiming equality in this division of labor. He proceeds to describe a
situation wherein he publically condemned Peter for hypocrisy.

When Peter initially had come to Antioch, where Barnabas and Paul
provided leadership, he apparently enjoyed table fellowship with gentile
Christians. Peter's initial comfort with this setting matches the description of his interactions with gentiles following his vision of the unclean

---

30. Paul's word for gentiles in 2:7 is ἀκροβυστία, which literally means foreskin.
Although this designation might seem indelicate for many English speakers today, it is
not an uncommon expression in the NT. For example, in Acts 11:3, Jewish Christians
in Jerusalem complain about Peter eating with gentiles, saying, εἰσῆλθες πρὸς ἄνδρας
ἀκροβυστίαν ἔχοντας καὶ συνέφαγες αὐτοῖς ("you came to men having a foreskin and
ate with them"; see similar uses of ἀκροβυστία in Rom 2:25–27; 3:30; 4:9–12; 1 Cor
7:18–19; Gal 5:6; 6:15; Eph 2:11; and Col 2:13; 3:11). In Gal 2:8–9, he uses τὰ ἔθνη.

animals in a sheet lowered from heaven and his subsequent stay with God-fearers in the household of Cornelius in Caesarea (Acts 10–11). Subsequently, however, complications arose in Antioch when messengers came from James. Paul does not state the nature of the message, but he does say Peter began to separate from gentile Christians. Paul publically confronted Peter over the matter.

> But when Cephas came to Antioch, I opposed him to his face, because he stood self-condemned; for until certain people came from James, he used to eat with the Gentiles. But after they came, he drew back and kept himself separate for fear of the circumcision faction. And the other Jews joined him in this hypocrisy, so that even Barnabas was led astray by their hypocrisy. But when I saw that they were not acting consistently with the truth of the gospel, I said to Cephas before them all, "If you, though a Jew, live like a Gentile and not like a Jew, how can you compel the Gentiles to live like Jews?" (Gal 2:11–14)

Paul's brief account leaves unsaid most of the details of the situation,[31] but his assertion in v. 11 that Peter stood condemned shows how grave he took the matter to be.[32] Paul saw Peter's actions as a denial of their previous agreement regarding the validity of the gentile mission.

However, Paul faced another serious problem. His readers would want to know why Barnabas did not side with Paul in this controversy. After all, Barnabas was heavily invested in taking the gospel message to gentiles and had worked alongside Paul for years. Yet he took Peter's side of the argument. Obviously, the situation was more complex than Paul indicates. Barnabas would not turn against him capriciously. What was it about the message from James that caused Barnabas to stop eating with gentiles? The matter must have been grave.

Scholars advance different theories regarding the content of the message from James.[33] Some claim that the delegates from Jerusalem

---

31. Paul's use of the imperfect form in v. 12 (συνήσθιεν) implies Peter had an ongoing practice of eating with gentiles. The use of two more imperfects in v. 12 seems to indicate Peter's process of separating himself from gentile Christians was not sudden (ὑπέστελλεν καὶ ἀφώριζεν). Most likely Paul would have used the aorist tense if Peter abruptly separated himself. In other words, Paul did not confront the situation immediately. Was he not in Antioch when Peter began to withdraw, or did his resentment grow until it reached the point he condemned Peter's actions? We simply do not know.

32. He uses the perfect passive participle κατεγνωσμένος of the verb καταγινώσκω.

33. For a detailed study of James and the transition of leadership in the Jerusalem church, see Bauckham, "James and the Jerusalem Church," 415–80.

were shocked by the casual way in which Jewish Christians in Antioch ate with gentiles, and they pressured Peter and the others to live more consistently with their Jewish heritage. But this hypothesis does not coincide with what we know about Barnabas. Perhaps James told Peter that word had reached Jerusalem he was eating with gentiles, which was causing turmoil among the more conservative Jewish Christians and was complicating the apostles' attempts to evangelize Jews. This scenario makes more sense. If true, then Peter and the other Jewish Christians in Antioch modified their eating habits because of a negative impact their actions were having on evangelization efforts in Jerusalem.

Another possibility is that James reported increased persecution of Jewish Christians by zealots in Judea. Beginning in the mid-forties, Jewish zealots became increasingly active, targeting those whom they saw as sympathizers with gentiles.[34] If this scenario is correct, Peter decided to cease table fellowship with gentiles as a way of protecting Jewish Christians in Judea from harm by zealots who would retaliate against Jews whom they believed were fraternizing with gentiles.

Whatever the situation, conditions were significant enough that Barnabas joined Peter and the other Jewish Christians. Paul labels their behavior hypocrisy, but the matter was more complex than he implies. Paul was inflexible. For him, it was a matter of principle. Barnabas, more pragmatic and sensitive to Peter's dilemma, rejected Paul's no-compromise stance. Barnabas viewed compromise as necessary in this situation. Although gentile evangelization was the main focus of his work, he was sympathetic to the problems faced by Peter, James and John. Paul felt betrayed by his former colleague.

Barnabas opposed Paul, with whom he had more in common. And Christian writers almost universally condemn his choice. Although scholars propose a variety of explanations for the nature of the debate to which Paul alludes in Gal 2:11–14, they consistently assume the validity of Paul's accusation that Barnabas was led astray by the hypocrisy of Peter and the other Jews. If we could hear Barnabas's version of events, however, we might reach a different conclusion. If all of the Jewish Christians in Antioch, including Barnabas, disagreed with Paul, something more than mere hypocrisy was at issue.

34. According to Josephus, Tiberius Julius Alexander (procurator of Judea from 46 to 48 CE) crucified James and Simon, sons of Judas of Galilee, because of their role in a tax revolt (*Ant.* 20.102). Josephus describes the zealots' aversion to paying taxes in *J.W.* 2.118; *Ant.* 18.23.

Compromise is not necessarily a negative word. In the course of human interactions, conflicts regularly arise. Although bridge-burners often make a larger impact on history than bridge-builders, their legacy frequently creates additional conflict. Mediators like Barnabas reduce hostility and facilitate long-term solutions that take seriously the concerns of both sides. In situations like the present-day, protracted conflict between Greek and Turkish Cypriots, the approach of Barnabas would be more constructive than a winner-take-all philosophy. Listening to the sad tales of the enemy, and feeling empathy instead of antipathy, leads to greater understanding and opens doors for creative solutions involving compromise by both sides.

Harold Evans beautifully makes this point. "At all levels of human experience—between nations, within nations, in industry and social relationships—bridge-builders are desperately needed to lead men out of the jungle of conflict, fear and suspicion into the garden of peace."[35] Unfortunately, I discovered that the New Testament image of Barnabas as a bridge-builder is largely lost in the history of traditions that developed about him. As later leaders created new histories of Barnabas, they did so as a means of addressing conditions in their own time periods.

35. Evans, "Barnabas the Bridge-Builder," 50.

CHAPTER FOUR

Early Creation of History
about Barnabas

One of the lovely aspects of living in Cyprus is the opportunity to learn directly from Eastern Orthodox Christians. Father Gennadios, the gracious abbot of the Monastery of Archangel Michael, explained much about Orthodox spirituality and told me the following regarding Barnabas: Barnabas's sister was the wife of the Apostle Peter; John Mark was Barnabas's nephew, because Mark's mother, Mary, was the sister of Barnabas; and Barnabas's brother was the first bishop of the British islands. As I listened, I knew I would spend a long time sorting out where such traditions arose. In all my years of studying the New Testament and the early church, I had never before heard this information.

The more we spoke with Cypriots about Barnabas, the more details we heard—including many names of individuals and explanations of who was related to whom. Of course, we heard a variety of claims—some of them contradictory. Most people told only a few things about Barnabas, but *all* mentioned the imperial privileges granted to Archbishop Anthemios because of Barnabas. They *all* explained that Barnabas appeared to Anthemios in the late fifth century and told the archbishop where to find his body. This assertion was the consistent thread that held together the diverse tapestry. But what is the source for this claim? Rarely did anyone mention the origins of the traditions—it was not a concern for them, no matter how fantastical the assertions.[1]

1. For a popularized presentation of traditions about Barnabas, see Stylianou, *Apostle Varnavas*. Although he typically cites where he gets material taken from the New Testament, he almost never states where he gets the later traditions.

The modern stories about Barnabas include material concerning his family of origin and his early years: He was born and raised in Salamis, Cyprus, to a rich, aristocratic family of Levites who moved to Jerusalem when Barnabas was an adolescent. There he became a friend of Saul of Tarsus when they were both students of Gamalial, studying the laws of Moses. We also heard that Barnabas was the brother of Mary, the mother of John Mark, who owned a house in Jerusalem where Jesus ate repeatedly. In Mary's home was an upper room where Jesus ate the last supper with his disciples, and in this same room the Holy Spirit descended on the day of Pentecost.

According to modern stories, Barnabas first met Jesus when he observed Jesus heal a man; and, thereafter, Barnabas became a disciple. Descriptions of Barnabas, which are absent in the New Testament, include the following: he spoke more with actions than with words; he was full of charm and love and had an imposing and majestic appearance, as evidenced by the people at Lystra calling him Zeus (Acts 14:12). Honestly, I sometimes ponder why legends about Barnabas include material about how handsome he was, given the claim that he was a virtuous, virgin apostle of Christ. I never figured out why traditions about monks need to stress their good looks.

Modern stories stress Barnabas's generosity (he sold his estates in Salamis and Jerusalem because of his love for Christ), his missionary activities (he preached the gospel in Rome and Alexandria while Jesus was still alive), and his positions of leadership (he was the leader of the 70 disciples sent out by Jesus in Luke 10:1, and he was selected along with Paul by elders at Antioch [during a Sunday supper] to go on the first missionary journey). Such stories fill in details missing from the account in Acts: The Holy Spirit spoke through the prophet Agabus to send the missionaries, and this meeting took place in the house of Nicephorus, who led Barnabas from Tarsus to Antioch. Additional details include the following: Barnabas, Paul, and John Mark boarded a ship owned by Kallinikos, whose daughter, Calliope, was abducted along with her nanny Euridice and sold as slaves to Sergius Paulus at Paphos. Calliope became a friend of Julia, daughter of Paulus; and Euridice took care of both girls.

I also heard that Barnabas led Paul and John Mark to Cyprus, because, as leader of the first missionary journey, he chose to go to his own country. That detail may be deduced clearly from the Acts narrative. But Orthodox story tellers delight in adding further names and connections.

The missionaries went first to the family home of Barnabas in Salamis, where they preached Jesus. His family, including his brother Aristovoulos, became Christians. We heard that Barnabas preached in his home synagogue at Salamis with mixed results. Those who believed his message began meeting at the home of Aristovoulos, whom Barnabas appointed to be an elder in the new church, and also Aristion. However, fanatic Jews, led by Ruvaim, came to Cyprus from Jerusalem and strongly opposed Barnabas and Paul.

All of these connections were new to me. I heard that Barnabas preached next in Kition, where Lazarus and Martha lived (Cypriots have another set of stories about Lazarus fleeing to Cyprus to escape vicious Jews in Jerusalem, and in Larnaca is the ancient Church of St. Lazarus with the supposed tomb of Lazarus). I also heard that Barnabas and Paul ordained Lazarus as an elder and established a church in Kition, but frenzied Jews forced them to leave. Along the road, Barnabas and Paul met Theonas (or Theodoros) and Iraklidios at Tamassos, men who immediately became Christians and renounced their estates. Iraklidios guided them to the Marathasa Valley, where St. John Lambadistis lived. We spent time in the lovely Monastery of St. John Lampadistis in Kalopanayiotis, where the man was supposedly baptized in the Marathasa River. Today there is a small chapel with holy water and wall paintings dedicated to Barnabas and Paul.

Modern stories add more details to the Acts account of Barnabas and Saul going to Paphos, where they met Sergius Paulus (for example, the Synagogue council summoned them to preach their gospel message and then judged them to be heretics and had them whipped). Sometimes physical objects are used to verify certain claims. For example, beside the remains of *Chrysopolitissa* Basilica in Paphos is a rock pillar where Paul was supposedly whipped with thirty-nine lashes. The pillar dates from many years after Paul, but people pay little attention to that detail. According to traditions, Sergius Paulus summoned Barnabas and Paul when he learned they were Roman citizens. Further additions include the belief that when Paulus became a Christian he returned Calliope to her parents.

FIGURE 12

**So-called Paul's Pillar is at the left—in front of the tree—
on the grounds of *Panagia Chrisopolitissa* in Paphos.**

Trajectories of sinless saintliness continue to the present day. We heard that Barnabas and Paul parted company over John Mark, but it was not out of any rancor but as a means of doing the work of Christ more effectively. The two apostles realized they could reach more countries for Christ if they went different directions, but they remained close friends.

Whereas Acts remains silent about the details of Barnabas returning to Cyprus with John Mark, traditions fill in many more details. For example, Aristion and Timon gave them hospitality at Kormakitis, and both of these men became Christians after Barnabas healed Timon. And Barnabas was consecrated bishop of Salamis and archbishop of Cyprus. Afterward, he was arrested in Salamis when Elymas incited a Jewish mob against him. They beat Barnabas and stoned him and prepared a fire to burn his body. While being stoned to death, Barnabas prayed for the Christians of Cyprus and also for the souls of his attackers. Miraculously, the fire blew out when the mob tried to burn his body, so Barnabas's relics remained intact (some Cypriots told us that Barnabas was burned, but God restored the body from the ashes). When the attackers left, Mark and friends came and buried the body underneath a carob tree. On his chest they placed his Gospel of Matthew, which Barnabas had translated into Greek from Matthew's Aramaic original. Mark then fled to Alexandria.

The stories go on to draw from traditions dating back to *Laudatio Barnabae apostoli*, recounting how Barnabas appeared 400 years later to Anthemios in a vision, during a time of great need. He revealed to Archbishop Anthemios the location of the saint's body under a carob tree and told him that a copy of Matthew would be on his chest. We also heard that, although the place of Barnabas's burial had long ago been forgotten, local people knew of the special nature of the location and called the carob tree the place of healing, because the sick would go to this place to be healed. In visions, Barnabas told Anthemios to take the Gospel of Matthew to Emperor Zeno, who would grant independence to the Church of Cyprus. Anthemios, acting in obedience to the vision, retrieved the relics and the Gospel of Matthew and took them to Zeno, who sided with Cyprus against Peter, Patriarch of Antioch, and confirmed the independence of the Church of Cyprus. He also granted the three imperial privileges to Anthemios and stored the Gospel of Matthew in the Church of St. Stephen in Constantinople. Anthemios then returned to Cyprus with money from Zeno and other wealthy contributors, and he built a beautiful church and monastery to honor Barnabas and to store his relics. Unfortunately, many years later, Arab raiders destroyed Salamis and stole Barnabas's body while looting the area.

Nearly all of these stories about Barnabas arose not from the New Testament but from later traditions that continued to develop over the centuries. We became increasingly aware that traditions about saints grow over time, with Christians making more and more connections between people in their stories by adding characters and events. Traditions are not static but evolve. My task was to track down the origins of the traditions about Barnabas and to document how (and, if possible, why) they developed.

Autocephalous Church of Cyprus

I quickly determined that documents from the early church contained little for me to analyze. Only a few texts written during the first centuries of the church even mention Barnabas. Compared with interest in the apostle Paul, the word *trifling* is appropriate. Over time, however, new claims about Barnabas appeared and became imbedded in tradition, regardless of the credibility of the source. But at first, Christian writers treated Barnabas like an appendage of Paul. During the second through the fifth centuries, when Christian writers cite texts related to Barnabas, typically their comments appear either in conjunction with Paul, who is their main focus of attention, or in arguments for Trinitarian beliefs. Only near the end of the fifth century does a text emerge that begins to transform Barnabas into a central character—and it occurs in response to a political situation of great concern to Cypriots: maintaining their ecclesiastical independence. Cypriots use the term *autocephaly*.

The Greek word αὐτοκεφαλία (*autokephalia*) means "self-headed" and refers to the Cypriot church being run by its own head, not by an archbishop located off the island. Greek Cypriots belong to the larger communion of Eastern Orthodox Churches, but they are *autocephalous* and appoint their own bishops and archbishops. They often connect the independence of their church to two decisions made in the fifth century. The first, a decree by the Council of Ephesus in 431, is well documented and clearly supports the independence of the Church of Cyprus. Canon 8 of this Third Ecumenical Council reads as follows.

> The Judgment of the same Holy Synod, pronounced on the peti-
> tion presented to it by the Bishops of Cyprus . . . [who] have
> reported to us an innovation which has been introduced con-
> trary to the ecclesiastical constitutions and the Canons of the
> Holy Apostles, and which touches the liberties of all. Wherefore,
> since injuries affecting all require the more attention, as they
> cause the greater damage, and particularly when they are trans-
> gressions of an ancient custom; and since those excellent men,
> who have petitioned the Synod, have told us in writing and by
> word of mouth that the Bishop of Antioch has in this way held
> ordinations in Cyprus; therefore the Rulers of the holy churches
> in Cyprus shall enjoy, without dispute or injury, according to
> the Canons of the blessed Fathers and ancient custom, the right
> of performing for themselves the ordination of their excellent
> Bishops . . . (*NPNF*², 14: 235)

Although the bishops attending the Council of Ephesus declared Cyprus to be independent, the patriarchs at Antioch did not give up their efforts to control the island. Toward the end of the fifth century, the matter came to another crisis point for the Cypriots. Again, they won the dispute, but details surrounding the edict made in their favor about 488 by Emperor Zeno are much murkier than decisions made by the Council of Ephesus. For over four centuries, Christian writers had paid little attention to Barnabas; but suddenly, in 488, he played a central role in a highly charged, political drama in Cyprus. Obviously, aspects of the story caught my attention. But first, here is a summary of how legends about Barnabas developed during the first four centuries.

Early Christian Writers Largely Ignored Barnabas

Non-canonical, Christian texts of the first century (e.g., 1 Clement, c. 95) never mention Barnabas. Even late in the second century, the massive, five-volume *Against all Heresies* by Irenaeus (c. 180) fails to reference Barnabas. Clement of Alexandria (c. 150–215), the head of the catechetical school of Alexandria (and teacher of the significant theologian Origen), occasionally quotes a strongly anti-Semitic document called the Epistle of Barnabas,[2] which he mistakenly believed Barnabas wrote. How this text became associated with Barnabas, a Jew from the tribe of Levi, remains a mystery.[3] The gentile author of the work makes outlandish claims, such as attributing circumcision to the delusion of an evil angel: " . . . the circumcision in which they trusted has been abolished. For he declared that circumcision was not of the flesh, but they erred because an evil angel was misleading them" (*Barn.* 9.4; K. Lake, LCL).

The pervasive use of allegory in the Epistle of Barnabas leads many scholars to believe its author was educated in Alexandria, Egypt; and several details in the text reveal he wrote between 80 and 135, decades after Barnabas died.[4] But someone along the line attributed the document to

2. *Stromata* 2.6.31 (subsection 2, line 1); 2.7.35 (sb. 5, ln. 2); 2.15.67 (sb. 4, ln. 1); 2.18.84 (sb. 3, ln. 1); 2.20.116 (sb. 3, ln. 4); 5.8.51 (sb. 4, ln. 2); 5.8.51 (sb. 4, ln. 2); 5.10.63 (sb. 1, ln. 1); 6.8.64 (sb. 3, ln. 2; *Fragmenta* frag. 4, line 4; frag. 13, line 7; frag. 70, line 6).

3. See Schürer, *History of the Jewish People in the Age of Jesus Christ*, 1:551–57.

4. The author looked back on the Roman destruction of the Jerusalem temple in 70, but he also believed the Romans would have the Jews rebuild the temple, indicating a time of writing prior to 135.

> I will also speak with you concerning the Temple, and show how the wretched men [Jews] erred by putting their hope on the building, and not on the God who made them, and is the true house of God. For they consecrated him in the Temple almost like the heathen. But learn how the Lord speaks, in bringing it to naught . . . "Heaven is my throne, and the earth is my footstool, what house will you build for me . . . " Furthermore, he says again, *"Lo, they who destroyed this Temple shall themselves build it."* That is what is happening now. *For owing to the war it was destroyed by the enemy; at present even the servants of the enemy will build it up again.* (*Barn.* 16.1–4; K. Lake, LCL; emphasis mine)

Expressing a belief that Jews would rebuild the temple after the Bar Kokhba

Barnabas, and thereafter many Christians simply accepted the title at face value. Tertullian (c. 160–225) mentioned the Epistle of Barnabas in his text *On Modesty* 7.20 and added that Christians generally accepted the Epistle of Barnabas—a belief that continued for many years. The important, fourth-century Codex Sinaiticus includes the Epistle of Barnabas at the end of its collection of New Testament texts.

Origen (c. 185–254) attributes the document to Barnabas, as did his teacher, Clement.[5] Yet the controversial and prolific Origen, in spite of the vast number of his writings, only mentions Barnabas a few times. His limited interest in the man is always connected with his comments about Paul.[6]

Legends about Barnabas begin to emerge during the third century in stories attributed to Clement of Rome, who lived in the first century. The Pseudo-Clementine *Homilies*, a fanciful account about Clement, probably written in Syria,[7] places Barnabas in Rome, preaching the good news about Jesus while Jesus was still alive in Israel (*Hom.* 1.9–13).[8] In the

---

rebellion (132–36 CE) is highly unlikely. According to Cassius Dio, the Roman legions slaughtered 580,000 Jews, destroying 50 fortified cities and 985 villages (*Hist. Rom.* 69.14, 3). Hadrian burned Torah scrolls, executed Jewish scholars, rebuilt Jerusalem as a Roman polis, erected a statue of Jupiter and another of himself on the temple mount, and forbade Jews from entering the city. So it appears the enigmatic Epistle of Barnabas was written after the death of Barnabas: following the Jewish rebellion of 66–70 but before the Bar Kochba rebellion ended in 136.

5. He quotes the Epistle of Barnabas in *Contra Celsum* 1.63 (c. 248 CE) as part of his refutation of Celsus (also *Philocalia* 18.9).

6. In *Contra Celsum* 2.1, while commenting on the situation of Paul confronting Peter about not eating with Gentiles, he quotes phrases from Gal 2:11–14, including Paul's comment about Barnabas's hypocrisy in siding with the other Jews—as well as what Gal 2:9 says about the pillars at Jerusalem extending to Paul and Barnabas the right hand of fellowship. In *Fragments on the Gospel of John* (*Fragmenta in evangelium Joanis [in catenis]*) 37, line 19 and 123, line 12), he quotes Acts 13:2. *Fragments in Luke* (*Fragmenta in Lucam [in catenis]* 158, line 9 speaks of God sending Paul and Barnabas to the Gentiles as an example of his idea of the wisdom of not working alone (also *Scholia on Luke* vol. 17 p. 352, line 18). His Commentary on the Gospel of Matthew 16.8, line 178, quotes Gal 2:10 while explaining a related point. In the fragments of Origen's *Commentary on 1 Corinthians*, section 15, lines 142–43, he cites Gal 2:10 about Paul and Barnabas going to the Gentiles, and section 28, line 6, comments on 1 Cor 9:4–5. Finally, in *Fragments on Psalms*, frag. on Ps 9:6, he references Barnabas when citing Acts 14:5 about Paul trying to prevent Gentiles from offering sacrifice to Barnabas and Paul. Not much, considering the volume of Origen's writings.

7. Wirbelauer, "Clemens," 425.

8. In the Pseudo-Clementine *Recognitions* 2.4, however, Clement meets Barnabas in Alexandria and listens to him preach in that city. Also, *Recognitions* 1.60 states that

story, Clement protects Barnabas from a mob and becomes a Christian after listening to Barnabas. Soon after the conversion, Barnabas directs Clement to go to Jerusalem to meet Peter (1.15–17; 2.4).

The fictitious nature of the Pseudo-Clementine *Homilies* is obvious both by the content and style of narration. Placing Barnabas in Rome during the time of Jesus matches no historical reality. Nevertheless, in spite of the fictional nature of the story, its claims became imbedded in church tradition. As a matter of fact, the description of Barnabas recited by Cypriots each week during sacred liturgy repeats what is now an assumed truth. Orthodox websites post the following English translation of this part of their liturgy pertaining to Barnabas.

> The great glory of Cyprus, the preacher of the world,
> The first amongst the Antiochians, the architect of Christian
>   calling,
> *The renowned pioneer of Rome*, and the divine hauler[9] of the
>   nations,
> The vessel of grace, the kinsman of the Holy Spirit,
> The travelling companion of the holy and great Apostle Paul,
> *First amongst the Seventy*, equal to the Twelve.
> Let us all the faithful piously come together and crown
>   Barnabas with hymns
> To have mercy on our souls.[10] (emphasis mine)

Once stated, even in a fictional account, the idea of Barnabas being the first to preach the gospel in Rome became permanent.[11] The line in the liturgy about Barnabas being the leader of the seventy disciples sent out

---

Matthias, one of the two men put forward as possible replacements for Judas as the twelfth apostle, was also called Barnabas—which seems simply to be a mistake in the manuscript. Acts 1:23 gives the name as "Joseph called Barsabbas." Pseudo-Clementine *Epistle on Virginity* 1.6.4 includes Barnabas in a list of men who prized purity.

9. The Greek word is actually σᾰγηνεύω, which means *to take fish with a drag-net* (σαγήνη). Symbolically it means "to sweep as with a drag-net" (Liddell and Scott, *Greek–English Lexicon*). "Divine fisher of nations" is a better English translation than "divine hauler of the nations."

10. The last line of the Cyprus version reads πρεσβευει γαρ κυριω ελεηθηναι τας ψθχας υμων ("for he is an ambassador/elder to the Lord to have mercy on our souls"), which reflects the Orthodox view that saints are intercessors.

11. Later, *Vitae prophetarum, index apostolorum discipulorumque Domini* (*textus Pseudo-Dorothei*) expresses this belief: "Barnabas, the one who ministered the word with Paul, first preached Christ in Rome, thereafter became bishop of Milan" (p. 135, line 17; *TLG*, AT). This text also identifies Mark in relation to Barnabas: "Mark, the cousin of Barnabas . . . became bishop of Apolloniada" (a city in Bithynia) (p. 141, line 11; AT).

by Jesus refers to Luke 10:1 ("After this the Lord appointed seventy others and sent them on ahead of him in pairs to every town and place where he himself intended to go") and developed many years after the composition of the Pseudo-Clementine *Homilies*. The belief regarding his leadership of the seventy, although much more plausible than the "first to preach in Rome" claim, emerged slowly, bit-by-bit.

Eusebius of Caesarea (c. 263–339), the first great church historian, wrote a wide variety of documents; but he also shows very little interest in Barnabas. With one exception, he only mentions Barnabas in his *History of the Church* (c. 325) with reference to the seventy.

> Now the names of the apostles of our Savior are plain to everyone from the Gospels, but *no list of the Seventy is anywhere extant. It is said, however, that one of them was Barnabas*, and of him the Acts of the Apostles has also made special mention, and so also has Paul when writing to the Galatians. (*Ecc. Hist.* 1.12.2; LCL; emphasis mine)

> . . . the Lord gave the tradition of knowledge to James the Just and John and Peter, these gave it to the other Apostles and the other Apostles to *the seventy, of whom Barnabas also was one.* (*Ecc. Hist.* 2.1.5, LCL; emphasis mine)

Eusebius does not claim Barnabas led the seventy disciples mentioned in Luke 10:1.[12] He merely acknowledges the tradition that Barnabas was among the seventy.[13]

Furthermore, Eusebius challenges the earlier belief that Barnabas wrote the Epistle of Barnabas: "Among the books which are not genuine must be reckoned the Acts of Paul, the work entitled the Shepherd, the Apocalypse of Peter, and in addition to them the letter called of Barnabas and the so-called Teachings of the Apostles" (3.25.4; LCL). Unlike Clement of Alexandria, Eusebius judges the Epistle of Barnabas to be pseudonymous (*Ecc. His.* 6.13.6; 6.14.1).[14] Many modern Cypriots, however, seem

---

12. Also, unlike Clement of Alexandria, Eusebius calls the Epistle of Barnabas pseudonymous in *Ecc. Hist.* 3.25.4. See also 6.13.6; 14.1 where, quoting Clement's *Stomateis*, he mentions Clement using disputed books, which include the Epistle of Barnabas.

13. Eusebius refers to Paul and Barnabas being sent with famine relief to Jerusalem in *Ecc. Hist.* 2.3.3; 2.8.2; and 2.12.3.

14. In *Ecc. Hist.* 7.25, Eusebius explores the authorship of the Book of Revelation. He explains that there were a number of men named John, one of whom was John Mark—whom he identifies as an assistant to Barnabas and Paul and states that John

totally unaware of this judgment. Only the scholars with whom I spoke seemed cognizant that Barnabas did not write the Epistle of Barnabas.

Barnabas, the Trinity, and Acts 13:2

As I translated passages from the fourth century, I noticed Christian authors seldom mention Barnabas, and when they do so it is primarily in connection with their arguments for the Trinity.[15] Athanasius of Alexandria (c. 298–373), a strong defender of Trinitarian Orthodoxy, mentions Barnabas in only three passages.[16] But his use of Acts 13:2 ("the Holy Spirit said, 'Set apart for me Barnabas and Saul for the work to which I have called them'") to argue for the Trinity strongly influenced later writers. Athanasius says the Spirit took divine initiative in setting apart Barnabas and Paul for the mission. The Spirit did not ask permission from God the Father or Jesus—which shows the Spirit is co-equal with the Father and the Son. Athanasius's use of Acts 13:2 became fairly common in Trinitarian arguments.

Epiphanius (c. 310-20-c. 403), a fierce defender of Orthodoxy, was bishop of Salamis in Cyprus for nearly 40 years, beginning in 365 or 367 (later he became the archbishop of Cyprus). He—not Barnabas—was the first Cypriot to be venerated on the island.[17] For many centuries Cypriot archbishops traced their authority to Epiphanius, not Barnabas. Among the hundreds of lead seals of Cypriot archbishops cataloged by Michael Metcalf,[18] many bear the image of Epiphanius; but only one bears what is possibly the image of Barnabas. Through the centuries, Epiphanius played a far more important role in the Cypriot church than did Barnabas. This forceful leader earned quite a reputation.

Mark did not write Revelation (7.25.15). Finally, in his commentary on Isa 1:63 he includes Barnabas in a list of men who were apostles.

15. For example, Gregory of Nyssa (c. 335–95) defended Trinitarian theology, saying that Peter, Paul, and Barnabas did not say the Father, Son, and Holy Spirit are three separate substances *(Ad Graecos ex communibus notionibus* 3.1, p. 21, lines 5, 19, 22; p. 23, lines 4; 14, p. 25, line 21; p. 25, line 21; p. 28, line 23; and p. 32, line 2. *Refutatio confessionis Eunamii* section 189, line 3 mentions being instructed by Paul, Barnabas, Titus, Silas and Timothy).

16. *Testimonia e scriptura* 28.41, line 38; *Synopsis scripturae sacrae* 28.404, line 56; and *De sancta trinitate* 28.1241, line 38.

17. Von Falkenhausen, "Bishops and Monks in the Hagiography of Byzantine Cyprus," 23.

18. Metcalf, *Byzantine Cyprus 491–1191*; and *Byzantine Lead Seals from Cyprus*.

FIGURE 13

Icon of Epiphanius hanging on a wall of the Monastery Church of Apostle Barnabas, which, under Turkish occupation, is now a museum.

Following Emperor Theodosius's bans on pagan worship in the 380s, Epiphanius persecuted the non-Christians of Cyprus and destroyed their temples. His zealous destruction of shrines and his powerful preaching made a massive impact on the island. His best-known work, *Panarion* (which means medicine chest), provided medicine for those infected with heresy.

Epiphanius lived for many years in Cyprus, so I anticipated that he would be quite interested in Barnabas. He was not. His writings show scant interest in Barnabas. He comments on the Cypriot apostle a few times, mostly regarding Paul and Barnabas receiving the right hand of fellowship from the Jerusalem apostles, and Barnabas being a Levite who was called Son of Encouragement (*Panarion* 1.366). However, Epiphanius mostly mentions Barnabas in his arguments for the Trinity, where he uses Acts 13:2 as an example of the Spirit's divine prerogative (*Panarion* 3.319, 331; *Ancoratus* 68.3).[19]

Nevertheless, an interesting detail does emerge in *Index discipulorum*, where Epiphanius provides a list of apostles and specifies where they were bishops and where they died. He adopts the belief put forward in the Pseudo-Clementine *Homilies* that Barnabas was first to proclaim Jesus in Rome, and he adds a claim that Barnabas was bishop of Milan: "Barnabas, the one who ministered the word with Paul, first preached Christ in Rome. And afterward he became bishop of Milan" (118, line 14; AT). In *Panarion* 1.232, he includes Barnabas in a list of men who were part of the *seventy-two* (instead of

19. Taking another tact, in *Ancoratus* (the well anchored man) Epiphanius argues that Peter extended to Paul and Barnabas the right hand of fellowship—three witnesses to one truth (9.13).

seventy). However, he seems unaware of any belief that Barnabas led the seventy. The fact that this influential leader of the Cypriot Church shows so little interest in Barnabas, one of the co-founding apostles of the Church of Cyprus, greatly surprised me.

Another strong supporter of Trinitarian belief, Gregory of Nazianzus (c. 329–389/390), was archbishop of Constantinople in the fourth century. Although a prolific writer, he only mentions Barnabas twice—in passing.[20] Basil of Caesarea (Basil the Great; 330–79) used his erudition to defend the Trinitarian belief expressed in the Nicene Creed (one substance, *homoousios*) but revealed virtually no interest in Barnabas.[21] In several passages, he quotes Acts 13:2 when defending the Holy Spirit as a co-equal part of the Trinity.[22] Similarly, Gregory of Nyssa (c. 335–94) mentions Barnabas when quoting Acts 13:2 to validate his belief in the Trinity, but he does not expound anything about Barnabas.[23] The dearth of information about the Cypriot apostle forced me to conclude he did not command much attention from theologians of this time period.

I found a few more traditions about Barnabas in the vast writings of John Chrysostom (c. 349–407). Chrysostom, who shows much more interest than previous writers in determining what actually happened in biblical stories, mentions the name Barnabas 111 times. Many of Chrysostom's hundreds of homilies expound the writings of Paul, and he mentions Barnabas primarily in relation to Paul. The vast majority of Chrysostom's references to Barnabas occur in his sermons on the Acts of the apostles—but, again, Barnabas is a secondary character. Chrysostom explains that Barnabas, the Son of Consolation, was a kind man (Acts 11:24), which he says is obvious in the incident of giving John Mark a second chance (Acts 15:37–39).

20. Once in his funeral oration for Basil (*Funebris oratio laudem Basilii Magni Caesareae in Cappadocia episcopi* [orat. 43] 32.3) and once in *In seipsum ad patrem et Basilium magnum* (orat. 10) 35.829.

21. Basil mentions Paul and Barnabas preaching the gospel (*Asceticon magnum sive quaestiones* 31.1032, lines 18–21) and quotes 1 Cor 9:5–6 (*Asceticon magnum sive quaestiones* 31.1128, line 39 and *Regulae morales* 31.752, line 52) Acts 15:36 (*Regulae morales* 31.832, line 8) and Gal 2:10 (*De baptismo libri duo* 31.1624, line 44).

22. *De spiritu sancto*; chapter 19, sec. 1, line 47; see also *Adversus Eunomium [libri 5]* 29, p. 720, line 45.

23. *Ad Graecos ex communibus notionibus* 3.1 p. 21 line 5; p. 22, line 19; p. 23, line 4, 14; p. 25, line 21; p. 28, line 23; p. 32, line 12; and *Refutatio confessionis Eunomii* 189, line 3.

Chrysostom's veneration of saints set limits on his explanations of potentially problematic New Testament texts. For example, when describing Paul's account in Gal 2:11–13 of publically denouncing Peter, Chrysostom explains away the entire event.[24] Regarding Barnabas siding with Peter against Paul, he says he thinks what really happened was that Peter went along with Paul's rebuke of Judaizing, merely pretending to be rebuked so Paul could teach others the truth about the gospel.[25] This tendency to make the saints more saintly grows over the centuries and is very much in evidence in Cyprus today.

What proved to be more interesting for my study, however, is Chrysostom's speculation that Barnabas was an old friend of Paul—which factored into his brave decision to take Paul to the apostles in Jerusalem.[26] Later authors pick up this idea and state it not as speculation but as fact. As the tradition grew further still, writers added that Barnabas was a student of Gamaliel and studied with Paul.

I was interested to see Chrysostom showing respect for Barnabas as a leader in his commentary on Acts. For example, he explains why the Jerusalem apostles sent Barnabas to Antioch instead of choosing Paul for the job: they did not yet recognize Paul's excellence. Chrysostom says Barnabas was the main leader at this early stage (60. p. 94, lines 17–52), and he notes that initially the Cypriot's name occurs first in the text of Acts, because Paul's light was not yet shining, and he had not yet worked miracles (60. p. 205, lines 35–36). In Chrysostom's Homily on 2 Cor 8:18, where Paul speaks of sending a famous preacher along with Titus to Corinth, Chrysostom speculates that Barnabas was the preacher, because Barnabas was such a great man (61. p. 523, line 43–p. 524, line 29).

Chrysostom notices that, after the incident in Paphos where Paul blinded the Jewish magician, Luke begins to place Paul's name first—before Barnabas (*Homily 30 on Acts 13:42*). When summarizing events in Acts 14:11–15, about gentiles in Lystra considering Barnabas to be Zeus and Paul to be Hermes, Chrysostom says Barnabas's physical appearance made him appear as the more esteemed of the two (60. 224, lines 55–56). This assessment of Barnabas's stature also became imbedded in tradition. Although the New Testament provides no physical description of either

24. *In illud: In faciem ei restiti* li., p. 383, line 46–p. 384, line 12.

25. Homily 2 on Galatians (*In epistulam ad Galatas commentarius* 61. p. 633, lines 47–55). Page 573, line 51 has a bit milder version of the explanation.

26. Ἐμοὶ δοκεῖ ὁ Βαρνάβας ἄνωθεν αὐτῷ εἶναι φίλος· διὸ καὶ πάντα διηγεῖται τὰ κατ᾽ αὐτόν.—*In Acta apostolorum* (*homilia* 1–55) 60. p. 167, line 17.

Paul or Barnabas, Cypriots today confidently describe Barnabas's lordly appearance. Their beliefs, however, stem from a more developed description of Barnabas presented in a speech delivered in the sixth century (which I will describe later).[27]

Barnabas Briefly on Center Stage in Cyprus

Although Barnabas played a lesser role in the history of Cyprus than Epiphanius, the heretic hunter, during a few times of political need Barnabas emerged as a focus of intense adoration. After receiving little attention for centuries, Barnabas suddenly appeared as a powerful force in the late fifth century, when Peter the Fuller, the Monophysite[28] patriarch of Antioch, sought to extend his rule over the Church of Cyprus.[29] Peter argued before Emperor Zeno in Constantinople that, "Christianity had been taken to Cyprus from Antioch, a church of apostolic foundation, and therefore Cyprus should be subject to Antioch."[30] This development troubled Cypriot bishops. They needed to counter Peter's claims, and they found a way through Barnabas.

Paul (Benedict) Englezakis, a Cypriot scholar, explains the changing ecclesiastical landscape of the late fifth century and its significance for the Church of Cyprus. At that time, the Orthodox patriarchs who resided in important cities such as Antioch and Alexandria were swallowing up smaller, autonomous provinces. These patriarchs reasoned that the church should adopt the political organizational structure of the Empire. Peter the Fuller argued that, because the governor who controlled Cyprus resided in Antioch, the patriarch whose ecclesiastical throne was in Antioch should control the Church of Cyprus.[31] The bishop's throne was called his

27. Theodoret of Syria (c. 393–c. 457) mentions the name Barnabas 31 times, but always in connection with points he makes about Paul. Other, more minor authors of this general time period occasionally mention Barnabas, but their sporadic comments add nothing new to my investigation, so I do not summarize them.

28. Monophysites believed Jesus had only one nature (from the Greek words *mono* = one, and *physis* = nature). Emperor Zeno espoused the position articulated by the Fourth Ecumenical Council of Chalcedon in 451 that Jesus had two natures, both divine and human. Peter the Fuller and the other Monophysites (some scholars prefer the word Miaphysite) believed that in Jesus of Nazareth the divine and human natures were totally merged into one.

29. For a detailed examination of this man, see Kosiński, "Peter the Fuller," 49–73.

30. Downey, "Claim of Antioch to Ecclesiastical Jurisdiction over Cyprus," 228.

31. Englezakis, "Epiphanius of Salamis," 36.

cathedra (Greek καθέδρα), and it was located in the bishop's main church, called a cathedral, which functioned as his administrative center.[32]

Englezakis also explains that, at the end of the fifth century, the emphasis of the Roman Church in the West on apostolic succession was influencing administrative structures of the Orthodox Church in the East. Apostolicity had become a principle of ecclesiastical organization. In a very telling observation, Englezakis says, "the Cypriot bishops, who until then had made no mention of St Barnabas, remembered their apostle.[33]

In this time of turmoil, with Antioch threatening their autonomy, the bishops of Cyprus discovered the importance of Barnabas for making the case that their church also had a legitimate apostolic founder—one who became their first archbishop and appointed bishops under him. They *had* apostolic succession, and the sudden appearance of a text called the Acts of Barnabas strengthened their case.

Either slightly before or soon after the claim arose that Archbishop Anthemios had discovered the tomb of Barnabas—and Anthemios's subsequent audience with Zeno in 488—an anonymous Cypriot wrote the Acts of Barnabas as if John Mark, the cousin and traveling companion of Barnabas, had written it during the first century. Of course, not a single author prior to the late fifth century ever mentioned the Acts of Barnabas, because it did not yet exist. The text responds to fifth-century Cypriot concerns with ecclesiastical independence from Antioch. It is clearly a forgery written to bolster the case that Barnabas, a respected apostle, founded the Church of Cyprus and ordained its first bishops. To advance his case, the author enhances the stature of both Barnabas and John Mark.

For example, the Acts of Barnabas vindicates John Mark of abandoning Paul and Barnabas on the first missionary journey, placing the blame for the rift between Paul and Barnabas completely on Paul. Whereas Acts 15:38 speaks of Mark "deserting" them in Pamphylia, Acts of Barnabas 2–4 exonerates Mark by having him say an angel told him not to go with Paul and Barnabas. Chapter 6 explains that Mark tried to clarify the situation for Paul, but Paul refused to listen. And whereas Acts 15:39 only says, "Barnabas took Mark with him and sailed away to Cyprus," the Acts of Barnabas invents details of this journey.

32. The area that he controlled was called his *see* (from the Latin *sedes*), meaning seat or throne or *diocese*.

33. Englezakis, "Epiphanius of Salamis," 38.

Another feature from the Acts of Barnabas that later proves to be important is when the author says Barnabas "received documents from Matthew, a book of the word of God, and a narrative of miracles and doctrines. This [scroll] Barnabas laid upon the sick in each place that we came to, and it immediately made a cure of their sufferings" (15, *ANF*). Such use of a holy relic to heal people would not seem odd to Christians in the late fifth century, but it would have been very peculiar when the Gospel of Matthew was written in the first century.

Historically speaking, the Acts of Barnabas responds to the dispute with Peter the Fuller over apostolic succession by emphasizing Barnabas's stature as a miracle-working apostle who established the church hierarchy of the island. The story describes the journey of Barnabas and Mark around Cyprus and their appointments of church officials. Especially important is the claim that they met Heracleius of Tamasus, renamed him Heracleides and ordained him as bishop over Cyprus (17). Thus, this account helped Cypriot bishops trace their offices back to Barnabas, not to Antioch—a point I heard repeatedly while in Cyprus.

In the Acts of Barnabas, Barnabas fearlessly proclaims the gospel; and when he preaches to Jews, he uses a scroll of Matthew's Gospel seemingly copied by Matthew himself. Speaking as if he were Mark, the pseudonymous author says, "We came to Salamis . . . to the synagogue near the place called Biblia; and when we had gone into it, Barnabas, having unrolled the Gospel [scroll] which he had received from Matthew his fellow-labourer, began to teach the Jews" (22, *ANF*). When later writers comment on this story, however, they usually claim *Barnabas* translated Matthew's Aramaic Gospel into Greek and used it for preaching. Partly, they are appropriating and adding to a tradition articulated about 185 by Irenaeus that Matthew wrote his Gospel in Aramaic (*Against All Heresies* 3.1).[34] Modern scholars, however, have demonstrated conclusively that the Gospel of Matthew was composed in Greek. There is also the problem of timing: Matthew was most likely written around 85, more than thirty years after Barnabas's death—at least the death described in the Acts of Barnabas.

The Acts of Barnabas emphasizes that Barnabas died a martyr. This account explains how ruthless Jews, led by a certain Barjesus, pursued Barnabas and murdered him.

---

34. According to Eusebius (*Ecc. Hist.* 3.39.16), Papias (c. 135) said Matthew wrote in the Hebrew language and others interpreted his words. So Papias might have been the earliest one to make this claim about Matthew.

> And Barjesus . . . brought together all the multitude of the Jews; and they . . . took Barnabas by night, and bound him with a rope by the neck; and having dragged him . . . out of the city . . . they burned him with fire, so that even his bones became dust. And straightway that night, having taken his dust, they cast it into a cloth; and having secured it with lead, they intended to throw it into the sea. (23, *ANF*)

During the night, however, Mark and two accomplices stealthily got the ashes and hid them in a cave, along with the scroll of Matthew (24). They hid from the Jews and finally managed to escape, boarding a ship to Alexandria, Egypt, where Mark remained and taught the gospel to many (25–26).

This version of the story, which has Barnabas's body reduced to ashes, later posed a problem with the church's claim of actually possessing the saint's body. Subsequent authors added new elements to explain why the body remained intact. Politically speaking, an important point to note is that the fifth-century Acts of Barnabas stresses the stature of Barnabas as a miracle-working apostle and martyr who established the Church of Cyprus and appointed its first bishops. Such details undermined Peter the Fuller's argument and strengthened the Cypriot case that their church had a legitimate apostolic founder. Another result was greater veneration for the Cypriot saint.

FIGURE 14

This stone relic box is part of a large church complex called Campanopetra, located by the sea east of the Monastery of Apostle Barnabas. The box apparently held the remains of a saint. A similar container probably held remains believed to be those of Barnabas.

For a time, Barnabas's stature rose to nearly equal that of Epiphanius. A late fifth- or early sixth-century inscription, painted on the wall of an underground cistern in ancient Salamis, connects these two saints. Joan du Plat Taylor first investigated the inscription[35] and translated it as follows.

> ΒΑΡΝΑΒΑΣ Ο ΑΠΟΣΤΟΛΟΣ ΣΤΙΡΗΓΜΑ ΗΜΟΝ
> Barnabas the Apostle is our foundation.
> ΕΠΙΦΑΝΙΟΣ Ο ΜΕΓΑΣ [ΕΠΑΡ]ΧΟΣ[36] ΗΜΟΝ
> Epiphanios our great governor.

Such veneration reaches its apex in a sixth-century speech that provides the first written account of Archbishop Anthemios going to Constantinople to appear before Emperor Zeno to argue for autocephaly. The contents of this speech lay the foundation for most modern Cypriot beliefs about Barnabas, so it is crucial for understanding developing traditions about Barnabas. Yet no one had ever produced an English translation—with good reason. Translating the document was difficult and labor intensive, because the speechwriter, a monk named Alexander, attempted to be as eloquent as possible. His complex vocabulary and syntax were a challenge to translate, but what he says and does not say about Barnabas are quite significant.

Sixth-Century Cypriot speech in Praise of Barnabas

Alexander, a monk at the Monastery of Apostle Barnabas near Salamis, penned his oration in praise of Barnabas around 550 CE. The Latin title used later to identify this text in the West is *Laudatio Barnabae apostoli*. In it, Alexander confesses that he long delayed writing the speech because of the daunting nature of the task; but he finally acquiesced to the will of the abbot of the monastery, who proposed the project. As a humble monk, Alexander feels compelled to assert his own unworthiness to recount the many virtues of Barnabas, but he nevertheless shows off his eloquence as he describes his hero. To allow for more precise references to parts of the speech, I opted to maintain the line breaks found in the critical edition of the Greek text. I also italicized all quotations of

35. "A water cistern with Byzantine paintings, Salamis, Cyprus," 97–108.

36. Rapp ("Epiphanius of Salamis," 177) believes the missing letters of the lacuna in the second line do not form the word [ΕΠΑΡ]ΧΟΣ (*eparch*), but rather [ΠΡΟΜΑ]ΧΟΣ (champion).

biblical passages for easy identification (for the complete translation of the speech, see Appendix B).

As the following quotation reveals, Alexander incorporates Moses's lament of his speaking problems in Exod 4:10 to bemoan his own inability to praise Barnabas properly.

> . . . How, therefore,
> shall I, a wretch, having been plunged under myriad passions,
> be able to swim the apostolic sea?
> For *I stammer to speak* articulately *and am slow of tongue, and* (30)
> *I am not eloquent*, in order that I might narrate the beyond human
> virtues of the divinely sweet Apostle Barnabas. For he
> successfully accomplished all the virtues exactly, as
> no one of the others had ever done. Because of this, I long
> delayed obedience, knowing that my own unworthy (35)
> narrative is insufficient for the most famous perfections
> of the man. (lines 27–37) [37]

In spite of his self-deprecation, Alexander provides the most complete compilation of beliefs about Barnabas to be written at his point in history. Because his speech contributes so significantly to what modern Orthodox Christians believe about Barnabas, summarizing its contents is an important part of charting the evolution of Barnabas traditions.

Alexander's encomium of Barnabas frequently uses ornate language, and overstatement is a standard element of his praise.

> Let him be praised by all creation, the one honored by the
> Father and called by the Son and perfected by the (70)
> Holy Spirit. Barnabas, the great orator of the
> church, the trumpet of the gospel proclamation, the
> voice of the Only Begotten, the lute of the Spirit, the
> instrument of grace. (lines 69–74)

Alexander continues to amass lavish descriptions of the many virtues of Barnabas, calling him the "intellectual paradise of God" (line 79), the "unshakeable tower" and "steward of the Orthodox creeds of the holy church of God" (lines 90, 99–100), the "highly revered pearl of virginity" (line 113), the "revered ornament of the Cypriots" (line 127), and the "unconquerable champion of the inhabited world" (line 128). Alexander

---

37. Translations of *Laudatio Barnabae apostoli* by Michael Cosby from the Greek text provided by the database *TLG* (*Thesaurus Linguae Graecae*), which is based on the print version of the critical text by Van Deun in "Encomium of Barnabas," 83–122.

laments that, although he tried very hard to praise Barnabas, he "did not even achieve an introduction" (line 134).

FIGURE 15

Excavated area in the older part of the Monastery Church of Apostle Barnabas complex near Constantia/Salamis. The stone shelf in the center probably supported a stone box like the one at Campanopetra, containing what were believed to be the remains of Barnabas.

Laudatio Barnabae provides considerable insight into how traditions about Barnabas had developed by c. 550. Alexander freely, indeed with relish, adds all sorts of details to fill in the gaps in the New Testament accounts of Barnabas. For example, he says Barnabas's parents took him to Jerusalem when he was a child, in order that he might study under Gamaliel; and there he and Paul became classmates (lines 177–80). Alexander claims Barnabas began to follow Jesus after observing the healing of the paralyzed man at the Sheep Gate in Jerusalem (lines 192–95; see John 5:1–9). He also says John Mark's mother, Mary, was Barnabas's aunt (lines 201–4) and when Barnabas brought Mary to Jesus, she professed faith in him as Savior and compelled Jesus to come to her home with his disciples to eat and rest (lines 205–15). In the upper room in her home,

Jesus celebrated the Passover with his disciples (lines 216–20). Alexander adds that Mark was the one who carried the jar of water and met Jesus' disciples and led them to the upper room for the last supper (lines 222–25). Furthermore, after his resurrection, Jesus appeared to Thomas and the other disciples in this upper room, and in this same room the disciples met on the day of Pentecost when the Holy Spirit descended (lines 229–36). All these claims, which Cypriots commonly rehearse today, embellish the New Testament accounts.

Alexander repeats the earlier claim that, when Jesus "commissioned the seventy disciples . . . the first and leader and head happened to be the great Barnabas" (lines 242–44; see Luke 10:1, 17). The monk then adds that, after hearing Jesus tell his disciples to sell their possessions, Barnabas sold all of his property but one field; and he sold the remaining field after the Lord's crucifixion and gave the money to the apostles (lines 254–70). Meanwhile, Barnabas sought to convert his friend, Saul; but Saul ridiculed Jesus, calling him "an ignoramus and a country bumpkin and a criminal" (line 276). However, after Saul's conversion on the road to Damascus, he contritely returned to Jerusalem. In his tearful confession to Barnabas, the penitent Saul not only praises Barnabas but also delivers a fully developed (and obviously anachronistic) statement of Trinitarian doctrine.

Alexander loves to add dialogue to his oration. Here Paul says to Barnabas,

> Forgive me, guide of the light and teacher (300)
> of the truth, for I know the truth in the experience of
> your words. For whom I blasphemed, calling the son
> of a carpenter,[38] I now confess him to be the only begotten *Son*
> *of the living God*,[39] consubstantial and like minded and sharing the
>   same
> throne, co-eternal and without beginning. *Who, being the radiance*
>   (305)
> *of the glory and the image of the substance*[40] of the invisible
> God, *in these last days, because of us and because of*
> *our salvation, he humbled himself, taking the form of a*
> *servant,*[41] that is to say a perfect man from the holy virgin

---

38. Matt 13:55.
39. Matt 16:16; John 16:69.
40. Heb 1:3.
41. Cf. the Christ hymn in Phil 2:6–11.

and Godbearer,[42] Mary, unmixed, unchanging, indivisible, (310)
inseparable. (lines 300–11)

The content of Paul's confession fits quite nicely with the creeds confessed
by Alexander and other Orthodox Christians in the sixth century, but the
Trinitarian formulations he adds to his selected phrases from the New
Testament would have played absolutely no role in any conversations
Paul ever had with Barnabas.

Alexander adds many dialogue elements to make his speech more
dramatic for his audience. Such invention was common in ancient literature, where authors wrote what they thought the speakers in their
stories would or should have said in the circumstances being narrated.
Consequently, such speeches often represented the authors' own (later)
viewpoints and therefore contained anachronisms—like Paul's Trinitarian formulae above.[43] Because Alexander wrote his speech to praise
Barnabas and glorify the saint, he felt considerable freedom to embellish
the account. Following the lead of others who wrote to praise the saints,
Alexander often creates details in his lavish praise of Barnabas.[44]

Sometimes, Alexander modifies previous legends. For example,
he repeats the tradition initially appearing in the Pseudo-Clementine

42. θεοτόκος.

43. Thucydides explains his method of composing speeches in *History of the Pelo-
ponnesian War* 1.22.1: "As to the speeches that were made by different men . . . it has
been difficult to recall with strict accuracy the words actually spoken, both for me
as regards that which I myself heard, and for those who from various other sources
have brought me reports. Therefore the speeches are given in the language in which,
as it seemed to me, the several speakers would express, on the subjects under consid-
eration, the sentiments most befitting the occasion, though at the same time I have
adhered as closely as possible to the general sense of what was actually said" (1.22.1; C.
F. Smith, LCL]). See also Lucian, *How to Write History* 58. For a detailed study of the
theological function of the speeches in Acts, as well as how they compare with the use
of speeches in other ancient literature, see Soards, *Speeches in Acts*.

44. Limberis, *Architects of Piety*, provides many examples of how Christian
hagiographers modified and invented details to accomplish their rhetorical purposes
(e.g., 46–47: "Gregory of Nazianzus, great scholar though he was, knew next to nothing
of the history of the Church in the third century . . . As in the case of Nyssen's *Life of
Gregory Thaumaturgus*, the panegyric is so full of invention it is obvious that he did
not know much about . . . Cyprian . . . Gregory is counting on his audience's lack of
acquaintance with Cyprian. His brilliant strategy uses their ignorance to his rhetorical
advantage as he shapes his composite martyr in order to fulfill his pastoral ambitions."
Because Alexander spoke at the Monastery of Barnabas, where his audience knew
more about the subject, he probably had less freedom than Nyssen to invent material.
But he certainly could embellish in his language of praise.

Homilies that Barnabas was first to preach the gospel in Rome; but he modifies the tradition so that Barnabas goes *after* Jesus' crucifixion but *before* Barnabas recruited Saul to help him at Antioch. He explains that Barnabas, after being commissioned to care for the church at Antioch, "went through all the cities and regions preaching good news until he came to the greatest city, Rome. For he before any other of the disciples of the Lord proclaimed in Rome the gospel of Christ" (lines 366–69). Alexander has Barnabas going from Rome to Alexandria, Egypt, to preach the gospel, and then preaching in other cities as he makes his way to Jerusalem (lines 381–84). From there, Barnabas travels back to Antioch and then goes to Tarsus to recruit Saul (lines 384–90). Why Barnabas would take such an extensive mission before going to Antioch as the apostles directed is not at all clear, but the evangelistic tour adds to the prestige of the apostle.

Alexander's praise of the saint leads him to revise the less laudatory first-century account of the debate between Barnabas and Paul found in the Acts of the Apostles. According to Acts 15:39, Paul and Barnabas sharply disagreed over the issue of taking Mark with them and parted company as a result. Alexander feels uncomfortable with what he would consider non-saintly behavior, so he explains away the entire incident. He warns his audience not to think the apostles argued and became angry at each other.

How, he asks, could those who had crucified the flesh with its passions be carried away by anger? How could the apostles, who insisted all anger and malice be removed from Christians, be guilty of this problem? He concludes that, because Scripture says to provoke one another to good works, the provoking the apostles did was to inspire each other with zeal for God. For "Paul was seeking precision, conspicuous apostolic perfection, but Barnabas was honoring benevolence" (*Laudatio* lines 460–62). Like Chrysostom before him, Alexander's view of saintly conduct imposed limits on his ability to interpret the behavior of the apostles. But he exhibits no constraints in his exaltation of the founder of the Church of Cyprus.

Although the New Testament never mentions Barnabas's physical appearance, Alexander emphasizes how good looking the man was.

> . . . his form was angelic and his appearance austere.
> And his eyebrows knit together, the eyes full of joy, not
> appearing grim, but inclining reverently downward. His mouth
> was noble and his lips handsome, with the sweetness of distilled honey

—for he never spoke excessively but controlled (himself)—; (475)
his walk was restrained and without conceit, and in general
the apostle Barnabas was always a pure pillar of Christ,
illuminating every virtue. (lines 471–78)

Creative Use of Scripture by Alexander the Monk

Alexander's appropriation of verses from the Bible is also interesting. In *Laudatio Barnabae*, he selects actions and words of various people in the Bible and uses these to describe Barnabas. One of his more creative uses of the New Testament is applying to Barnabas the description of the elderly widow, Anna, in Luke 2:37: "He did not separate himself from the temple, ministering night and day by fasts and prayers" (line 185).

A more extensive example of Alexander's use of Scripture occurs when he combines parts of Paul's farewell speech to the Ephesian elders in Acts 20:18–35 with a compilation of material drawn from 2 Cor 5:10 (Rom 14:10), 1 Thess 2:12; 5:2, 14, 22; 1 Cor 7:31; 2 Tim 4:1; Jas 5:7–8; Phil 2:15; 2 Pet 3:14; 2 Tim 4:6–8; and Acts 20:36–38 in order to compose a speech for Barnabas to deliver to Christians in Salamis prior to his martyrdom. The two columns below show sections of Alexander's speech from lines 486–521 alongside the New Testament passages he used for each part of his account.

But the holy apostle of Christ, Barnabas, after gathering all the brothers, *said to them, "You understand how I was with you the* entire *time,*	[Paul] sent a message to Ephesus, asking the elders of the church to meet him. When they came to him, *he said to them: "You yourselves know how I lived among you the entire time"* . . . (Acts 20:17–18).
admonishing and encouraging each one to remain in the grace and *in the faith* of our Lord Jesus Christ, and *to keep his commands and to do them* and *to be separated from every evil deed.*	. . . *urging and encouraging you and pleading that you lead a life worthy of God* (1 Thess 2:12; compare 1 Thess 5:14 *admonish . . . encourage*) . . . hold fast to what is good; *abstain from every form of evil* (1 Thess 5:22).

For it is necessary for all of us to stand before the judgment seat of Christ, in order that each might give account for the things done through the body, unto which things he practiced, whether good or evil.	*For all of us must appear before the judgment seat of Christ, so that each may receive recompense for what has been done in the body, whether good or evil* (2 Cor 5:10).
For the form of this world is passing away,	*For the present form of this world is passing away* (1 Cor 7:31).
and the Lord *is about to come from heaven to judge the living and the dead.*	*. . . Christ Jesus, who is to judge the living and the dead* (2 Tim 4:1).
Therefore, do not be careless, knowing *that in an hour you do not expect,* our Lord *comes.*	*. . . you also must be ready,* for the Son of Man is *coming at an unexpected hour* (Matt 24:44; compare 1 Thess. 5:2: . . . you . . . know . . . that the day of the Lord will come like a thief in the night).
Therefore, *bear hardship patiently* and in hope *establish your hearts, because the coming of the Lord is near.*	Be *patient,* therefore, beloved, until the *coming of the Lord . . .* You also must be *patient. Strengthen your hearts, for the coming of the Lord is near* (Jas 5:7–8).
. . . Therefore *make haste that you might be found blameless* and *without blemish in that day . . .*	*. . .* you may be *blameless and innocent, children of God without blemish* (Phil 2:15; also 1 Thess 3:13: that you may be *blameless . . .* at the coming of our Lord Jesus with all his saints).
For I am already being poured out as a libation and my time of departure is imminent, as our Lord Jesus Christ revealed to me. *I have fought the good fight. I have finished the race. I have kept the faith. Now the crown of righteousness is laid up for me, and not only for me, but also to all the ones* who struggle because of his name."	*I am already being poured out as a libation, and the time of my departure has come. I have fought the good fight, I have finished the race, I have kept the faith. From now on there is reserved for me the crown of righteousness, which the Lord, the righteous judge, will give me on that day, and not only to me but also to all who have longed for his appearing* (2 Tim 4:6–8).
And after saying these things, he prayed with all of them. And all appropriately wept,	*When he had finished speaking, he knelt down with them all and prayed. There was much weeping* (Acts 20:36–37).
because the apostle had said that *"The time of my departure has come."*	*. . . the time of my departure has come* (2 Tim 4:6).

Sometimes Alexander revises earlier traditions—such as the burning of Barnabas's body. According to Acts of Barnabas 23–24, Mark collected the remains of Barnabas—which were reduced to ashes by those who murdered him—hid the ashes in a cave, and then set sail for

Alexandria. In Alexander's account of Barnabas's martyrdom, however, the large fire built to incinerate the body Barnabas failed to accomplish his murderers' plan.

> And after . . . interrogating him
> closely, they led him during the night outside of the city and there (540)
> the lawless ones stoned him to death. And kindling a great
> fire, they threw the blessed one there until no remains of
> his body were to be found. But, in the providence of God, the body
> of the apostle remained unharmed and the fire damaged
> nothing of it. And Mark, in obedience to the arrangements given to
>   him, (545)
> went outside the city to the west with certain brothers
> in secret, where they collected the remains of Saint Barnabas. And
> after burying the remains in a cave about five stadia from the city,
> they withdrew, *after making great lamentation over him.*[45]
> *And in that time great persecution came upon (550)*
> *the church in* Salamis, *and all were scattered.* (lines 539–51)

Alexander appropriates the last three lines of this text from Acts 8:1–2, which describes the persecution of the Jerusalem church following the death of Stephen: "That day a severe persecution began against the church in Jerusalem, and all except the apostles were scattered throughout the countryside of Judea and Samaria. Devout men buried Stephen and made loud lamentation over him."

Addressing Political Concerns when Praising Barnabas

Regarding events closer to his own historical setting, Alexander seems quite aware of the various Byzantine rulers of the fifth century—as well as the christological controversies in the eastern Mediterranean world. His completely disparaging description of Peter the Fuller, Patriarch of Antioch, is consistent with the antagonism Cypriots still feel toward the man. And his lengthy condemnation of Peter the Fuller's actions and theology shows that the Patriarch of Antioch was a significant foe of the Church of Cyprus (lines 587–677).

Alexander glorifies Barnabas for thwarting Peter's attempt to annex Cyprus. He also eulogizes Archbishop Anthemios and explains how Barnabas appeared three times on three consecutive nights to this pious man, instructing him where to find the saint's relics under the carob tree

45. This phrase is also used in 1 Macc 2:70; 4:39; 9:20; 13:26.

and exhorting him not to fear going to Constantinople (lines 704–57). Here, in about the year 550, we have the first written account of Barnabas appearing to Anthemios and the subsequent discovery of the saint's body (lines 758–72). Alexander explains how Anthemios went to Constantinople and saved Cyprus by explaining to the assembled leaders there that he had in his possession the complete relics of Barnabas, as well as the Gospel of Matthew copied by Barnabas himself. Emperor Zeno, much impressed that a saint had appeared during his own reign, ruled in favor of Anthemios and promised patronage to the Cypriot archbishop (lines 773–809).

According to *Laudatio Barnabae,* Zeno requested for his own collection the Gospel of Matthew found on Barnabas's breast, and he had the wooden cover of this Gospel adorned with gold (810–16). The detail about a wooden cover reveals another historical problem, because it indicates the document was a codex—not a scroll. The codex, a precursor of the book, was initially used for informal writings. During the time of Matthew and Barnabas, Christian authors still used scrolls for documents such as the Gospels.

> The codex made of papyrus or parchment apparently evolved from sets of thin wooden boards, either whitened to receive writing with ink or slightly hollowed and filled with wax to receive writing with a stylus, and then hinged along one edge. Such sets of writing tablets *(tabellae, pugillares)* had long been used as notebooks for jotting memoranda, keeping accounts, doing school exercises, or making rough drafts. The term codex derives from them: *caudex* or *codex* meant originally "a piece of wood." When sheets of papyrus or parchment were substituted for wooden tablets the codex became lighter, easier to handle, and far more capacious. Yet it retained its purely functional status as a notebook and was not immediately regarded as a proper book, that is, a medium of literature . . . The first mention of the codex as a medium of literature, and thus as a book proper rather than a notebook, is found in epigrams of the Roman poet Martial in the late 1st century c.e.[46]

During the second century, Christians began to appreciate the practicality of codices for copying and disseminating writings. A codex was much more portable than a scroll and allowed readers to locate particular

---

46. Gamble, "Codex," 1067–68.

passages with greater efficiency—which aided in teaching and in missionary proclamation of the gospel message.

By the fifth century, use of codices had a long history. All the collections of biblical books were produced in this form, and Christians would naturally associate a copy of a Gospel with a codex. So when Anthemios appears before Zeno with a codex of the Gospel of Matthew, it does not seem to be an issue with Zeno. Nor was this detail a problem for Alexander and his audience at the monastery. They were all familiar with codices and evidently not aware of the fact that early Christians like Barnabas did not use codices. In other words, Anthemios took a forged copy of the Gospel of Matthew to Zeno, and the deception worked.

Alexander wrote *Laudatio Barnabae* not only to praise the saint but also to legitimize the island's ecclesiastical independence—thus continuing events set in motion in the late fifth century.[47] Michael Metcalf comments, "The invention of St Barnabas, during the reign of Zeno (474–91), came at an opportune moment as the hierarchy in Cyprus struggled to avoid renewed subjection to the nearby patriarch."[48] Regarding Anthemios presenting a codex of Matthew to Zeno, Metcalf observes, "One permits oneself to smile at the archbishop's deception . . . All this was high politics: the archbishop had been fighting, shrewdly enough, for his freedom, and that of his hierarchy, from Antioch."[49]

G. W. Bowersock, however, speculates that Zeno was not duped by Anthemios but was directly involved in the deception for his own political reasons.

> The physical appearance of Barnabas after four centuries in his grave allowed the court at Constantinople finally to put an end to a rivalry it can have had no interest in continuing. Let there be no mistake: the miraculous entry of the person of Barnabas in Cypriot politics had to have been programmed at the highest levels of government. In terms of foreign policy, it allowed Cyprus to be detached from the political orbit of Syria, where the non-Chalcedonian forces—the Monophysites—were gaining alarming strength. The autocephaly of Cyprus was part of a

47. Downey, "The claim of Antioch to ecclesiastical jurisdiction over Cyprus," 228, states, "Alexander's encomium . . . is obviously a tendentious document to support Cyprus' claim to autocephaly." He believes Anthemios's vision of Barnabas and the discovery of the saint's body was a deliberate scheme to fend off Antioch's claim on the island.

48. Metcalf, *Byzantine Cyprus*, 308.

49. Metcalf, *Byzantine Cyprus*, 309.

deliberate restructuring of the power balance of the Byzantine state. This was necessary precisely because the economic and geographical position of the island could tip any balance. The Orthodox Christians of Cyprus had their own reasons for separation, but it should never be forgotten that Zeno had his. He was under no compulsion to react as he did to the gospel on the breast of Barnabas.[50]

Regardless of who formulated the plan to discover Barnabas's relics, Anthemios benefitted in several ways from the transaction. Alexander explains that Zeno sent Anthemios back to Cyprus with a generous donation to build a large church to honor Barnabas on the site where the saint's body was discovered (*Laudatio* lines 818–24). Other wealthy individuals also contributed to the donation, and Anthemios got right to work on the immense project. Alexander's description of the church and accompanying monastery provides helpful information regarding the design of the complex, including an aqueduct that brought abundant water to the site (lines 823–43). Metcalf provides an important summary of the situation.

FIGURE 16

Monastery Church of Apostle Barnabas—built in the eighteenth century. Following the conquest of northern Cyprus in 1974, Turkish officials converted the church into a museum and still forbid Orthodox Christians from holding liturgy in the building.

50. Bowersock, "International Role of Late Antique Cyprus," 18.

> Archbishop Anthemius [Western spelling of Anthemios] quickly built a basilica dedicated to St Barnabas, at the place of the invention, with gifts from Zeno and from the notables of Constantia. It is said to have been surrounded by stoas, gardens, cells, aqueducts, and hostels 'for refreshing foreign visitors'. Here we have a substantial investment in the cult of St Barnabas, and a presumption that it would attract large numbers of pilgrims, and not just from within Cyprus . . . Anthemius may have had his eye on pilgrims travelling to or from the Holy Land, and pausing in Constantia. We see what facilities were deemed desirable, at the beginning of the sixth century, in providing for the better class of pilgrims.[51]

Toward the end of his oration, Alexander asks Saint Barnabas to "intercede on our behalf to the one you love, Christ the only begotten Son and Word of God. Thus he might rescue *us from the present evil age* and *grant* us to *find* forgiveness of sins and *mercy* and consolation *in that* fearful *day* when *he comes to judge the living and the dead*" (lines 873–78; quoting Gal 1:4, 2 Tim 4:1, and 1 Pet 4:5). Alexander also asks Barnabas to bless the archbishop, the saint's holy successor at the monastery, and to protect the fatherland from every foe (lines 879–97).

What About the Imperial Privileges?

Modern Cypriot beliefs about Barnabas listed at the beginning of this chapter rely heavily on the information contained in *Laudatio Barnabae apostoli*. It is the primary source for the claims regarding Barnabas appearing to Anthemios, the discovery of the saint's relics, Anthemios's journey to Constantinople and appearance before Zeno, and Anthemios's triumphant return to Cyprus to build the church and monastery to honor Barnabas.

Most Orthodox beliefs about Barnabas either come directly from or are expansions of claims made in Alexander's elaborate, sixth-century speech in which he freely invented many narrative details in his zeal to honor the saint. The information about Barnabas added by later writers mostly involves creating additional connections, such as specifying the names of the saint's family members, providing the name of the owner of the ship on which Barnabas, Saul, and Mark sailed to Cyprus, adding the story of the ship owner's daughter and nanny being abducted and sold as

---

51. Bowersock, "International Role of Late Antique Cyprus," 18.

slaves to Sergius Paulus, formulating the names of significant converts in Cyprus who became church leaders, and stating the names of Jews who persecuted and killed Barnabas.

As I translated Alexander's complicated speech, however, I became eerily aware that it says absolutely nothing about the core conviction we consistently heard from Cypriots: Zeno gave imperial privileges to Anthemios. *Nothing!*

Alexander the Monk lived at the center of veneration of Barnabas, in the large monastic complex built under the supervision of Anthemios with funds from Emperor Zeno and other wealthy donors (beginning c. 488). Writing c. 550, Alexander had available all the existing details pertaining to the controversy with Peter the Fuller over the autocephaly of the Church of Cyprus. He would certainly have known about imperial privileges if Emperor Zeno had granted them to Anthemios. Indeed, if the privileges had been granted, Alexander would undoubtedly have embellished them quite effectively to bolster his case for Cypriot autocephaly. But he does not mention them, because they did not exist. The complete absence of the imperial privileges, the central belief that modern Cypriots learn about Barnabas, forced me to conclude that someone invented them after the time of Alexander the Monk. But who? And when? For what purpose? My attempts to unravel this mystery led me down unforeseen paths in my effort to uncover the origin of the legend of the imperial privileges.

CHAPTER FIVE

Creation of the Imperial Privileges

In light of the effusive description of Anthemios in the sixth-century *Laudatio Barnabae apostoli*, I expected subsequent Cypriot literature to contain routine references to this archbishop who ensured their *autocephaly*. I was wrong. Anthemios falls into a literary black hole, not mentioned in writings again for hundreds of years. Authors in the following centuries occasionally reference Barnabas and Epiphanius or Barnabas and Zeno, but never Anthemios.

Anthemios is extremely important to the heritage of modern, Cypriot Orthodox Christians. They regularly repeat the story of his discovery of Barnabas's relics and his triumphant journey to Constantinople to appear before Zeno. Yet I discovered he was largely irrelevant for Cypriots throughout most of their Christian history. As my research progressed, it became clear I could take nothing for granted while investigating this mystery. Evidence simply did not support what Cypriots told me with sincere confidence about Anthemios. Especially revealing was the fact that Alexander the Monk said nothing in *Laudatio Barnabae* about Emperor Zeno granting imperial privileges to Anthemios and his successors. The origin of the story had to be later.[1]

Barnabas and the Ecclesiastical Independence of Cyprus

Peter the Fuller's failed attempt to bring Cyprus under his jurisdiction precipitated a rediscovery of Barnabas by Cypriot Orthodox leaders. The

---

1. In this chapter, I give my translations of the relevant passages from ancient sources so readers can see the evidence on which I base my conclusions. In footnotes, I provide the Greek texts so historians have the primary sources readily available for analysis.

fifth and sixth centuries saw a resurgence of interest in Barnabas, and stories about him spread outside the island. Several sixth- and seventh-century texts show an awareness of traditions connecting Barnabas with Epiphanius.

In the sixth century (perhaps a few years earlier than Alexander the Monk's *Laudatio Barnabae*), Theodorus Anagnostes, a lector (reader) at Hagia Sophia Church in Constantinople, wrote his *Historia Ecclesiastica*, a history of the church from 439–518. Although his book does not survive, later writers quote it in their own histories. In one such quotation, Theodorus briefly mentions the discovery of Barnabas's body under a carob tree, having on his chest the copy of the Gospel of Matthew written with his own hand. Theodorus states that, because of this discovery, the Cypriots prevailed over Antioch and remained autocephalous. He also mentions Zeno storing Barnabas's Gospel of Matthew at the palace in the Church of St. Stephen in Constantinople.[2] But he makes no mention of Anthemios or the imperial privileges that Zeno supposedly granted to this Cypriot archbishop.

A seventh-century book written by Leontios, Bishop of Neapolis in Cyprus, attests to the popularity of Barnabas at this time. In his *Life of St. John the Almsgiver* (Patriarch of Alexandria from 606 to 616),[3] Leontios says John journeyed to Constantia in Cyprus (c. 619) and there paid homage to the relics of both Epiphanius and Barnabas (some ancient authors refer to the site as Constantia, while others use the older name Salamis). In a brief comment, Leontios states that John the Almsgiver called Barnabas the *praiseworthy apostle* and Epiphanius the *miracle worker* (*thaumaurge*).[4] However, such interest in Barnabas waned for centuries.

Reports of Barnabas's connection with the ecclesiastical independence of the Cypriot church surfaced sporadically; and,

---

2. Βαρνάβα τοῦ ἀποστόλου τὸ λείψανον εὑρέθη ἐν Κύπρῳ ὑπὸ δένδρον κερατέαν, ἔχον ἐπὶ στήθους τὸ κατὰ Ματθαῖον εὐαγγέλιον ἰδιόγραφον τοῦ Βαρνάβα. ἐξ ἧς προφάσεως καὶ περιγεγόνασι Κύπριοι τοῦ αὐτοκέφαλον εἶναι τὴν κατ᾽ αὐτοὺς μητρόπολιν καὶ μὴ τελεῖν ὑπὸ Ἀντιόχειαν. τὸ δὲ τοιοῦτον εὐαγγέλιον Ζήνων ἀπέθετο ἐν τῷ παλατίῳ ἐν τῷ ἁγίῳ Στεφάνῳ (*Historia Ecclesiastica* [*exerpta et fragmenta*] 3. 436; Greek text from *TLG*. See *Historia Ecclesiastica* [*Patrologia Graeca* 86a: cols. 183–84] for printed text).

3. Also known as John the Almoner or John the Merciful.

4. Βαρνάβα τοῦ πανευφήμου ἀποστόλου καὶ Ἐπιφανίου τοῦ θαυματουργοῦ (*Vita Sancti Johannis Eleemosynarii* [*Patrologia Graeca* 93: cols. 1613–68]). See *Bibliotheca hagiographica graeca*. Ancient texts more frequently connect Epiphanius with his rule of Cyprus, not with his reputation as a miracle worker. Rapp, "Epiphanius of Salamis," 177n47, gives a longer list of sources.

not surprisingly, details became garbled. The geographer George of Cyprus wrote his *Description of the Roman World* in the early seventh century, and he connected Barnabas's relics with Cypriot autocephaly in the following way: "The eparchy of Cyprus has continued, having sovereignty for itself, because here the holy apostle Barnabas was found, having the Gospel of Mark on his chest."[5] Because George's work survives in a compilation assembled in the ninth century, it is unclear whether George was himself confused over which Gospel was found on the chest of Barnabas, or whether the ninth-century compiler (or even an earlier copier) mistakenly substituted "Mark" when copying the text.

Also in the ninth century, a monk in Constantinople, George the Chronographer, recorded some of the details of the story found in *Laudatio Barnabae*:

> During the rule of Zeno, the body of Barnabas was discovered by revelation in Cyprus, in the city of Constantia, under a carob tree, having on his chest the Gospel of Matthew written by the hand of Barnabas. Because of this revelation and the advice of the apostle, the Cypriots prevailed over the contentious Peter the Fuller, who tried to bring the Church of Cyprus under the control of Antioch, and remained autocephalous under the rule of the Metropolitan of Cyprus. Zeno placed this Gospel of Matthew in the palace in the Church of St. Stephen. Every year it is read aloud on the holy and great fifth [day of Passover].[6]

Although George the Chronographer accurately recounted elements of the story, he made no mention of Anthemios—and still nothing is known of imperial privileges.

Over the three centuries that Arab raiders periodically devastated the coastal cities of Cyprus (649–965), the elegant Monastery of Apostle

5. *Georgii Cyprii Descriptio Orbis Romani*, 56, line 1096.

6. AT of the Greek text in *TLG* (printed text in *Patrologia Graeca* 121: cols. 673–74): Ἐπὶ τῆς αὐτῆς βασιλείας Ζήνωνος, Βαρνάβα τοῦ ἀποστόλου τὸ λείψανον εὑρεθὲν ἐξ ἀποκαλύψεως ἐν Κύπρῳ (ἐν πόλει Κωνσταντίᾳ) ὑπὸ δένδρον κερατέαν, ἔχον ἐπὶ στήθους τὸ κατὰ Ματθαῖον Εὐαγγέλιον ἰδιόγραφον τοῦ Βαρνάβα. Ἐξ ἧς προφάσεως τῇ ἀποκαλύψει καὶ εἰσηγήσει τοῦ ἀποστόλου περιγεγόνασι Κύπριοι τῷ Κναφεῖ Πέτρῳ φιλονεικοῦντι, ὑπὸ Ἀντιόχειαν τελεῖν τὰς κατὰ τὴν Κύπρον ἐκκλησίας, καὶ αὐτοκέφαλον εἶναι τὴν κατὰ Κύπρον μητρόπολιν. Ὅπερ Εὐαγγέλιον τὸ εὑρεθὲν ἀποθέμενος Ζήνων ἐν τῷ παλατίῳ ἐν τῷ ναῷ τοῦ Ἁγίου Στεφάνου (κατ᾽ ἐνιαυτὸν ἀναγινώσκεται τῇ ἁγίᾳ καὶ μεγάλη ε᾽). Georgius Monachus, *Chronicon Breve* (110:761, lines 25–37). For further reading on George's work, see Adler and Tuffin, *Chronography of George Synkellos*. Lines 816–18 of *Laudatio Barnabae apostoli* also mention the *fifth* day: "For during the great fifth (day) of Passover each year, they read the Gospel in the chapel of the palace."

Barnabas near Constantia was reduced to ruins. We may only speculate on the extent of the losses with respect to writings about Barnabas. Existing evidence, however, reveals no development of Barnabas traditions during this time.

Barnabas in Books about the Saints

As my search for Barnabas traditions progressed into tenth-century texts, I gained greater appreciation for books devoted to recounting stories about saints. Orthodox Christians call such a collection of traditions a *Synaxarion* or *Menologion*. These books arrange stories about the saints according to the days of the year, with each saint having a name day specified in the calendar. For example, June 11 is the name day of both Bartholomew and Barnabas, and for this day the *Synaxarion* presents information concerning these two saints. Because the authors of such books collect and organize information from earlier sources, their descriptions provide a valuable resource. The problem is that these authors do not indicate where they obtained their material.

The most detailed modern collection of traditions about the saints that I saw in Cyprus was multi-volume set entitled *The Synaxarion: The Lives of the Saints of the Orthodox Church,* by Makarios, Hieromonk of Simonos Petra (published in 2005). His books blend an amazing collection of historical data and legends. Volume 5 is only for May and June, and it alone is 690 pages long. The volumes represent an immense amount of work, a careful synthesis of Orthodox beliefs about the saints.

Hieromonk Makarios's *Synaxarion* provides much more detail than the single volume devotional guides found in many Orthodox homes. His attitude toward the historicity of his sources seems to be very fluid. For example, in his remarks regarding Bartholomew for June 11, Makarios describes Bartholomew preaching the gospel message to peoples in the East. In a candid comment acknowledging the challenges posed by the diversity presented in his sources, he says, "But, as with the other Apostles, the sources are fairly contradictory and very unclear about the itinerary of his mission."[7] His candor, however, does not mean he systematically analyzes stories about the saints to determine their historical credibility. He asserts with credulity, for example, that those who murdered Bartholomew placed the martyr's body into an iron coffin and threw it into the sea. Makarios says God intervened and caused the

---

7. Makarios, *Synaxarion,* 5:451n2.

coffin to float to "the island of Lipari in Sicily, where his relics worked many miracles."[8] Such stories abound in these books that honor the saints.

In spite of the detailed nature of his work, Makarios seldom references where he gets his information. Most Orthodox readers seem not to ponder the historical accuracy of stories about saints. They read them with reverence and use the accounts as guides to venerate the saints. One of our Orthodox friends keeps her copy on a coffee table in her living room and each morning faithfully reads about the saints who are honored on that day.

Because the writing of these books goes back many centuries, I began to explore older editions for clues to the development of traditions about Barnabas. In the tenth century, Symeon *Logothetes* (or *Metaphrast*) compiled ten volumes of material about the saints. What he says and does not say are interesting, because the role of politics affects the way he venerates Barnabas. Symeon states that, during the reign of Zeno, Barnabas's remains, and a copy of Matthew written by Barnabas, were discovered under a carob tree. He adds that, on the basis of this discovery, Cyprus was not under Antioch but under Constantinople. He concludes by saying Zeno kept the Gospel in the imperial palace in the Church of St. Stephen.[9] Unlike previous writers, he does not mention Cypriot autocephaly with the discovery of Barnabas's relics—which is understandable in light of his assertion that Constantinople had jurisdiction over Cyprus. Such connections between politics and veneration of saints are fascinating.

Michael IV, Byzantine emperor from 1034 to 1041, also produced a *Synaxarion*. His comments about Barnabas reveal greater awareness than his predecessors of the story line in *Laudatio Barnabae apostoli* and are very unusual in mentioning Anthemios. Michael recounts the discovery of Barnabas's body during the reign of Emperor Zeno, following the appearance of the apostle in a nocturnal vision to Anthemios. As in *Laudatio Barnabae*, this text has Barnabas telling Anthemios to go outside the city five stadia to the west, where he would find his body and a copy of the Gospel of Matthew. However, the account omits the end of the story

---

8. Makarios, *Synaxarion*, 5:452.

9. Ζήνων ἡδοναῖς ἀτόποις καὶ πράξεσιν ἀτόποις ἐσχόλαζεν· ἐφ' οὗ τὸ τοῦ ἀποστόλου Βαρνάβα λείψανον εὑρέθη ἐν Κύπρῳ ὑπὸ δένδρον κερατέαν, ἔχον ἐπὶ στήθους τὸ κατὰ Ματθαῖον εὐαγγέλιον ἰδιόγραφον τοῦ Βαρνάβα, ἐξ ἧς προφάσεως γέγονε μητρόπολις, καὶ μὴ τελεῖν ὑπὸ Ἀντιόχειαν ἀλλ' ὑπὸ Κωνσταντινούπολιν. τὸ δὲ τοιοῦτον εὐαγγέλιον Ζήνων ἀπέθετο εἰς τὸ παλάτιον ἐν τῷ ἁγίῳ Στεφάνῳ. *Chronicon* (*sub nomine Leonis Grannatici vel Theodosii Melisseni vel Julii Pollucis—redactio A + B operis sub titulo Epitome fort. Sub auctore Trajano Patricio*) 117, lines 15–21; TLG.

in *Laudatio Barnabae*, which tells of Anthemios returning to build the church in honor of Barnabas. And still there is no hint of Zeno granting imperial privileges to Archbishop Anthemios.[10]

Confused Versions of the Barnabas Story

With respect to material about Barnabas, the authors of history books were no more discerning in their use of earlier sources than were the authors of *Synaxaria*. But that was no surprise. Ancient historians commonly combined legendary material with more factual accounts in their narratives—or just made up material when they felt like it. An interesting dynamic exists in the way authors' religious and political views shape the way they tell their stories. For example, like Symeon *Logothetes,* George Kedrenos, in his eleventh-century *Concise History of the World* (*Compendium Historiarum*), claimed Cyprus was under the jurisdiction of Constantinople. His confused summary of the Barnabas story speaks of a cherry tree instead of a carob tree and makes no mention of autocephaly.[11] Furthermore, George Kedrenos says nothing about Anthemios—a trend until the eighteenth century.

Moving forward in time, brief versions of the Barnabas story surface sporadically—typically diverging in some way from the account in *Laudatio Barnabae*. The twelfth-century Byzantine writer Nilus Doxapatris again confused which Gospel was on the saint's chest: "The island of Cyprus, which remained autocephalous for all times, and being subject to no throne of greater sovereignty, but being unconditionally

---

10. From the Greek text of *Sanctorum Bartholomaei et Barnabae vitae e Menologio Imperiali deprompta Menologii Imperiales* (*TLG*, lines 201–41; print version in Van Deun and Noret, *Hagiographica Cypria*).

11. "the remains of the holy Apostle Barnabas were found in Cyprus, placed under a cherry tree, having upon the chest the Gospel of Matthew written by the hand of the holy Apostle Barnabas, for which reason thereafter the Cyprus metropolis has emerged, not under the control of Antioch but under the control of Constantinople. And Zeno placed this Gospel in the palace, in the Church of St. Stephen, in Daphne" (AT from *TLG*). The Greek text is as follows: τὸ τοῦ ἁγίου ἀποστόλου Βαρνάβα λείψανον εὑρέθη ἐν Κύπρῳ, ὑπὸ δένδρον κερασέαν ἱστάμενον, ἔχον ἐπὶ τοῦ στήθους τὸ κατὰ Ματθαῖον εὐαγγέλιον ἰδιόγραφον αὐτοῦ τοῦ ἀποστόλου Βαρνάβα. ἐξ ἧς προφάσεως ἔκτοτε γέγονε μητρόπολις ἡ Κύπρος, καὶ τοῦ μὴ τελεῖν ὑπὸ Ἀντιόχειαν ἀλλ᾽ ὑπὸ Κωνσταντινούπολιν. τὸ δὲ τοιοῦτον εὐαγγέλιον Ζήνων ἀπέθετο ἐν τῷ παλατίῳ, ἐν τῷ ναῷ τοῦ ἁγίου Στεφάνου ἐν τῇ Δάφνῃ (*Compendium Historiarum* 1:618, line 5; published Greek text in *Patrologia Graeca* 121: cols. 673–74).

free because the Apostle Barnabas was found in her, having on his bosom the holy Gospel According to Mark."[12]

In the thirteenth century, Joel the Chronographer explained that Cypriot autocephaly was based on the discovery of Barnabas's relics and the Gospel of Matthew, but he made no mention of Anthemios—neither did he mention imperial privileges.[13] Also in the thirteenth century, Pseudo-Zonaras, the Lexicographer, correctly identified the Gospel as Matthew in his brief version of the discovery of the relics during the reign of Zeno, but he said nothing about autocephaly or Anthemios.[14] In the fourteenth century, the historian Nikephorus Kallistus Xanthopulus of Constantinople mentioned the story of Barnabas and included Cypriot autocephaly in his account. But, like most of his predecessors, he did not mention Anthemios.[15]

So, although Anthemios is extremely important in contemporary Cypriot consciousness, he seems to have been almost completely unknown for Christian writers after the time of Alexander the Monk (c. 550) until well into the 1600s. Perhaps the fact that there was as yet no tradition about Zeno granting imperial privileges to Anthemios diminished the need to include him in the story of autocephaly.

12. AT from *TLG* (print version in *Patrologia Graeca* 132: cols. 1097–98). The Greek text is as follows: ἡ νῆσος Κύπρος ἣ ἔμεινεν αὐτοκέφαλος παντελῶς καὶ μηδενὶ θρόνῳ τῶν μεγίστων ὑποκειμένη, ἀλλ᾽ αὐτεξούσιος οὖσα διὰ τὸ εὑρεθῆναι ἐν αὐτῇ τὸν ἀπόστολον βαρνάβαν ἔχοντα ἐπιστήθιον τὸ κατὰ Μάρκον ἅγιον εὐαγγέλιον (Nilus Doxapatris, *Notitia patriarchatuum* 10, line 12–11, line 3).

13. καὶ Βαρνάβα τοῦ ἀποστόλου τὸ λείψανον εὑρέθη ὑπὸ δένδρον κερασίαν, ἔχον ἐπὶ στήθους τὸ κατὰ Ματθαῖον εὐαγγέλιον ἰδιόγραφον τοῦ Βαρνάβα. ἐξ ἧς προφάσεως παραγεγόνασι Κύπριοι τοῦ μὴ τελεῖν ὑπὸ Ἀντιόχειαν τὴν κατ᾽ αὐτοὺς μητρόπολιν. ὅπερ εὐαγγέλιον ἀποτεθὲν παρὰ Ζήνωνος ἐν τῷ παλατίῳ εἰς τὸν ναὸν τοῦ ἁγίου Στεφάνου ἀναγινώσκεται κατ᾽ ἐνιαυτὸν τῇ ἁγίᾳ μεγάλῃ πέμπτῃ (*Chronographia compendiaria*, 43, lines 6–12, *TLG*; printed text in *Patrologia Graeca* 139: cols. 263–64).

14. ἐπὶ Ζήνωνος βασιλέως εὑρήθη ἐν Κύπρῳ τὸ λείψανον Βαρνάβα τοῦ Ἀποστόλου· ἔκειτο δὲ ἐπὶ τὸ στῆθος αὐτοῦ τὸ κατὰ Ματθαῖον ἅγιον εὐαγγέλιον ἔχον πτυχία θύϊνα (*Lexicon*, alphabetic letter Θ, 1063, line 4, *TLG*).

15. τὸ λείψανον Βαρνάβα τοῦ ἀποστόλου εὑρέθη ἐν Κύπρῳ ὑπὸ δένδρον ὃ Κεράτιον λέγεται κείμενον· οὗ ἐπιστέρνιον τὸ θεῖον καὶ ἱερὸν Εὐαγγέλιον Ματθαίου τοῦ εὐαγγελιστοῦ ἐτύγχανεν ὄν, χερσὶν οἰκείαις τῷ Βαρνάβᾳ γραφέν. Ἐκ ταύτης τοίνυν προφάσεως καὶ Κύπριοι τὸ καταρχὰς περιγεγόνασιν αὐτοκέφαλον ἔχειν τὴν κατ᾽ αὐτοὺς μητρόπολιν, καὶ μὴ τελεῖν ὑπὸ Ἀντιόχειαν ᾗ καὶ ὑπέκειτο πρότερον. Ἐκράτυνε δ᾽ ἐπὶ μᾶλλον τοῦτο καὶ Ἰουστινιανὸς ὕστερον ἐπὶ δόξῃ τῆς γαμετῆς Θεοδώρας Κύπρον λαχούσης πατρίδα (*Historia Ecclesiastica* 16. 37, lines 32–45, *TLG*; printed text in *Patrologia Graeca* 147: col. 193). The *TLG* data search revealed that Nikephorus mentioned Barnabas 19 times in *Historia Ecclesiastica*.

Rediscovery of Anthemios

For 800 years differing versions of the story of the discovery of Barnabas's relics occasionally appeared in Christian writings. But among the surviving texts, only the sixth-century *Laudatio Barnabae apostoli* by Alexander the Monk and the eleventh-century praise of Barnabas by the Byzantine emperor Michael IV included Anthemios in the story. And never, ever, was there any mention of Zeno giving imperial privileges to the Cypriot archbishop and his successors. During the entire Lusignan occupation of the island (1192–1489), no writer mentioned the privileges.

Time Line

c. 47	Barnabas and Paul bring Christianity to Cyprus.
c. 488	Pseudonymous *Acts of Barnabas* depicts Barnabas as a martyr and the founder of the Church of Cyprus.
c. 550	*Laudatio Barnabae apostoli* glorifies Barnabas and recounts the discovery of his relics by Anthemios and the subsequent reaffirmation of autocephaly by Zeno. No mention of imperial privileges.
550–1191	During this entire time period, Byzantine Emperor Michael IV (ruled 1034–1041) is the only other writer to mention Anthemios, and he makes no mention imperial privileges.
1192–1489	No writers during the rule of the Lusignan dynasty mention the imperial privileges.
1489–1560	No one until near the end of Venetian rule over Cyprus says anything about imperial privileges.
1560	Florio Bustron mentions the archbishop's scepter—the first known reference to one of the imperial privileges later associated with the Cyprus archbishops.
1571	Ottoman Turks conquer Cyprus.
1660	Ottomans make Archbishop Nikephoros the ethnarch of Cyprus and delegate tax collection responsibilities to him.
1788	Kyprianos reports that Zeno gave three imperial privileges to Anthemios.

In my research, as a matter of fact, by November 2011, the earliest Greek text I had found that actually mentions the imperial privileges granted to Anthemios was the *Chronological History of Cyprus* published by the Archimandrite Kyprianos in Venice in 1788.[16] Kyprianos drew details from *Laudatio Barnabae apostoli*, lacing his description of Peter, the patriarch of Antioch, with the defamatory statements asserted c. 550 by Alexander the Monk—many of which modern Cypriots repeat regularly. Kyprianos provided a summary of Barnabas appearing to Anthemios (whose name he misspelled Anthemitos) in a vision. But what he states in addition to *Laudatio's* description is revealing.

> The king placed the archbishop of Salamis over all Cyprus, and he honored its high priest with imperial privileges: that he might bear clearly the scarlet mantle in the sacred rites, that he might carry the imperial scepter instead of the shepherd's staff, and make his signature with red, and the archbishop be magnified *autocephalos*, and that he is not submissive to any of the patriarchs.[17]

Kyprianos focused interest on Barnabas and Anthemios and their role in Cypriot *autocephaly*, and his influence on the understanding of history in Cyprus is immense. Many modern Cypriots cite Kyprianos as authoritative, although his history falls far short of the standards of modern historiography. Of course, his approach to telling history was typical of authors during his time. The contemporary problem arises with accepting his material as historically accurate.[18]

16. Another Greek manuscript that mentions the privileges actually predates Kyprianos's history, but I was not aware of it until several years later. More about that text later.

17. AT of the Greek text in Κυπριανος, ΙΣΤΟΡΙΑ ΧΡΟΝΟΛΟΓΙΚΗ ΤΗΣ ΝΗΣΟΥ ΚΥΠΡΟΥ, 151.

18. Chris Schabel laments the way modern Cypriots uncritically trust Kyprianos as if he were a reliable source. Two particularly revealing articles by Schabel are "Knight's Tale," esp. 4, 16–17, 27; and "Myth of Queen Alice."

FIGURE 17

**Icon of Barnabas on a wall in the Monastery Church of Apostle Barnabas.
Dated 1921, this icon depicts Barnabas seated on a royal throne,
wearing a crown and a lavish, red cape, and holding an ornate scepter.**

Kyprianos's 1788 history of Cyprus plays a very significant role in modern, Greek Cypriot beliefs about Barnabas and the saint's connection to ecclesiastical power on the island. His contribution to the Cypriot Orthodox Church's self-understanding is enormous, for he articulated the story of Zeno giving imperial privileges to Anthemios. But Kyprianos did not invent the story of the archbishop's imperial privileges. Two icons from 1673 and 1691 depict imperial privileges, the 1676 Deed of Election of Nektarios of Paphos mentions one, and journal entries published by foreign travelers to Cyprus in the seventeenth and eighteenth centuries mention them. However the earliest written comment is an obscure statement made in 1560.

I learned about the 1560 text when I consulted with Christopher Schabel, Professor of Medieval History at the University of Cyprus in Nicosia. I told Schabel that I was puzzled by the fact that the earliest Greek author I had found thus far who mentioned the privileges was Kyprianos. In an email dated November 23, 2011, he called my attention to non-Greek texts that predated Kyprianos by several centuries:

> Etienne de Lusignan, ca. 1570, mentions that the archbishop was allowed to wear red. Earlier in the 16th century Florio Bustron had said that the emperor granted the archbishop of Cyprus the *"baston imperiale, con il pomo in cima, et il capello con la croce rossa di supra."*[19] So the imperial sceptre was also known. These writers are not Orthodox. My guess is that this is indeed an old tradition from before 1191.[20]

Because I cannot translate sixteenth-century Venetian dialects, I needed to be sure that I understood the comment by Bustron. I really should have waited to consult with an expert in ancient Venetian dialects, but scholars in Cyprus were busy at the time—and the date for my Fulbright lecture was fast approaching.

So, I emailed my former colleague, Joseph Huffman, who is a Medievalist. He drew on his knowledge of Latin and translated the text as follows: "An imperial scepter with an orb[21] on top, a cape with a red cross on the upper portion." Huffman became interested in the matter, looked up the text by Bustron, and added the rest of the sentence: "and many other immunities for the perpetual honor of this blessed and holy island." After I returned home from Cyprus, I collaborated for a brief time with Huffman and shared with him my discoveries about the lack of any mention of the archbishop's special privileges in ancient texts.

After reflecting on the passage, Huffman concluded that Bustron was describing an imperial scepter topped with an orb and a cross (a *globus cruciger*). He claimed that there was no evidence prior to Bustron

---

19. Schabel got the text from *Chronique de l'ile de Chypre par Florio Bustron*, 32: "*Et li concesse il baston imperiale, con il pomo in cima, et il capello con la croce rossa di supra, et molte altre immunità a honor perpetuo di questa isola benedetta et santa.*"

20. I.e., before French crusaders took over Cyprus.

21. Literally, an apple (*il pomo*).

of any ruler having a scepter topped by a *globus cruciger*—it was a new innovation.[22] For several years, I believed this assertion, but eventually I realized the claim was wrong by at least 460 years! And there were other problems.

Florio Bustron and the Archbishop's Privileges

Florio Bustron, a politically well-connected man from a noble family, functioned as a counselor to the Venetian governors of Cyprus; but he wrote his chronicle of the history of the island while in Venice—not in Cyprus. Bustron's chronicle is widely read by Cypriots, and a PDF of the entire document is readily available for free download.[23] His story about Barnabas and the saint's successors in Cyprus includes material that originated in the sixth-century speech by Alexander the Monk, *Laudatio Barnabae apostoli.* However, in his short and confused account, Bustron says that Barnabas was born in Kyrenia—instead of Salamis as previous authors specified. And, in a huge overstatement, he claims that Barnabas converted the island to Christianity. He also states that the governor of Salamis, a man named *Igemone*, murdered Barnabas—instead of a Jewish mob as specified in the Acts of Barnabas and *Laudatio Barnabae.* Bustron catalogues some of the Cypriot archbishops after Barnabas; but, oddly enough, he lists the archbishop succeeding Barnabas as Epiphanius, who ruled 365–403, thus skipping over three centuries.

Bustron explains that Anthemios (whose name he spells *Anthimius*) went to the emperor to defend himself against the contention of Peter, Patriarch of Antioch, who had insisted that he should control Cyprus because an apostle, Paul, founded the Church of Antioch. According to Bustron, Anthemios argued that Cyprus also had an apostolic founder—Barnabas—and that he (Anthemios) knew by divine inspiration that the saint's relics were in Salamis, with a copy of Matthew on his chest. Whereas previous accounts claimed that Anthemios first discovered the relics and then took them to the emperor, Bustron says that the emperor sent prelates to Cyprus and *they* discovered the body of Barnabas with the

---

22. "The Donation of Zeno: St Barnabas and the Origins of the Cypriot Archbishops' Regalia Privileges," 246–50.

23. https://archive.org/details/chroniquedelleoobustuoft. The British Library has in its archives an eighteenth-century copy of Bustron's book (Ms. 8630).

Gospel of Matthew on his chest. Bustron goes on to say that Anthemios was allowed to maintain his position as head of the Church of Cyprus.

Interestingly, Bustron never specifies the name of the emperor, Zeno. He explains that the emperor gave money to Anthemios to build a large church to honor Barnabas, and then he makes his statement about the emperor granting to the archbishop an imperial scepter and a special hat and many other immunities—whatever that means. But he does not recount the later legend that Emperor Zeno granted to Archbishop Anthemios three imperial privileges.

Bustron was, of course, familiar with the ancient symbolism of the *globus cruciger*. He would have seen it in multiple locations around Cyprus. For example, in the ancient apse of the Church of *Panagia Angeloktistis,*[24] a short distance west of Larnaca, Cyprus, is a sixth-century mosaic of the Virgin Mary holding Jesus. In this mosaic the archangels Michael and Gabriel stand on either side of Mary and Jesus. Each angel holds in his left hand a scepter and in his right hand a globe with a cross on it, which he offers to Jesus.

FIGURE 18

Sixth-century mosaic in the Church of *Panagia Angeloktistis* depicting Mary holding Jesus. The archangels Michael and Gabriel each offer a *globus cruciger* to Jesus.

24. Παναγία της Αγγελόκτιστης. *Panagia* refers to the all holy virgin Mary, and *Angeloktistis* means "built by angels." According to a legend, angels built the church.

The globe symbolized universal dominion. Ancient Roman statues of Jupiter sometimes depicted him holding a scepter in one hand and an orb in the other hand—symbolizing his authority over all the earth. Roman emperors appropriated this imagery to enhance their own rule, and Christian emperors placed a cross on the orb, producing what was called the *globus cruciger* to symbolize Christ's sovereignty over the world—exercised, of course, through the Christian emperor.

Bustron wrote when the Ottoman Turks continued to expand their territory. He published his book for Venetian readers in 1560,[25] and he died in 1570, during the Ottoman siege of Famagusta. Huffman believes that Bustron invented the idea of placing a *globus cruciger* atop an imperial scepter as part of a failed attempt to stir up the Venetians to launch a new Crusade to save Cyprus from the Turks.

According to Huffman, the political motivation behind Bustron's idea of placing a *globus cruciger* atop an imperial scepter bears similarities to the notorious Donation of Constantine. In the mid-eighth or early-ninth century, a monk forged a document in which the fourth-century Emperor Constantine supposedly made a land grant to the pope and also granted him the right to wear imperial regalia (wear a crown, carry an imperial scepter, wear purple robes, etc.).[26]

Although Huffman admits, "One cannot postulate from silence, and so we shall never know for sure," he goes on to say, "It is quite plausible that Bustron turned to Cyprus' apostolic founding saint just as the papacy had turned to the power of St Peter."[27] He moves further into speculation when he states, "And so it is not too much to conclude that the regalia privileges of the archbishops of Cyprus have their historical origins in Florio Bustron's 'Donation of Zeno' [who] called upon an ancient Cypriot hero in a new way . . . to secure Latin defence of the island."[28] If such high stakes were involved in this so-called donation of Zeno, why did Bustron not at least mention Zeno's name? Did he even know Zeno's name? Although Bustron had access to archives in Cyprus, many questions arise regarding how much he actually used them. I see no evidence in his

25. *Historia overo Commentarii de Cipro.* Bustron used some material from an earlier manuscript owned by Francis Amadi.

26. Huffman, "Donation of Zeno: St Barnabas and the Origins of the Cypriot Archbishops' Regalia Privileges," 251–54.

27. Huffman, "Donation of Zeno: St Barnabas and the Origins of the Cypriot Archbishops' Regalia Privileges," 253.

28. Huffman, "Donation of Zeno: St Barnabas and the Origins of the Cypriot Archbishops' Regalia Privileges," 254.

mangled account of Anthemios that Bustron was creatively motivating Venetian readers to defend Cyprus. Nevertheless, in a subsequent article, Huffman moves from speculation to certainty, asserting that the tradition of the imperial privileges "was the invention of Florio Bustron."[29]

Huffman declares, "the 'baston imperial, con il pomo in cima' combines them [scepter and orb] in a manner unheard of anywhere else in Christendom. . . . it was customary for the orb to be held in one hand and the sceptre in the other; these two objects were never combined to create a new insignia."[30]

Multiple problems exist with Huffman's claims. First, Florio Bustron was absolutely *not* the first person in history to invent the idea of placing a *globus cruciger* atop an imperial scepter. In 1100 CE, Emperor Henry IV (German "Heinrich IV") commissioned an illuminated Gospel as a wedding gift for his sister Judith upon her marriage to Władysław I Herman, Duke of Poland. One of the paintings in this manuscript depicts Henry in the middle, his father Henry III on the left, and his son Conrad on the right. Each man holds a scepter topped with a *globus cruciger*.

FIGURE 19

Henry III, Henry IV, and Conrad of Germany. Photo from the manuscript
Ewangeliarz Emmeramski **(AKKK, Ms 208, fol. 2v) used by permission of the Krakow Cathedral Archives (***Archiwum i Biblioteka Krakowskiej Kapituly Katedralnej***)**

29. Huffman, "Donation of Zeno: St. Barnabas and the Modern History of the Cypriot Archbishop's Regalia Privileges," 714.

30. Huffman, "Donation of Zeno: St Barnabas and the Origins of the Cypriot Archbishops' Regalia Privileges," 249–50.

A photo of this painting provides the cover image of the biography *Henry IV of Germany,* written by I. S. Robinson.[31] Furthermore, the same painting adorns the cover of Gerd Althoff's biography of the same emperor: *Heinrich IV.*[32] In other words, the existence of a painting from 1100 showing Henry IV holding a scepter topped with a *globus cruciger* is not an obscure matter. Even the Wikipedia article on Henry IV includes a photo of him from the painting in the illuminated Gospel. King Henry had a royal scepter topped with a *globus cruciger* 460 years before Florio Bustron wrote his brief comment about the Cyprus archbishops.

FIGURE 20

Playing card produced in Paris by Jacques Vieville in the 1600s.

Other images readily available for free download on the Internet reveal that the precursors of tarot cards made in France in the 1600s depict both the emperor and the empress holding scepters topped by a *globus cruciger.* I cannot imagine that Bustron's mention in 1560 of the scepter of the archbishop of Cyprus could have exerted such widespread cultural influence that artists of French playing cards began to depict the emperor and empress holding such scepters.[33]

31. Robinson, *Henry IV of German,* 1056–1106.

32. Althoff, *Heinrich IV.* A photo of the complete painting of Henry III, Henry IV and Conrad II provides the cover image for Althoff's book, *Family, Friends and Followers.*

33. The oldest surviving cards of this type date to the mid 1400s. Philippo Maria Visconti, Duke of Milan, and his son-in-law Francesco Sforza, who succeeded Visconti as duke, commissioned Bonifacio Bembo to produce these playing cards. At this time the cards were still called Trionfi, which means triumph or trump; and their style and meaning exercised much influence over later cards. These early cards show the emperor holding a staff with nothing on the top. However, cards produced by the following people in France depict both the empress and the emperor as holding scepters topped with a *globus cruciger*: Jean Noblet (Paris, c. 1650); Jacques Viéville (Paris, c. 1650); Jean Dodal (Lyon, c. 1701); and Nicolas Conver (Marseille, c. 1760).

Ironically, Huffman bases his assertion that Bustron invented the idea of placing a *globus cruciger* atop an imperial scepter on his own faulty translation. In a personal email to me dated Feb. 2, 2018, Daniele Baglioni, a linguist at the University of Venice who is an authority in ancient Venetian dialects—and also an expert in Medieval Cyprus—explained Bustron's meaning of *cap(p)ello*:

> Both in 16-th century Italian and in coeval Venetian the basic meaning of the word is 'hat'. Metaphorical uses indicating 'top' or 'cover' are quite rare . . . I had a look at the entire sentence ("Et li concesse il baston imperiale, con il pomo in cima, et il capello con la croce rossa di supra, et molte altre immunità a honor perpetuo di questa isola benedetta et santa") and it seems clear to me that both the *capello* and the *molte altre immunità* ('many other immunities') are direct objects of the verb *concesse* 'he granted'. Consequently, this would be . . . my new translation: 'He granted him the imperial scepter with a knob on it, and a hat with a red cross on the upper portion, and many other immunities etc." . . . I would be rather sure that the cross is on the hat and not on the scepter.[34]

Baglioni's translation indicates that Bustron described the archbishop's scepter as having only a knob on top. The red cross was on the archbishop's hat, not on his scepter.

In spite of Bustron's confused account of Barnabas and Anthemios and the discovery of the saint's relics, his comment about the archbishop receiving an imperial scepter is interesting. I have found no author prior to him who made such a statement. And, although he never specifies the name of Emperor Zeno, he does associate the gift of the scepter with an emperor. I seriously doubt that Bustron came up with this idea on his own. More likely, a tradition already existed in 1560 that included an early version of the archbishop's privilege of an imperial scepter—and, perhaps, something about his clothing. However, the scepter described by Bustron was not the modern version that is topped by a *globus cruciger*, and Bustron certainly did not invent the idea of such a scepter. Bustron's muddled narration does not inspire confidence, but the beginning of a legendary connection between the Cyprus archbishop's imperial regalia and a gift from an emperor to Anthemios appears in the literary record for the first time with Bustron. How much before 1560 this link existed is impossible to tell, due to the lack of sources. But it is there in embryo. And that is significant.

34. Daniele Baglioni, email message to Michael Cosby, Feb. 2, 2018.

Excursus on the Insignificance
of the Color Red in Icons of Barnabas

One of the imperial privileges of the Cyprus archbishop is the right to wear red/scarlet (or purple), so I explored the possibility that the use of red in artwork might reveal more about the origin of these privileges. Once I examined the paintings in Cypriot churches, however, I concluded that this idea was a dead end. Well before the time Florio Bustron mentioned special privileges of archbishops, paintings of Barnabas depicted the apostle wearing red garments.

Because Huffman draws false conclusions about the development of the imperial privileges based in part on the color of Barnabas's robes in a few icons,[35] I need to correct some of his assertions. For example, he uses as evidence an icon of Barnabas painted c. 1550 and currently on display in the Byzantine Museum adjoining the Archbishopric in Nicosia. Because the icon slightly predates Bustron's description of the archbishop, and the icon does not depict Barnabas wearing imperial regalia, Huffman concludes this absence of regalia further demonstrates that prior to Bustron there was no belief in imperial privileges.[36]

In fact, the absence of regalia in this icon proves nothing. Few icons or frescos in Cyprus show Barnabas holding an imperial scepter. Today, even after centuries of Cypriot belief in the archbishops' imperial privileges, Cypriot artists continue to depict Barnabas in the traditional manner, with no signs of imperial regalia other than a red or purple cloak—which does not distinguish him from other saints. The Byzantine Museum, located adjacent to the Archbishopric, the epicenter of veneration of Barnabas as the saint who instigated Zeno's conferral of the imperial privileges on the archbishop, proudly displays the c. 1550 icon of Barnabas, although it lacks any hint of a scepter with a *globus cruciger* or a pen and red ink. The icon depicts Barnabas wearing a reddish robe, and the absence of a scepter and a quill and red ink poses no cognitive dissonance whatsoever for Greek Orthodox Cypriots.

---

35. See Huffman, "Donation of Zeno: St. Barnabas and the Modern History of the Cypriot Archbishop's Regalia Privileges," 742–43.

36. Huffman, "Donation of Zeno: St Barnabas and the Origins of the Cypriot Archbishops' Regalia Privileges," 250. For a full-page photograph of this icon, see *Cyprus: Island of Saints: A Devotional Journey*, 17. A PDF of this book is available free for download: https://docplayer.net/40884182-Cyprus-island-of-saints-a-devotional-journey.html. The non-color photograph in the book does not reveal that Barnabas wears a red robe in the icon.

Indeed, when the Very Reverend Archimandrite Gabriel, the Abbot of the Holy Monastery of Apostle Barnabas who fervently believed in the archbishop's imperial privileges, painted his modern icon of Barnabas, he depicted the saint wearing a purple robe, an archbishop's omophorion (a vestment like a stole or shawl with crosses on it),[37] and holding a book— presumably the Gospel of Matthew according to traditions dating back to the fifth century. Aside from the purple robe, however, nothing in the icon suggests imperial privileges. Actually, most modern icons and mosaics of Barnabas do *not* depict him displaying the archbishop's imperial regalia, in spite of the pervasive belief in Cyprus that Barnabas helped Anthemios receive imperial privileges from Zeno in the late fifth century.

FIGURE 21

1550 icon of Barnabas. © Byzantine Museum and Art Gallery of the Archbishop Makarios III Foundation. Photo used by permission.

37. Bishops wear the omophorion about their neck and shoulders and draped down the front of their bodies. This band of cloth with crosses on it symbolizes the bishop's pastoral care of his people.

FIGURE 22

Modern icon of Barnabas painted by the Archimandrite Gabriel,
Abbot of the Monastery of Apostle Barnabas.

In the ancient churches of Cyprus, frescos and icons abound with
red. It was a favorite color of the artists. St. George nearly always wears a
red cape, and the same is common with St. Mamas riding the lion. Mary,
mother of Jesus, wears red. St. Marina wears a vivid red robe. Mary Mag-
dalene sometimes wears red. Paul often wears red. Many saints and angels wear red. Artists depicted Barnabas wearing red long before anyone
began to speak of imperial privileges.

In the late fifteenth-century church of *Panagia Chrysokourdaliotissa*
is a beautiful fresco of Barnabas in a niche so dark you cannot see it unless you know to turn on a particular light. This fresco predates Florio
Bustron's comment about the archbishop, and in it Barnabas wears a red
robe and a bishop's omophorion. He holds an ornate book in his left hand
(presumably the Gospel of Matthew) but no scepter or quill with red ink.

FIGURE 23

Fifteenth-century fresco of Barnabas in *Panagia Chrysokourdaliotissa*.
Photo taken by permission (in very low light).

In St. Nicholas of the Roof, a church built in the eleventh century
and so named because of its steeply pitched roof, is a lovely fresco of
Barnabas from the 1300s. He wears a red robe under a purple outer
drape, and he holds in both hands a scroll (presumably Matthew). But he
does not wear a bishop's omophorion with crosses on it, and there is no
hint of imperial regalia.

FIGURE 24

Fourteenth-century fresco of Barnabas in St Nicholas of the Roof.
Photo taken by permission.

The Church of *Panagia tou Araka* near Lagoudera dates to the twelfth century and is one of the most important Byzantine churches in Cyprus. An inscription above the north entrance of the church indicates that money for the frescos was donated in December 1192. But because the frescos in the apse and the bema use a different style, they probably were painted prior to 1192; and this art contains a fresco depicting Barnabas and Epiphanius. Predictably, the red in the under-robes of both Barnabas and Ephiphanius does not distinguish their clothing from the other saints depicted around them in the bema. Barnabas holds a book in his left hand and wears a bishop's omophorion with crosses on it, but he shows no signs whatsoever of imperial privileges.[38]

38. Paul Englezakis provides in an article on Epiphanius a black-and-white photo of this fresco in "Epiphanius of Salamis, the Father of the Cypriot Autocephaly," 40. Richard the Lionheart conquered Cyprus in 1191 and sold it to Guy de Lusignan in 1192, so this fresco predates the French crusaders' rule over Cyprus.

In the monastery church of St. John Lampadistis, which has no fresco of Barnabas, one section has well-preserved frescos from the 1200s. I was immediately struck with how much red they contain. Another set of frescos in this same church dates to the early 1400s, and red also abounds in these. For example, a section of the east vault depicts scenes from Christ's trial and crucifixion. The scene of Jesus before the high priest depicts the high priest wearing a red robe. Jesus wears a more subdued, reddish under-robe in this panel—but the soldiers who arrested him have the same, red color robes under their armor. The scene of Jesus before Pontius Pilate shows Pilate wearing a red cape. A panel depicting Jesus' triumphant entry into Jerusalem shows a man wearing a red robe kneeling before Jesus—and a young boy throws his red robe on the road before Jesus, who is riding a donkey into Jerusalem.

Some of the frescos in the church of *Panagia Asinou* date to 1105/1106 (455 years before Florio Bustron's history of Cyprus). Their colors are still vivid, and red was a favorite color for the artist of these frescos also. Even Judas wears a red robe when betraying Jesus with a kiss. Depending on context, ancient artists used red to designate royalty, special position, or wealth.[39]

A small fresco with a defaced image of Barnabas may be seen in the semi-circular apse under the windows of the bema in the front of *Panagia Asinou*—paired with a similar painting of Epiphanius. Each saint holds a gilded book in his left hand, and each wears a white omophorion with large, black crosses on it. The fresco is faded, but the color of Barnabas's robe appears to be red.[40]

39. For a technical article documenting the expensive nature of red dye, see Munro, "Medieval Scarlet and the Economics of Sartorial Splendour," 13–70.

40. For examples of the pervasive use of red in Cypriot artwork, see books like *Icons of Cyprus* by Anastasios Papageorghiou. The lavish photos in this large format book show the pervasive use of red by ancient artists in icons from the 700s through the 1500s—all but two of them painted prior to Bustron's comment in 1560. What I still find stunning is the lack of images of Barnabas in ancient Cypriot artwork. In all the icons shown in *Icons of Cyprus*, for example, there is only *one* small image of Barnabas on page 110 in an icon of Christ with selected apostles and saints depicted on either side of him.

FIGURE 25

Barnabas fresco in a semi-circular apse under the windows of the bema in
Panagia Asinou. Barnabas is the defaced image on the left. Epiphanius is
depicted on the right. Photo courtesy of Ourania Perdiki.

Thus, the presence of red/scarlet in frescos and icons of Barnabas
provided no benchmark for my research. The true significance of what
art reveals about the origins of the archbishop's special privileges comes
from two icons painted a century *after* Bustron, during Ottoman occupation of Cyprus. I will describe these icons in the next chapter—but first, a
word about a sixteenth-century Frenchman.

Excursus on Étienne de Lusignan

During the Turkish invasion of Cyprus in which Florio Bustron died
defending the island in 1570, Étienne de Lusignan (1537–1590), a Do-
minican priest, was writing a book on geography.[41] Étienne came from
the French royal family that had ruled Cyprus from 1192 to 1489, prior to
Venetian control of the island. He fled Cyprus during the Turkish invasion

41. Huffman provides detailed information on Étienne de Lusignan ("Donation
of Zeno: St Barnabas and the Origins of the Cypriot Archbishops' Regalia Privileges,"
254–59), and here his comments lack the speculation found in his presentation on
Florio Bustron.

and published his book in Naples in 1573.[42] Étienne's description of Cyprus contains an emotional reminder to readers that the French brought the true light of Catholicism to Cyprus and kept this light burning for 300 years until the Venetians took over the island. He adds poignantly, "Later, alas, it fell and was extinguished, having sunk like a pearl into the wickedness of the enemy of Christianity, so we can rightly say along with the Prophet, 'The crown of our leaders has fallen, woe to us who have sinned!'"[43] By applying words from Scripture to his own time, he appropriates a biblical statement to condemn lack of effort to regain Cyprus. His quotation appears to be a misappropriation of Lam 5:16: "The crown has fallen from our head; woe to us, for we have sinned!" (NRSV). But regardless of his dubious use of Scripture, he applies the words to his own time and condemns failure to defend Cyprus as sinful.

Étienne de Lusignan argues for the survival of Cyprus by describing it as the sacred island God loves. He goes so far as to call it an extension of the Holy Land.[44] To motivate Latin Catholics to action, Étienne cites the ancient tradition of Barnabas being the first to preach the gospel message in Rome and another tradition of Barnabas being the first bishop of Milan. Then he directly appeals to the Latins to save Cyprus.[45]

> So you can imagine . . . how much Christianity owes to Cyprus. But what will we say about you, Holy Rome, which have received the first principle of your holiness mainly from Barnabas? And you, Milan, which received such grace from him . . . ? Here you see, therefore, how Cyprus is Christ's friend and a true province of the Holy Land, because it was the main reason that Rome was sanctified as head of the world.[46]

42. *Chorograffia et breve Historia universale dell'isola de Cipro principiando al tempo di Noè per in sino al 1572.* A PDF of this book is available as a free download: https://archive.org/details/chorograffiaetbroolusi. Modern Cypriot scholars regularly study Lusignan's book, and its contents are widely known and quoted.

43. From Pelosi, *Lusignan's Chorography of Cyprus*, 1–2.

44. "Therefore, you, sacred island with a double holiness, do not have to suffer and to be desperate in the present time. Take as example our holy mother Jerusalem in every respect, and you can hope in the fact that you will be soon consoled. And you [monks] . . . have carried the fruits of Jerusalem to Cyprus and called it a province of the Holy Land. It is indeed connected with the Holy Land, sanctified and producing fruits . . . " (*Chorograffia* 31).

45. Here Huffman's thesis is cogent, because Étienne overtly makes his case for a crusade to save Cyprus.

46. *Chorograffia* 32.

Étienne says nothing about Cypriot archbishop's imperial privileges in his argument for why Catholics in France and Italy should take up arms once again and liberate the Holy Land, including Cyprus, from Turkish domination. Étienne argues that Rome and Milan owe a great debt to Barnabas and should therefore save Cyprus, but he makes no mention of Bustron's comment written a decade earlier about the Cyprus archbishop having special privileges. They simply are not part of his argument. Perhaps he knew nothing about Bustron's remark; perhaps he simply chose not to include it. Either way, his appeal failed. No crusade materialized to save Cyprus. The Ottoman Turks continued to control the island. And, during Turkish rule, in another twist of history, the legend of the archbishop's three imperial privileges developed and grew to maturity under Islamic overlords.

CHAPTER SIX

Development of the Imperial Privileges

Ottoman conquest of Cyprus brought a reversal of fortune for the Orthodox Church. The Turks abolished Catholic rule and made Orthodoxy the official Christian religion on the island. They allowed Greek Cypriots to keep their churches, but they converted Latin churches into mosques.

FIGURE 26

Interior of the Gothic Cathedral of St. Nicholas in Famagusta.
This church was converted to a mosque in 1571.

Over the next century, Ottoman forms of governing the island slowly modified in response to Cypriot complaints about corrupt Turkish administrators. In 1660 the Turkish government officially recognized then Archbishop Nikephoros as the *ethnarch* (political leader) of the Greek Cypriots and gave to him responsibility for tax collection. This official recognition further established Nikephoros's position as a power broker and provided increased impetus for him and his inner circle to develop the legend of the archbishop's imperial privileges.[1]

The archbishop's already significant administrative authority increased with his official recognition as the *ethnarch* of the Orthodox community. During this time of limited autonomy under Ottoman rule, Orthodox leaders apparently cultivated the claim that in the fifth century Zeno had given to Archbishop Anthemios three imperial privileges. Perhaps ironically, under Islamic rule they appealed to their Byzantine past as a way of enhancing the archbishop's present prestige. And it worked. By the time Archimandrite Kyprianos wrote his *Chronological History of Cyprus* in 1788, the privilege of Cypriot archbishops signing documents in red ink was a well-established tradition recognized by Ottoman rulers.[2]

During the decades surrounding 1660, the legend of Archbishop Anthemios receiving from Emperor Zeno the privileges of wearing a red/scarlet (or purple) cape, carrying an imperial scepter, and signing his name with red ink was crystalizing. In 1673, Archbishop Nikephoros

---

1. Huffman incorrectly asserts that after 1571 the Greek Orthodox leaders of Cyprus had to reinvent their past and their church structure because they had been under Catholic domination for centuries ("Donation of Zeno: St. Barnabas and the Modern History of the Cypriot Archbishop's Regalia Privileges," 716). In fact, they already had four bishops, one of whom had a cathedral in Nicosia and functioned as the *defacto* archbishop. For centuries after 1571, they chose not to return to the 14 bishops they had had prior to the thirteenth century when Catholic leaders imposed increased restriction on the Orthodox Church of Cyprus. Following the Ottoman conquest of Cyprus and the increased religious autonomy of the Orthodox Church, they had no need to make structural changes to their ecclesiastical system, let alone reinvent it.

2. For an English translation of this passage from Kyprianos's *Chronological History of Cyprus,* see *Excerpta Cypria,* 353–54. The scanned version of Cobham's collection of translated excerpts from multiple ancient sources is available on-Line in a fully searchable PDF: https://archive.org/details/excerptacypriamaoocobhuoft

I draw freely from the online PDF of this valuable 1908 collection, which Cypriots study regularly. Indeed, its contents are widely known on the island—even among students in secondary schools. However, in "Donation of Zeno: St. Barnabas and the Modern History of the Cypriot Archbishop's Regalia Privileges," 713–45, Huffman presents more detailed information than I do on some of the ancient authors that we both quote; so where appropriate, I footnote his work. During my tenure as a Senior Fulbright Fellow in 2011, I had personal conversations with Cypriot scholars whom Huffman later cited in his article.

commissioned Leontios, a monk from Limassol, to depict an early version of the privileges in an icon of Barnabas. The Holy Monastery of Machairas in the mountains southwest of Nicosia possesses this icon of Barnabas painted by Leontios.[3] A monk at Machairas told me that the icon was packed in a storage closet, so I could not personally examine it. However, the monks at the monastery provided a digital photograph of the icon and gave their permission for me to publish it. Leontios's signature and the date 1673 are prominent at the bottom right of the icon, which shows Barnabas sitting on a throne (*cathedra*), wearing a red cape and a bishop's *omophorion*. Nothing pertaining to Anthemios or Zeno appears in the icon—although it is possible that the artist presupposed the legend about Zeno granting them. Leontios depicts the privileges as coming directly from angelic messengers.

FIGURE 27

1673 icon of Barnabas by Leontios. Photo used by permission of the Holy Monastery of Machairas.

3. Hadjichristodoulou, "Map of Cyprus in a Cypriot Icon," provides a good summary of the education and career of Leontios, including other icons he was commissioned to paint (see esp. 337, 339–42; 344n1).

One of several indicators of western influence on Leontios is the fact that, under the feet of Barnabas, symbolizing his heavenly rule over the island, is a map of Cyprus based on a map published in Venice in 1570 by Paolo Forlani.[4] Christodoulos Hadjichristodoulou, with whom I discussed my research while in Cyprus in 2011, points out in his 2004 article that Leontios added this map after he finished the icon—which is clear from the uncharacteristic way the southern coast of Cyprus goes over the original gold band across the bottom of the icon. [5]

The icon depicts Barnabas holding a book in his left hand, which I expected to be the Gospel of Matthew to match the traditions dating back to the fifth-century Acts of Barnabas. However, the text displayed on the book held by Barnabas is from Luke 10:16: "And the Lord said to his disciples, 'The one who hears you hears me, and the one who rejects you rejects me.'"[6] The quotation makes sense, because it comes from Jesus' exhortation to the seventy disciples he sent before him in Luke 10:1. For many centuries, Cypriot Orthodox tradition has affirmed that Barnabas was the leader of the seventy. But the quotation from Luke 10:16 does not connect the icon with the legend about Anthemios discovering the Gospel of Matthew on the chest of Barnabas and taking the codex to Emperor Zeno.

Hadjichristodoulou explains the icon's depiction of Barnabas as follows:

> The Apostle Barnabas is, then, shown to be blessing his homeland of Cyprus, as its missionary, protector and saviour *par excellence,* and the Archbishop of the day, his successor on the throne. St Barnabas was established as the patron saint of the Autocephalous Church of Cyprus in the late fifth century, when the Roman doctrine of apostolicity on apostolic sees made

---

4. Hadjichristodoulou, "Map of Cyprus in a Cypriot Icon," 340–43. Hadjichristodoulou's article contains photographs of Forlani's map, which was circulated widely from 1570 through the early 1700s.

5. Hadjichristodoulou, "Map of Cyprus in a Cypriot Icon," 340. Huffman references Hadjichristodoulou's article in "Donation of Zeno: St. Barnabas and the Modern History of the Cypriot Archbishop's Regalia Privileges," 719. His comment "now the red (or scarlet) mantle is also included" is ill founded, as I have shown above regarding the widespread use of the color red in frescos and icons predating and postdating Bustron.

6. ΕΙΠΕΝ Ο ΚΥΡΙΟΣ ΤΟΙΣ ΕΑΥΤΟΥ ΜΑΘΗΤΑΙΣ Ο/ΑΚΟΥΩΝ ΥΜΩΝ ΕΜΟΥ ΑΚΟΥΕΙ ΚΑΙ Ο ΑΘΕ[ΤΩΝ ΥΜΑΣ ΕΜΕ ΑΘΕΤΕΙ].

its appearance in the East and was at that time declared to be a principle of ecclesiastical organisation.[7]

Further describing this icon, Hadjichristodoulou says,

> Two archangels are shown in the two upper corners, doing reverence and proffering to the saint a mitre, an imperial sceptre (!), a gold inkstand with cinnabar [i.e., red ink], and an archiépiscopal royal staff and the melon (globe of the world), imperial privileges, which were given, according to tradition, to the Archbishop of Cyprus.[8]

Unfortunately, the paint on the old icon is degraded. The digital photo given to me by monks at Machairas does not have sufficient clarity to confirm the details specified by Hadjichristodoulou. The angel on the left bears a miter, but the nature of the other gifts is not decipherable.

Pertaining to this same 1673 icon, Veronica della Dora, in a 2012 article, explained that Leontios painted his icon during "the seventeenth century, at the peak of Western Renaissance cartographic production, as well as of Ottoman expansion." She observed that icons with maps such as this one arose "from networks of exchange between different worlds" and "can be read as the results of processes of hybridization between Orthodox and Western visual traditions."[9] She argued that Western influence caused Eastern Orthodox artists to add concerns for mapping regions of the world to their interests in artistic mapping of the heavens. [10]

7. Hadjichristodoulou, "Map of Cyprus in a Cypriot Icon," 339.

8. Hadjichristodoulou, "Map of Cyprus in a Cypriot Icon," 339. If Hadjichristodoulou's description is correct, I am curious as to why the angels would offer to Barnabas both an imperial scepter and a staff topped by a *globus cruciger*. Cypriot archbishops carry one scepter topped by a *globus cruciger*.

9. Della Dora, "Windows on Heaven (and earth)," 86. Huffman references della Dora's article in "Donation of Zeno: St. Barnabas and the Modern History of the Cypriot Archbishop's Regalia Privileges," 720–21.

10. Della Dora, "Windows on Heaven (and earth)," 91. Della Dora's description of Barnabas follows the normal storyline in Cyprus: "Leontios's icon of Saint Barnabas (1673), for example, depicts the enthroned patron saint and founder of the Autocephalous Church of Cyprus resting his feet on a map of the island (Figure 4). Saint Bar-nabas was one of the seventy disciples Christ sent out two by two during His earthly ministry. Born of a wealthy Cypriot Levite family, Barnabas traveled and preached the Gospel with Paul and Mark on missionary journeys. According to the Orthodox hagiographic account, the saint was martyred by the Jews in his home country in A.D. 61 and buried in the city of Salamis, on the east coast of the island. The location of his grave was revealed by Barnabas to Archbishop Anthemius of Cyprus through visions in A.D. 478, during the reign of Emperor Zeno. At that time Patriarch

Building on Hadjichristodoulou's article, della Dora connects the icon with modern beliefs about Emperor Zeno and Anthemios.

> On Leontios's icon, the apostle is portrayed in red episcopal gar-
> ments and in a blessing gesture. With his other hand he holds a
> copy of the Gospel (which he was said to have personally copied
> and been buried with). In the two upper corners, the two arch-
> angels offer Barnabas a miter, an imperial scepter, a gold ink-
> stand with cinnabar, and an archiepiscopal staff topped by the
> globe of the universe,[11] that is, the imperial privileges that were
> first given by Zeno to the Archbishop of Cyprus. Barnabas's
> iconography reflects the traditional Byzantine iconography of
> the *Majestas Domini* [Christ in Majesty], with Christ enthroned
> in the universe and resting His feet on the Earth. As an apostle,
> Barnabas is a reflection of Christ on earth. And this is echoed
> in the inscription on the Gospel he holds: "He that heareth you
> heareth me; and he that despiseth you despiseth me." The Lord
> sits in the heavens and blesses the earth and the universe; Bar-
> nabas sits in heaven and blesses the island of Cyprus, his home-
> land, archdiocese, and site of martyrdom.[12]

Della Dora is unaware of the late date of the appearance of the imperial privileges, and her identification of the Gospel in Barnabas's hand as Matthew needs clarification because the quotation is from Luke 10:16. Also, whether or not Leontios had in his mind the modern belief that Zeno gave the privileges to Anthemios when he painted the icon is unclear from the details he included in his painting. Perhaps della Dora assumes the presence of Zeno and Anthemios in the mind of Leontios because she herself is familiar with the fully developed story. But her analysis of the political function of the icon provides important insights.

Della Dora describes the historical forces that led Nikephoros to commission the icon, and she explains the significance of where this struggling archbishop chose to display the icon in an effort to buttress his faltering authority. Nikephoros briefly lost his position as archbishop

---

Peter of Antioch was trying to extend his rule to include Cyprus, which had been recognized as autocephalous, under an independent archbishop since A.D. 431. The recovery of the relics of Saint Barnabas proved the apostolic foundation of the Church of Cyprus, and its autocephaly was therefore confirmed by the emperor against the claims of the Patriarch of Antioch" (91).

11. In private correspondence, della Dora told me that she did not personally have access to the icon but relied on Hadjichristodoulou's description.

12. Della Dora, "Windows on Heaven (and earth)," 92–93.

due to a theological dispute,[13] and the year after he regained his position as archbishop, he commissioned Leontios to paint the icon of Barnabas. Nikephoros hung this icon of Barnabas on his episcopal throne in Nicosia as a visual means of solidifying his position as the legitimate successor of Barnabas.[14] Again we see political maneuvering—this time via artwork—on the part of an archbishop to strengthen his leadership position.

Della Dora adds that, eighteen years later, another icon makes an even stronger connection between Barnabas and an archbishop. An icon dated 1691, and currently on display in the Byzantine Museum in Nicosia, shows in miniature Archbishop Iakovos I (James I) standing at the bottom left of the icon. Wearing his royal vestments, Iakavos raises his hands in prayer to the much larger Barnabas,[15] who is seated on his throne and also wearing royal clothing.

13. "In 1662 Archbishop Nikephoros of Cyprus visited Constantinople to obtain relief for his overtaxed faithful. Ten years later he was threatened with deposition on the grounds that he had held communion with the ex-patriarch Parthenios IV, who had been exiled to Cyprus after having returned to the ecumenical throne for the third time in 1671. On presenting himself in Constantinople to Patriarch Dionysios IV (Parthenios's rival), asking forgiveness and pleading that he had been misled by the false reasoning of the ex-patriarch, Nikephoros was pardoned and reinstated as the legitimate archbishop of the island." (Della Dora, "Windows on Heaven (and earth)," 93).

14. Della Dora, "Windows on Heaven (and earth)," 93–94.

15. In 110 n30, della Dora provides the following information on the inscription at the bottom right of the icon:

The inscription reads: "Εν δόξη παριστάμενος Θεώ τω Παντοκράτωρα, Βαρνάβα Κύπρου καύκημα, εκτενώς ικετεύω του δυσωπείν του σωτήρα υπέρ του αχρίου. Του αξίωσε με τότε της δεξιάς του μερίδος. + Δεήσις και πολλού πόθου του Μακαριωτάτου Κύπρου Κυρίου Ιακώβου 1691 XY" (in Anastasios Papageorgiou, *E autokephalos Ekklesia tes Kyprou: Katalogos tes ektheses* [Nicosia: Byzantine Museum of the Archbishop Makarios III Institute, 1995]). Leontios, a priest-monk at the archiepiscopal court, was the leading ecclesiastical portraitist of his time on Cyprus. His subjects also include Iakovos I and Christodoulos II (1682–1685?), the two successors of Nikephoros's successor, Hilarion. See Hadjichristodoulou, "Map of Cyprus in a Post-Byzantine Cypriot Icon," 340.

My translation of the Greek inscription is as follows: "By the glory present in God the Almighty (*Pantakrator*), by Barnabas the boast of Cyprus, I fervently supplicate in order to beg of the savior on behalf of the worthless. Make me worthy of the right hand of the portion/share. + Prayer and great longing of the most blessed Lord of Cyprus, James."

FIGURE 28

1691 icon of Barnabas. © Byzantine Museum and Art Gallery of the Archbishop Makarios III Foundation. Used by permission.

The angel at the top right of the icon offers to Barnabas a scepter topped by a *globus cruciger*. However, the angel at the top left does not offer an inkpot with red ink as Huffman asserts.[16] The left angel clearly offers to Barnabas a miter that matches the one worn by Archbishop Iakovos I at the lower left of the icon. Although the red ink privilege is not depicted in this 1691 icon, the absence of the quill and ink does not necessarily indicate that the artist was unaware of this privilege. Artists

16. Huffman, "Donation of Zeno: St. Barnabas and the Modern History of the Cypriot Archbishop's Regalia Privileges," 723. Huffman also states that Archbishop Iakovos is *kneeling* before Barnabas, but the photograph clearly shows the archbishop *standing*.

do not need to depict everything they believe about a subject when they paint an icon of the individual.[17] The matter remains unclear.

What is clear is that twelve centuries after the time Anthemios met Zeno in 488 and supposedly received the privileges from the emperor, the legend of the privileges was becoming part of the Cypriot Greek Orthodox narrative under Ottoman rule. By the end of the seventeenth century, these symbols of earthly power were a created history.

Time Line

1560	Florio Bustron mentions the Cyprus archbishop carrying an imperial scepter topped by a knob.
1571	Ottoman Turks conquer Cyprus and make Orthodoxy the official Christian presence on the island.
1660	Ottomans make Archbishop Nikephoros the ethnarch of Cyprus and delegate tax collection responsibilities to him.
1673	Leontios paints an icon depicting Barnabas as both the spiritual and terrestrial ruler of Cyprus, receiving special privileges from two archangels.
1676	Deed of Election of Nektarios of Paphos states that Zeno granted to the archbishop of Cyprus the privilege of signing his name with red ink.
1788	Archimandrite Kyprianos recounts the story of Barnabas and specifies three imperial privileges given by Zeno to Anthemios.

Created History Takes Roots

Scholars miss things, and I am no exception. After I had translated Greek texts about Barnabas that spanned eighteen centuries and thought I was the first one to notice the late date of the archbishop's special privileges, I learned that a Cypriot scholar briefly commented on the privileges thirty years before I commenced my research. In 1981, Paul (Benedict) Englezakis published in Greek an article about Archbishop Kyprianos's inkstand. Almost as an aside, he states the following:

17. Another complication that lurks in the background is the possibility of later modification of an earlier painting. I am assuming that what the 1673 and 1691 icons depict is original, but I cannot state with complete assurance that the originals have not been altered. When specialists restore ancient icons and frescos, they sometimes discover that earlier versions lie beneath the outer layers of paint. Future restoration efforts on these icons could reveal that monks updated them to represent beliefs that were current in their own times. However, other evidence from this time period confirms what the icons depict.

With regard to the legend of the privileges bestowed by Zeno, here it is sufficient for us to note that the ancient sources make no reference to them—not even the Cypriot monk Alexander, from whom almost everything is drawn—and the first written evidence of such a thing which we possess dates only from 1676.[18]

Englezakis cites the 1676 Deed of Election of Nektarios of Paphos, which specifies that the ancient Emperor Zeno revered the throne of the archbishop of Cyprus and honored him with the privilege of signing his name with red ink—a privilege shared by no other patriarch.[19]

I see no evidence that Englezakis compiled all the data as I have done, and I do not know how many of the texts that I found and translated he actually read. But he obviously made his observation based on familiarity with the ancient sources. The *TLG* database that I used does not contain the Deed of Election of Nektarios. Englezakis, however, was familiar with manuscripts contained in the Patriarchate Archive in Constantinople.

Englezakis believed that the custom of the archbishop of Cyprus signing his name in scarlet ink became permanent at the beginning of the seventeenth century. But he traced its origins back to the Greek bishops of Cyprus using red wax seals in the thirteenth century, during the period of French rule over the island—which is an intriguing possibility.[20] According to Englezakis, the archbishop's scepter "was

18. Englezakis, "Archbishop Kyprianos's Inkstand," 269. When Englezakis published this article in 1981, I was just beginning my PhD studies at Emory University. Two of his coworkers published an English translation of his article in 1995—after his untimely death.

19. Englezakis, "Archbishop Kyprianos's Inkstand," 269. Footnote 25 cites the Deed of Election of Nektarios, Proedros of Paphos in K. Delikanes (The Official Church Documents Kept in the Codex of the Patriarchate Archive, Constantinople, 1904), and provides the following quotation: "῏Ωτινι . . . φιλοδορούθμεθα . . ., πλὴν τῆς ὑποκλαπείσης λάθρα ματαίας τοῦ βασιλικοῦ σκήπτρου κατακρήσκεως, ὅπερ, ὡς μόνῳ τῷ Ἀποστολικῷ ἡμῶν Θρόνῳ πεφιλοτιμημένον ὑπὸ τῶν ἀοιδίμων πάλαι βασιλέων Ζήνωνος καὶ Ἰουστινιανοῦ τοῦ Μεγάλου μετὰ τῆς ἐρυθρᾶς ὑπογραφῆς, οὐδένα συγκοινωνὸν τοῦ μεγίστου τούτου προνομίου ἀποδεχόμεθα (nothing is said about the *mandyas*)."

20. Englezakis, "Archbishop Kyprianos's Inkstand," 270. Footnote 26 states, "In the forged synodical deed of 1295, *Boundaries with God's help of the holy fathers who are bishops in Cyprus in the year 6308 from Adam*, it is said that the bishop of Karpasia and archbishop of Cyprus may have a seal 'with red wax because he sits on the archiepiscopal throne.'" But Englezakis explains that the archbishops did not sign documents

first used liturgically by Orthodox bishops at the end of the sixteenth and the beginning of the seventeenth century," and he adds, "The oldest representation known to me of the archiepiscopal sceptre of Cyprus is on the reliquary of the head of St John Lampadistis at Kalopanagiotes, dating from the archiepiscopate of Nikephoros (1614–74)."[21]

I verified in 2019 the presence of a depiction of a scepter topped by a *globus cruciger* on the reliquary of St. John Lampadistis donated by Archbishop Nikephoros, but the monks at the Monastery Church of St. John Lampadistis in Kalopanagiotes would not allow me to photograph it (although photographs of the reliquary are readily available on the Internet). One panel of the metal reliquary, which supposedly contains the skull of St. John Lampadistis, depicts Archbishop Nikephoros kneeling, with arms outstretched in a gesture of supplication; and he wears a miter with a cross on top.[22] Behind Nikephoros, seeming to stand by itself, is a scepter topped by a *globus cruciger*.[23] Thus, Nikephoros, whom the Turks made *ethnarch* of Cyprus in 1660, appropriated for his own regalia a scepter topped by a *globus cruciger* and made effective use of this imperial privilege.

Englezakis revealed no awareness of Florio Bustron's 1560 comment about the archbishop carrying an imperial scepter with a knob on top. However, he was well aware that, when Nikephoros was named *ethnarch* in 1660, the imperial scepter topped by a *globus cruciger* was part of the archbishop's regalia—as the depiction on the reliquary of St. John Lampadistis reveals. The second half of the seventeenth century was apparently

---

with red at that time. That privilege was the emperor's alone. "The false synod of 1295 bestowed it on the third ranking bishop, in the synod's view, the bishop of Solea and Nicosia, the second ranking bishop, the bishop of Paphos, having received the privilege of black wax. All these are inventions under Western influence. As is known, in the Byzantine period the archbishops of Cyprus sealed their more official documents with lead bulls."

21. Englezakis, "Archbishop Kyprianos's Inkstand," 271n28: "See K. Myrantheus, Ὁ ἅγιος Ἰωάννης ὁ Λαμπαδιστής, Nicosia, 1969, illustr. 20."

22. A miter of this type does not appear to be what Florio Bustron had in mind when he described the archbishop's hat (not miter) as having "a red cross on the upper portion." He probably meant a bishop's hat with a cross stitched on it; but, given the nature of his description of Barnabas and Anthemios, I hesitate to state with confidence his intended meaning.

23. Above the figure of Nikephoros is the following Greek text: ΝΙΚΗΦΟΡΟΣ ΑΡΧΙΕΠΙΣΚΟΠΟΣ ΚΥΠΡΟΥ ("Nikephoros Archbishop of Cyprus"). Two photographs of this silver and gilded reliquary may be seen in Papageorghiou, *Monastery of Saint John Lampadistis in Kalopanayiotis*, 60 (figs. 68, 69).

a seminal time for the development of the legend of the archbishop's imperial privileges.

Regarding Zeno granting to Anthemios the privilege of signing his
name in red ink in c. 488, Englezakis points out that a law enacted by
Emperor Leo I (father-in-law of Zeno) in the year 470, and later incorporated into the Justianic code (*Codex Just.* I, 23:6–a.470), strictly forbade
anyone but the emperor from signing documents in red ink—"on pain of
confiscation of property and death." Leo's law also forbade granting this
right to anyone else. Consequently, by law Zeno would *not* have granted
this privilege to Anthemios.[24] Use of red ink was a jealously guarded right
of the emperor alone.

Englezakis believed that the myth of the the archbishop's imperial
privilege of signing documents in red ink developed not under Byzantine
rule but under the Ottoman Turks as a means of giving more hope to
the Orthodox Christians of Cyprus.[25] Ottoman rulers did not share the
Byzantine custom of the emperor alone using red ink, so they did not see
it as a threat to their sovereignty; nor did they explore the historical basis
for the anachronistic claim of Cypriot clergy regarding their archbishop.
Apparently, the Cypriots successfully convinced the Turks that their
archbishop was heir also to terrestrial power over the island.[26]

Michalis Michael has built on the work of Englezakis, strengthening
the argument that the three imperial privileges of the Cyprus archbishops
did not emerge until Ottoman occupation of the island, when the archbishops of Cyprus began to connect legendary symbols of a Byzantine
past as a means of strengthening their standing under their Ottoman rulers in the seventeenth century.[27] Like Englezakis, Michael does not appear
to be aware of the 1560 comment by Bustron regarding the archbishop's
scepter and other privileges. How beliefs about the privileges developed

---

24. Englezakis, "Archbishop Kyprianos's Inkstand," 272. Englezakis provides more
detailed information on ancient sources regarding this practice.

25. Englezakis, "Archbishop Kyprianos's Inkstand," 273.

26. What still puzzles me, however, is how the Cypriot clergy convinced the Orthodox patriarchs in surrounding regions to believe the legend of Zeno granting to
Anthemios the imperial privileges.

27. "Βυζαντινά σύμβολα ὀθωμανικῆς πολιτικῆς ἐξουσίας: ἡ περίπτωση τῶν
προνομίων τῶν Ἀρχιεπισκόπων Κύπρου," 315–32. He has also published other articles that focus on the same material: "Orthodox Institution of Ottoman Political
Authority"; "Kyprianos, 1810–21"; "Local Authorities and Conflict"; "Myth and Nationalism"; and "Loss of an Ottoman Traditional Order."

between 1560 and 1660 is unclear, but by the end of the 1600s they were part of the Cypriot Orthodox national identity. Shortly after this time, foreigners travelling to Cyprus began to mention the archbishop's imperial regalia.

Seventeenth- and Eighteenth-Century Travelers Mention the Privileges

Cypriot Orthodox archbishops communicated claims of imperial privileges not only to their Ottoman overlords but also to foreigners visiting from other countries. During the seventeenth and eighteenth centuries, journal entries of those who traveled to Cyprus or Turkey occasionally include information about Barnabas.[28]

Of course, one needs to exercise caution when reading journals. Accounts of travelers reflect the cultural bias and interests of the individuals making observations. And, what one traveler considers important, another might not even notice. Traveling Monks predictably describe monasteries and relics. Pilgrims visiting Cyprus on their way to the Holy Land might walk for days through the countryside but never mention the crops or animals or people of a region. Instead, they recount stories about famous icons that perform miracles (like the icon of the Virgin Mary at Kykkos) or which monastery has a piece of the holy cross.

Businessmen and diplomats, however, tend to notice things like the inefficiency or greed of local leaders, the construction of the homes of rich and poor and how well maintained the structures are in villages and cities. They mention relics and ruins of ancient churches and recount stories they hear from locals, and they observe the kinds of crops produced and the amount of land that could be cultivated but is not. However, pilgrims and politicians alike mention the excellent wines of Cyprus, and often they complain about the fetid pools of water in certain areas that breed disease and are a threat to the health and life of visitors to the island.

If these intrepid travelers actually had lived in Cyprus and had grown more familiar with the people and customs, they would have modified their comments. Also, to be fair, details easily become muddled

---

28. See Huffman, "Donation of Zeno: St. Barnabas and the Modern History of the Cypriot Archbishop's Regalia Privileges," 713–45, for greater detail on some of these accounts. To access many of the ancient accounts directly, see *Excerpta Cypria*: https://archive.org/details/excerptacypriama00cobhuoft.

when writing or rewriting descriptions of places or events days, weeks, months, or years after the fact. Memory blurs details, and even with the best intentions, filling in the particulars at a later time often results in mistakes. Yet, the observations of travelers do provide a mosaic that allows modern readers to glimpse the reality faced by Cypriots during the centuries described.

The journal entries provided in *Excerpta Cypria* reveal differences between descriptions of Cyprus made when the French and Venetians controlled the island and when the Turks controlled it. The Lusignans, the French Crusaders who ruled Cyprus 1192–1489, lived on the island. It was their home, and they made improvements, built grand structures, and took pride in their surroundings.[29] The Venetians, who controlled Cyprus 1489–1571, built roads and bridges, and fortified cities. But journals of travelers during Venetian rule express more complaints about Venetian treatment of Cypriots.[30] However, *all* the journal entries made during Ottoman rule abound in caustic comments about the Ottomans, who settled Turks on the island but mostly used it to generate tax revenue[31] and showed little interest in improving Cyprus.

29. E.g., L. Von Suchen visited Cyprus sometime between 1336–1341 (see *Excerpta Cypria* p. 18 regarding the publication of his journal entries). Describing Cyprus under the Lusignan Dynasty, he gives a glowing description: "From Rhodes we sail to Cyprus, an island most noble and fertile, most famous and rich, surpassing all the islands of the sea, and teeming with all good things . . . It is productive beyond all other lands." He describes Nicosia as a very healthy, capital city where many wealthy nobles live and spend much time hunting and participating in tournaments. He also speaks of wealthy merchants who do a thriving trade with shipping of goods, and he adds that pilgrims headed for Jerusalem also bring a lot of commerce to Cyprus (*Excerpta Cypria*, 20).

30. E.g., Martin von Baumgarten made a pilgrimage to the Holy Land and visited Cyprus (1508). He complains that Nicosia and Famagusta are the only two nice cities, and, in spite of abundant resources the people are poor. He claims that Cypriots have to work two days a week for the state, and get fined if they cannot do their work. "Besides, all the inhabitants of Cyprus are slaves to the Venetians, being obliged to pay to the state a third part of all their increase or income. . . And which is more, there is yearly some tax or other imposed on them, with which the poor common people are so flayed and pillaged, that they hardly have wherewithal to keep body and soul together" (*Excerpta Cypria*, 55).

31. E.g., John Macdonald Kinnier, who worked for the East India Company, visited Cyprus from January 2–24, 1814 and criticized both the Turkish government and the Orthodox clergy: "The evil consequences of the Turkish form of government are nowhere more apparent than in Cyprus, where the Governor, who is appointed yearly by the Capudan Pasha, the ex-officio proprietor of the island, has recourse to

Under oppressive Ottoman rule, Cyprus archbishops told the legend of their imperial privileges enough times that it became an essential part of the Greek Cypriot narrative. They connected their privileged position on the island to an imaginary, distant past. And the Turks were not the only foreigners who believed the story.

In 1678 (five years after Leontios painted the icon of Barnabas receiving imperial privileges and two years after the Deed of Election of Nektarios of Paphos, which mentions signing with red ink), Paul Rycaut, the British consul in Smyrna, Turkey, emphasized the Cyprus archbishop's unique privilege of signing documents with red ink. By this time the Cypriot clergy had successfully communicated to people living in Turkey their story about Barnabas, Zeno, Anthemios, and the archbishop's privileges.

Rycaut's version of the story of Barnabas was confused, but he knew the basics about Emperor Zeno granting to Anthemios the privilege to sign documents in red ink—a privilege shared by no other patriarch in the Orthodox Church. He even heard that the Church of Cyprus was once subject to the Patriarch of Antioch, but that the Eighth Canon of the Council of Ephesus (431 CE) condemned any interference in Cyprus by Antioch.[32]

---

every method of extortion; so that the Turks would labor under the same grievances as the Christians were not the latter, in addition to the demands of the government, compelled to contribute to the support of a number of lazy and avaricious monks. All affairs connected to the Greeks are under the superintendence of the Archbishop and Dragoman of Cyprus (an officer appointed by the Porte) who are accountable to the Mutessellim for the contributions, miri, &c. . . . the Greek peasantry, who are the only industrious class, have been so much oppressed by the Turks, monks and bishops, that they are now reduced to the extremity of indigence, and avail themselves of every opportunity to emigrate from the island." He goes on to say that the governor and archbishop—who at that time was Kyprianos—buy most of the corn from the farmers and then either export it or sell it back to Cypriots at higher cost (*Excerpta Cypria*, 414).

32. In his account he mistakenly connects Emperor Justinian (ruled 527–565) to Cypriot autocephaly, claiming Justinian granted the imperial privileges and Emperor Zeno later confirmed them. Rycaut also erroneously says that Justinian's mother was a Cypriot, and he misspells Barnabas. See Rycaut, *Present State of the Greek and Armenian Churches, Anno Christi 1678*, 89: "The island of Cyprus was in its ecclesiastical government subjected once to the Patriarch of Antioch but afterwards by the Council of Ephesus as canon the eighth, and the same again confirmed by the grace and favour of Justinian the Emperour (whose mother was a Cypriot by birth) this church was made absolute and independent of any other, and a privilege given to Anthemius, the Archbishop in that age, to subscribe his name to all publick acts in red letters, which was an honour above that of any Patriarch, who writes his name or firm in

Published reports of what travelers heard about Barnabas while they were in Cyprus frequently contain mistakes. For example, J. Heyman toured the Middle East from 1700 to 1709 and kept a journal of his travels. Years later, his nephew, John Heyman, a Dutch professor of Oriental languages, compiled these notes and combined them with journal entries by Egmond van der Nijenburg, who traveled through the Middle East from 1720 to 1723. Heyman's account is almost comical. After explaining

---

black characters, that which was afterwards confirmed by the authority of Zeno the Emperour: this favour and indulgence was granted in honour to the Apostle Barnaby, who primarily governed this diocese (sic), where now his sepulcher remains" (quotation from Cobham, *Excerpta Cypria,* 234).

Rycaut's awareness that the Eighth Canon of the Council of Ephesus acknowledged the autocephaly of the Cypriot Church is interesting, because others of his time who describe the archbishop and Cyprus make no mention of the Council of Ephesus. The text of the eighth Canon is as follows:

> The Judgment of the same Holy Synod, pronounced on the petition presented to it by the Bishops of Cyprus:

> Our brother bishop Rheginus, the beloved of God, and his fellow beloved of God bishops, Zeno and Evagrius, of the Province of Cyprus, have reported to us an innovation which has been introduced contrary to the ecclesiastical constitutions and the Canons of the Holy Apostles, and which touches the liberties of all. Wherefore, since injuries affecting all require the more attention, as they cause the greater damage, and particularly when they are transgressions of an ancient custom; and since those excellent men, who have petitioned the Synod, have told us in writing and by word of mouth that the Bishop of Antioch has in this way held ordinations in Cyprus; therefore the Rulers of the holy churches in Cyprus shall enjoy, without dispute or injury, according to the Canons of the blessed Fathers and ancient custom, the right of performing for themselves the ordination of their excellent Bishops. The same rule shall be observed in the other dioceses and provinces everywhere, so that none of the God beloved Bishops shall assume control of any province which has not heretofore, from the very beginning, been under his own hand or that of his predecessors. But if any one has violently taken and subjected [a Province], he shall give it up; lest the Canons of the Fathers be transgressed; or the vanities of worldly honour be brought in under pretext of sacred office; or we lose, without knowing it, little by little, the liberty which Our Lord Jesus Christ, the Deliverer of all men, hath given us by his own Blood. Wherefore, this holy and ecumenical Synod has decreed that in every province the rights which heretofore, from the beginning, have belonged to it, shall be preserved to it, according to the old prevailing custom, unchanged and uninjured: every Metropolitan having permission to take, for his own security, a copy of these acts. And if any one shall bring forward a rule contrary to what is here determined, this holy and ecumenical Synod unanimously decrees that it shall be of no effect. (*NPNF*[2], 14: 234–35)

the controversy regarding the independence of the Cyprus church in the fifth century,[33] he states the following:

> In the mean time, an affair happened which occasioned a great deal of talk. The monks of a certain convent, whether in building or repairing it, by accident found a coffin, and in it a body with a leaden plate on it, signifying that in this coffin was deposited the body of the apostle St Barnabas. About the neck of the saint was also a chain fastened to a leaden box, which was found to contain an Arabic copy of St Matthew's Gospel, written by St Barnabas himself on parchment. The clergy of Cyprus very dexterously availed themselves of this discovery, sending to the Emperor Zeno both the sacred relics and the manuscript; with which present that devout prince was so pleased that he gave a charter to the church of Cyprus, declaring it independent of any patriarch.[34]

One can scarcely imagine how Heyman got the details so confused. Interestingly, he mentioned nothing about imperial privileges; but a few years later an Orthodox pilgrim from Ukraine specified them.

Vasyl Hryhorovyč-Bars'kyj, born in Kiev in 1701,[35] visited Cyprus on four occasions between 1726 and 1736. His fourth time on the island, September 1734–August 1736, was by far the most extensive. His journal entries describe the many monasteries that he visited, and he drew pictures of some with pen and ink.[36] I saw reproductions of his sketch of

33. "Anciently, a very great contest happened in this island about jurisdiction: the Archbishop pretended to be independent of any patriarch, whereas the Patriarchs of Antioch and Alexandria no less violently insisted that this church was subordinate to them. The pretentions of the three contending parties were laid before the Grecian Emperor at Constantinople for his decision" (Cobham, *Excerpta Cypria*, 249).

34. Cobham, *Excerpta Cypria*, 249.

35. Alexander Grishin explains that Bars'kyj began his studies at the Kiev Academy in 1715 or 1716, but because of a large ulcer on his leg, he did not finish his studies. In 1723, he journeyed to the western Ukraine city of L'viv for medical treatment, where he experienced what he believed to be a miraculous cure; and he vowed to go on a pilgrimage of thankfulness. At the time, he was still poorly educated. Bars'kyj tried to attend a Jesuit academy in L'viv, but he was denied admission because he was Orthodox. During his two decades of travel, however, he became increasingly more educated, and his journals reflect a growing maturity of intellect. By the end of his life, he was a well-respected scholar. See p. 4 of Grishin's introduction to *A Pilgrim's Account of Cyprus: Bars'kyj's Travels in Cyprus*.

36. For descriptions of his travels to monasteries, see Grishin, *Pilgrim's Account of Cyprus*, 25–103. Eighteen plates at the end of Grishin's book provide reproductions of Bars'kyj's drawings. The drawing of Apostle Barnabas Monastery is Plate 16.

the Monastery of Apostle Barnabas near Salamis in a number of Cyprus museums.

In 1734, Archbishop Philotheos recruited Bars'kyj to teach Latin to students in Nicosia, but a devastating earthquake in April 10, 1735, terminated his teaching career. After the earthquake came a time of lawlessness in which Turks murdered many Greek Cypriots, and Archbishop Philotheos and Bars'kyj both fled to the mountains for safety from the chaos in Nicosia.[37] In spite of his close association with Archbishop Philotheos, Bars'kyj's account of events surrounding the discovery of the relics of Barnabas is somewhat confused.

> In the beginning this was the Episcopal Seat of the Apostle Barnabas. Behind the church altar outside the church, there is a hole full of clean water, with a chapel built on top of it, and there is a stone staircase, and it was here, so they relate, that they found the handwritten manuscript of the Gospels of the Evangelist Saint Matthew, which were later presented as a gift to pious Emperor Justinian. For this the emperor granted the archbishops of Cyprus autonomy and the right to wear crowns on their heads similar to those of patriarchs and to carry a staff with a golden apple on top, to sign their names in red ink and to be addressed as 'Most Holy.'[38]

I have visited the tomb of Barnabas multiple times, and there is no spring of water underneath the present chapel built over the tomb—so that part of his description puzzles me.[39] Why Bars'kyj says the Gospels of Mat-

---

37. Grishin, *Pilgrim's Account of Cyprus*, 27. Bars'kyj has nothing good to say about the Turks. Sprinkled throughout his descriptions of Cyprus are vitriolic condemnations of how the Turks abuse Christians, impose crushing taxes, steal their land, and desecrate Orthodox churches. He states that "Many of the high towers crumbled, and others were destroyed to their foundations. Following this, there was an increase in crime, and many Christians that year were murdered by the Turks, and a reign of horror was unleashed on the world."

38. Grishin, *Pilgrim's Account of Cyprus*, 96.

39. In 1738, the English traveler Richard Pococke visited the monastery of Barnabas, and he also mentioned a well by the supposed tomb:
> … there is a monastery and a large church dedicated to St Barnabas, which seems to have been a fine building; the church has been ruined and rebuilt; the foundations of the east end of the old church remain in three semicircles. About half a furlong east of this church there is a descent by several steps to a sepulcher grot cut in the rock, with niches for bodies on three sides of it: here, they say, the body of St Barnabas was deposited, who was a native of this island, and suffered martyrdom at Salamis in the time of Nero. At the entrance of the grot there is a well of water that is a little salt, and a small chapel is built

thew, I do not know; and why he said Emperor Justinian (ruled 527–565) instead of Emperor Zeno is a mystery to me.

But Bars'kyj believed that an emperor allowed the Cyprus archbishop to wear a miter, carry a staff topped by a knob, sign his name in red ink, and to be called most holy. Although he got the name of the emperor wrong, he obviously heard a story about the granting of special privileges to Cyprus archbishops. And, unlike later travelers from Europe who kept journals of their experiences in Cyprus and wrote derogatory things about Orthodox priests, Bars'kyj, a committed Orthodox Christian, wrote consistently complimentary descriptions of Cypriot clergy.[40]

In spite of inconsistencies in the various journal entries regarding the archbishop's privileges, evidence suggests that Cypriot Orthodox clergy during the seventeenth and eighteenth centuries did, in fact, articulate a narrative (narratives?) regarding Anthemios, Zeno, and the imperial privileges. Travelers to Cyprus often failed to get details correct when listening to stories about matters that were foreign to them. And, perhaps, some of the Orthodox clergy of Cyprus were still unclear on particular details. But frescos in the National Cathedral of St. John show that by the mid 1700s the story had crystalized into its modern form.

---

over the grotto, which does not seem to be of any great antiquity. (Cobham, *Excerpta Cypria*, 256–57)

40. For example, he says of Archbishop Philotheos, "I saw in him a man who was wise, benevolent, virtuous, and well spoken, and one who was dedicated to teaching." (Grishin, *Pilgrim's Account of Cyprus*, 25). When describing Archbishop Philotheos presiding over a special liturgy at the Monastery of Machairas, he states the following.

His dress is similar to that of a patriarch, with the only difference being that the patriarch wears an embroidered cape and in his hands holds a staff and in charters is referred to as 'most holy and most blessed,' while the archbishops of Cyprus are dressed in a very light red cape and hold a staff in their hands with a handle in the shape of an apple, or as they call it, a sceptre, and write their names in the charters with red ink, a right given to them by Greek emperors. They have absolute power, like the patriarchs, and write their names and are generally referred to as 'most holy,' but never as 'most blessed.' (Ibid, 86)

Bars'kyj did not specify that the archbishop's scepter had a *globus cruciger*, but he listed the rest of the special privileges.

FIGURE 29

Cathedral of St. John in Nicosia

Archbishops Crystalize
the Myth of the Imperial Privileges

In 1662, Archbishop Nikephoros (two years after being named *ethnarch*) directed construction of the Church of St. John in Nicosia, and today the Archbishopric stands next to this church. Archbishop Sylvester renovated St. John in 1720 and consecrated it as the national cathedral of Cyprus. The rather plain and unimpressive exterior of the Cathedral of St. John (something demanded by the Turks) differs dramatically from the ornate interior of the structure. Under Archbishop Philotheos (ruled 1734–1759), artists covered the walls and ceiling of the cathedral with frescos. Among these frescos is a four-panel unit that depicts the story of Barnabas appearing in a vision to Archbishop Anthemios, of Anthemios uncovering the tomb of Barnabas, of Anthemios presenting the Gospel of Matthew to Emperor Zeno, and Emperor Zeno granting to Anthemios the imperial privileges. A representative of the Holy Archbishopric of Cyprus granted permission for me to photograph this prominently displayed fresco, which reveals that, by the mid-eighteenth century, Orthodox clergy had expanded the events described in *Laudatio Barnabae apostoli* (c. 550) to include the legend of Zeno conferring all three privileges to the archbishop.

FIGURE 30

Fresco in St. John's Cathedral of the Barnabas–Anthemios legend.
Photo taken by permission of the Holy Archbishopric of Cyprus.

Later that century, in his 1788 *Chronological History of Cyprus*, Archimandrite Kyprianos published the version of the story of the privileges that survived and flourishes today in Cyprus. In this history, Kyprianos admitted he knew little about the time between the Ottoman conquest of Cyprus in 1571 and the conferral of civic power on the archbishop in 1660 by the Porte, the official Turkish governing body.[41] But

41. Porte is the Turkish word for gate, and it refers to the gate that led into the complex of buildings in Constantinople (now Istanbul) where the central Ottoman government officials met to conduct business. Porte (also called the Sublime Porte) designates the Ottoman government. Kyprianos reports the following:

> . . . the first appointed bishops of Cyprus—concerning whom we have but dim and vague information—and their successors up to 1660, do not appear to have mixed themselves in the civil affairs of the *rayahs* [Turkish word meaning flock, which designates the tax-paying underclass Cypriots—whom officials fleeced], that is to say, in the matter of their taxes . . . It is however quite clear that the local bishops were recognized by the Porte, because they could not assume jurisdiction over their flocks and churches without an imperial *berat*. (Cobham, *Excerpta Cypria*, 353)

According to Turkish history professor Nejdet Gök, "In Ottoman diplomatics, *berat* is a kind of document issued by the sultan in order to grant a privilege (or to make an appointment of a dignitary), or to confer the right to possession of a property

when members of the Porte made the Cypriot archbishop the *ethnarch* of Cyprus and delegated to him the power and the responsibility to collect taxes, they further elevated the archbishop's status in society.

While describing the archbishop's role in negotiating with Turkish authorities on behalf of the Greek Cypriots, Kyprianos described the red-ink imperial privilege that distinguished Cypriot archbishops from other Orthodox leaders—a privilege recognized by the Porte as being of ancient origin.[42]

In another section of his history, Kyprianos articulated all three of the archbishop's imperial privileges. After rehearsing the sixth-century narrative written in *Laudatio Barnabae apostoli* regarding Anthemios winning Zeno's approval in Constantinople, he added the relatively recent tradition about the archbishop's privileges.

> And the king placed the archbishop of Salamis over all Cyprus, and he honored its high priest with royal privileges: that he might bear clearly the scarlet mantle in the sacred rites, that he might carry the royal scepter instead of the shepherd's staff, and make his signature with red, and the archbishop be magnified *autocephalos*, and that he is not submissive to any of the patriarchs.[43]

In yet another statement—one destined to be of immense importance—Kyprianos went beyond connecting Barnabas with the ecclesiastical independence of Cyprus and praised him with highly nationalistic

---

belonging to the state, (sic) it can be both an official approval of an act and an order for third parties to comply with an act" ("Introduction of the *Berat* in Ottoman Diplomatics," 141).

42. Kyprianos explained that ". . . the Porte . . . receives very graciously their [the archbishops'] *arz* or petition about taxes, and all the complaints they may make, if so they be sent to it direct under their seals, the Archbishop's name being written in Turkish in red ink, (his seal alone is found imprinted in the Imperial *qayd* or register in red ink, while all the seals which accompany it, including those of the Patriarchs, are impressed in black ink). So that we may conclude that the Ottoman Porte was certainly assured after the conquest, the fact being of course confirmed by the Patriarch, that the Archbishop of Cyprus enjoyed *ab antiquo* [from ancient times] the privilege, given him by the sovereign on account of the loyalty and devotion of himself and his flock, and which he preserved without a break up to the present day, to sign and seal with red ink: and this same vermillion seal is recognized by the Porte and by all its subjects. And I do not believe that any other red seal will be found in the registers" (Cobham, *Excerpta Cypria*, 353–54).

43. AT of the Greek text from Κυπριανός, ΙΣΤΟΡΙΑ ΧΡΟΝΟΛΟΓΙΚΗ ΤΗΣ ΝΗΣΟΥ ΚΥΠΡΟΥ, 151.

rhetoric. Although the New Testament presents Barnabas as a skilled negotiator, Kyprianos and his successors saw in Barnabas the ideal of a saint who fights for God and country.

> I doubt whether any other Apostle so defended his native land and proved himself such a patriot as our Barnabas, who during his life freed his fellow-countrymen from the abominable worship of idols by teaching them the true faith of our Lord Jesus Christ, and after his death delivered the holy Church of his native land from the oppression of the ambitious and grasping clergy of Antioch, and raised it to such an eminence that it was the envy of even those of the highest rank in the hierarchy. Truly and without doubt the veritable Son of Consolation he, I mean Barnabas, fulfilled in all respects the injunction: "Fight for faith and Fatherland." Under what an obligation then we Cypriots are to the deliverer of our souls, to the benefactor and originator of our Church's renown, let us each decide for himself; and let us celebrate the patron and protector of his native land both in the present life and in the one to come.[44]

The Archimandrite Photios S. Constantinou's quotation of these words of Kyprianos in his 2005 statement regarding Barnabas[45] illustrates the impact of Kyprianos's history on Cypriots. The phenomenon of patriotic priests fighting against foreign occupiers has a long history in Cyprus. Many frescos and paintings on their church walls and ceilings depict warrior saints. Although icons do not depict Barnabas as a warrior saint, Kyprianos's description of him as a model of fighting for the fatherland provided a foundation for later Greek Cypriot beliefs.

---

44. Translation by Hackett, *History of the Orthodox Church of Cyprus*, 25.
45. In Stylianou, *Apostle Varnavas*, 103–4, 106.

FIGURE 31

**Modern painting on the wall of a church in Nicosia, depicting two warrior saints.
Many such paintings and frescos decorate the walls of churches in Cyprus.**

In 1810, another monk, also named Kyprianos, became the arch-bishop of Cyprus.[46] Most Greek Cypriots consider Archbishop Kyprianos to be a holy martyr for the Orthodox faith and for the cause of Greek independence (an ethnomartyr), but this belief is also a created history. Research by Cypriot scholars such as Englezakis and Michael reveals that the execution of Kyprianos had far more to do with his success in

46. People sometimes mistakenly assume that the archimandrite historian and the archbishop are one and the same person, so caution is needed in this matter. The archimandrite was born near Limassol about 1735 and died around 1803. The archbishop, born in 1756, was from Strovolos, near Nicosia, was a monk at Machairas until 1783, became archbishop in 1810, and was executed by the Turks in Nicosia in 1821.

amassing political power than it did with his Orthodox beliefs. Contrary to the often repeated, modern narrative about Kyprianos, he was *not* part of the Greek liberation movement but sought to exercise his power *within* the Ottoman government framework. And, as Englezakis detailed in his article, "Archbishop Kyprianos's Inkstand," Kyprianos designed his elaborate inkpot to depict the three imperial privileges he so jealously guarded and used to emphasize his civic power.

Foreign Travelers to Cyprus describe Opulent Archbishops

Shortly before Kyprianos became archbishop of Cyprus, a Spaniard named Don Domingo Badia-y-Leyblich travelled around the Middle East in 1806, "announcing himself as Ali Bey el Abbassi, son of the Othman Bey of Aleppo, prince of the Abbassids, and directly descended from Abbas, son of Abd El Motalleb and uncle of Mohammad."[47] The book describing his experiences was published in French in 1814 and in English translation in 1816 under the title *Travels of Ali Bey*.[48]

Don Domingo was aboard a ship caught in a violent storm and driven off course, landing after three days of hardship at the port city of Limassol, Cyprus, on March 7, 1806.[49] Once there, he decided to visit sites on the island and, traveling northeast, he arrived in Nicosia after a few days.[50] Once in the city, he stayed in the palatial home of "the Dragoman of Cyprus, the principle officer of the Greek community in the island."[51] Later, he went to the "palace of the Archbishop" where he was met at the gate by "the archimandrite and the steward, with twenty or thirty servants."[52]

47. Cobham, *Excerpta Cypria*, 391.

48. Cobham, *Excerpta Cypria*, 391. The 1816 English translation was not available to the editor of *Excerpta Cypria*, so he used instead the French version published in 1814 and translated this section into English from it.

49. Cobham, *Excerpta Cypria*, 391.

50. He said that Nicosia as a city was capable of housing a population of 100,000 but had only about 1,000 Turkish families and 1,000 Greek families. He described Nicosia as a desert with large gardens but also "great open spaces full of ruins and rubbish." Cobham, *Excerpta Cypria*, 393.

51. Cobham, *Excerpta Cypria*, 394.

52. Cobham, *Excerpta Cypria*, 395.

In his account of meeting the archbishop, Don Domingo said the old man's legs were so painfully swollen that he had to be carried by others. This archbishop, Chrysanthos, complained about "the terrible vexations he had suffered last year at the hands of the Turkish rebels." Yet Don Domingo's description of the archbishop indicates that this frail old man exercised considerable political power, some of which he delegated to the dragoman.[53] At this time, the dragoman (or *divan tercümani*), named *Hadjigeorgakis Kornesios*, had immense power in Cyprus and reported directly to the Ottoman government in Constantinople. Dragomen were tasked by Turkish authority to be official translators between Turks and Greeks, and these diplomats became wealthy.

Don Domingo explained that, in 1804, Kornesios fled to Constantinople because of a Turkish uprising in Nicosia. A mob of disgruntled Turks took over the city, "behaved atrociously to the Archbishop and other Greeks" and "killed those who refused to give them money." They descended on the opulent home of Kornesios and looted it. He was, however, able to convince Turkish authorities in Constantinople that he was in the right, and they sent armed forces to restore order in Cyprus. The pasha in charge finally quelled the revolt and beheaded several of the Turkish rebels. Don Domingo adds, "This event has humiliated the Turks, and given the Greeks a certain air of boldness and even independence."[54] Trouble was definitely simmering and occasionally boiling over.

Don Domingo emphasized that "In spiritual matters the Archbishop of Cyprus is an independent Patriarch, and has no relations whatever with the Patriarch of Constantinople." He added that the archbishop of Cyprus appointed his own bishops and other officials and also granted marriage licenses. However, his description of the Orthodox bishops is not flattering.

---

53. Don Domingo wrote that "The Archbishop of Cyprus, an independent Patriarch in communion with the Greek Church, is also the prince or supreme spiritual and temporal chief of the Greek community in the island. He is responsible to the Grand Seigneur [Grand Vizier] for the taxes and conduct of the Greek Cypriots. To avoid entering into the detail of circumstances, and to excuse himself of the burden of part of the temporal administration, he has delegated his powers to the *Dragoman of Cyprus*, who has thus become the chief civil authority: he has practically the rank and attributions of a prince of the community, because the Turkish Governor can do nothing to a Greek without the participation and presence of the Dragoman, who is also entrusted with the duty of laying at the foot of the Grand Seigneur's throne the wishes of his fellow-Christians" (Cobham, *Excerpta Cypria*, 395).

54. Cobham, *Excerpta Cypria*, 395–96.

> The Greeks are extremely respectful and submissive towards their bishops: in saluting them they bow low, take off their cap, and hold it before them upside down. They scarcely dare speak in their presence. It is true that for this community of slaves the bishops are rallying points. It is through them that it preserves some kind of existence, so that it suits the people to give their prelates political importance. . . [The bishops] parade in their houses and followers a princely luxury (sic); they never go out without a crowd of attendants, and to ascend a flight of stairs they must needs be carried by their servants. [55]

Don Domingo wrote that the Greek Cypriots paid large fees to their bishops, who became rich: "handling the taxes brings enormous gains to the spiritual heads of the people, who suffer in silence lest a worse evil befall them." Evidently, some of the Orthodox clergy were as guilty of fleecing Greek Cypriots as were the Turkish authorities.

Don Domingo's description of the bishops' attire is interesting: "Bishops wear a little violet riband round the head, and often dress in cloth of the same colour. Other priests generally wear black."[56] Apparently, the wearing of red or purple by bishops was somewhat common at the time. Sporting this color was not limited to the archbishops as a part of their special privileges.

A decade later, John Macdonald Kinneir, "Captain in the service of the Honourable East India Company," visited Cyprus (January 2–24, 1814). In 1818, he published *Journey through Asia Minor, Armenia and Koordistan.*[57] His book summarizes a view that British control of Cyprus would benefit Great Britain in a variety of ways.

> The possession of Cyprus would give to England a preponderating influence in the Mediterranean and place at her disposal the future destinies of the Levant. Egypt and Syria would soon become her tributaries, and she would aquire an overawing position in respect to Asia Minor, by which the Porte might at all times be kept in check, and the encroachments of Russia, in this quarter, be retarded, if not prevented. It would increase her commerce in a very considerable degree. . . It is of easy defence; and under a liberal government would, in a very short space of time,

55. Cobham, *Excerpta Cypria*, 396.

56. Cobham, *Excerpta Cypria*, 396.

57. Cobham, *Excerpta Cypria*, 412. His title also included the following: "Town Major of Fort St George, and Political Agent at the Dunbar of His Highness the Nabob of the Carnatic." I never grow accustomed to such pretension.

amply repay the charge of its own establishment, and afford the most abundant supplies to our fleets at a trifling expense.[58]

Obviously, the British were looking at the value of controlling Cyprus for many decades before they actually procured it from the Ottomans. And the fact that British naval bases still exist on Cyprus reveals the continued strategic location of the island.

John Macdonald Kinneir spent time with Archbishop Kyprianos, and he speaks of the pomp, prestige, and power of the man. Kyprianos was astute and politically ambitious—and had well established contacts in Constantinople with the Turkish government.

> The Archbishop, dressed in a magnificent purple robe, with a long flowing beard and a silk cap on his head, received me in the vestibule, and ordered an apartment to be prepared for me in the palace, a large and straggling building, containing upwards of a hundred chambers. These are all required for the accommodation of the bishops, priests, and their attendants; for the Archbishop, both in power and affluence, is the second personage on the island. All affairs connected with the Greeks are under his immediate cognizance and management; and consequently when the Governor is desirous of making a new arrangement regarding that class, or of levying contributions, he has recourse to the Archbishop, who has lately usurped the whole authority, and seldom even deigns to consult the dragoman. From the humble situation of an obscure deacon he raised himself, by extraordinary means, to the episcopacy: he borrowed immense sums of money from the rich, which he lavished on the poor; securing in this manner the votes of his creditors, that they might be repaid, and those of the others in expectation of future reward. [59]

Kinneir also reports political tensions between the archbishop and the dragoman.

> In the morning the dragoman paid me a visit, and in the evening I returned it: he was a Greek of a good family at Constantinople, and formerly attached to the English army in Egypt. It was not difficult to perceive that a jealousy subsisted between him and

---

58. Cobham, *Excerpta Cypria*, 412.
59. Cobham, *Excerpta Cypria*, 416.

the Archbishop, whom he accused of avarice and ambition, and a desire of intermeddling in matters that did not concern him.[60]

Such maneuvering for political power put Archbishop Kyprianos on a collision course not only with the Turkish elite on the island but also with affluent Greeks.

William Turner, who in 1812 was part of the staff of Sir Robert Liston, the British ambassador to the Porte, later trekked around Cyprus as part of his tour through the Middle East. His made numerous observations of the dreadful Turkish rule of Cyprus, but he also regularly criticized Greek behaviors. In his journal,[61] dated October 17, 1815, he recounted his audience with Archbishop Kyprianos in Nicosia and reported that charges of greed and corruption had been brought against the man. Turner said that the archbishop "received us very hospitably," and added that

> he is the primate of the island and is so respected by the Greeks that he shares the supreme power with the Agha [Turkish officer]. His enemies in Constantinople having declared that his tyranny and rapacity rendered his name odious to the Cypriotes, the Porte has sent two Turks (whom we found with him) to inquire into the affair: but he has escaped from the snare by procuring a declaration from the Greeks that they are content with him, and by giving presents (without which no declaration would avail him) to the messengers.[62]

Was Kyprianos corrupt or the victim of jealousy? Or both? More about that later. Turner went on to report that Kyprianos "told me that he was independent of all the four patriarchs, for the following cause":

> In the time of the latter Byzantine Emperors of Constantinople the church there having no authentic copy of the Gospel of S. Matthew, issued orders for the seeking of one throughout the Empire. The priest of a convent near Famagosto dreamed that if he dug under his church in a spot pointed out, he should find it. Next day he obeyed the injunctions of the Angel who had appeared to him in a vision, and found the tomb of S. Barnabas, with the Gospel of S. Matthew laid on the bosom of the dead saint. The Archbishop wrote this to Constantinople, whence the

60. Cobham, *Excerpta Cypria*, 417.

61. *Journal of a Tour in the Levant,* published in London in 1820 (see Cobham, *Excerpta Cypria*, 424).

62. Cobham, *Excerpta Cypria*, 437.

royal galleys were immediately sent, on board of which he carried the treasure to the capital, and in return for his present he
was made independent, and presented with a red vest, which he
still has the prerogative of wearing, and allowed the privilege of
writing with red ink, which he has ever since continued. He has
a third privilege, that of bearing the arms of the Greek Church
(very like the Russian Eagle) on his chair, like a Patriarch.[63]

I am mystified by how Turner's story of Barnabas became so convoluted.
But in spite of Turner's confused account of the fifth-century discovery of
Barnabas's body, the British traveler clearly heard from Kyprianos about
the imperial privileges of the archbishop—although he speaks of an eagle
on the archbishop's chair, not an imperial scepter.

Turner goes on to recount a brief tour around Nicosia and his dinner with the opulent Kyprianos.[64] In his journal entries, Turner reports
with distaste a variety of behaviors he witnessed in Cyprus. He expressed
contempt for the priests, whom he described as greedy and unscrupulous. In one entry he states,

these Greek priests, everywhere the vilest miscreants in human
nature, are worse than usual in Cyprus from the power they
possess. They strip the poor ignorant superstitious peasant of
his last para, and when he is on his deathbed, make him leave
all to their convent, promising that masses will be said for his
soul.[65]

In another derrogatory observation, Turner says,

Cyprus, though nominally under the authority of a Bey appointed by the Qapudan Pasha, is in fact governed by the Greek
Archbishop and his subordinate clergy. The effects of this are

---

63. Cobham, *Excerpta Cypria*, 437.

64. "After sitting and smoking half an hour with the archbishop, we went to look
at the church of S. Sophia, built by the Venetians, and now converted into a mosque,
which stands at the centre of the city. It is built in the Gothick style. . . and the Turks
have broken the wall in three or four places, to make doors. . . . [Turner further describes the rundown condition of Nicosia.] We returned to the convent and supped
with the Archbishop, whom I was astonished to see, contrary to the custom of the east,
sit himself at the head of a long table in a great armchair covered with red cloth. He
said that there were 5000 houses in the city, but we were not inclined to believe that
there are more than 3500, and many of these are so wretchedly small as to be little better than hovels . . . We slept well on the divan, which the Greeks made into a tolerable
bed for us" (Cobham, *Excerpta Cypria*, 437).

65. Cobham, *Excerpta Cypria*, 449.

seen everywhere throughout the island, for a Greek, as he seldom possesses power, becomes immediately intoxicated by it
when given him, and from a contemptible sycophant is changed
instantaneously to a rapacious tyrant.[66]

Turner had significant issues with Cypriot clergy, including Archbishop
Kyprianos.

Records kept by other travelers reinforce Turner's description of
the opulence of Kyprianos and the general squalor of the Greek Cypriot
population. The picture emerging from these travelogues is potentially
disturbing. Don Domingo depicts the bishops in Nicosia as greedy. William Turner and John Macdonald Kinneir describe Archbishop Kyprianos as opulent and power hungry. And quests for power can end badly.

In 1853, some forty years after John Macdonald Kinneir's visit to
the island, Louis Lacroix, a history professor in France, published his Îles
de la Grèce. Lacroix provides a fascinating history lesson on the political
power of the archbishop—and the bloody results.

> The Archbishop of Nicosia, who had the title of ri'aya-vekili, as
> representing the Christian subjects of the Porte, had annexed
> pretty well the whole administrative authority, and not only had
> made himself independent of the Muhassils,[67] but generally de-
> termined on their appointment and recall. From his palace the
> Archbishop administered the whole island, filled up the offices
> in every district, assessed the amount of the annual contribu-
> tions, sent the sums for which the island was farmed out to
> the Grand Vezir, or the Imperial Treasury. Certain privileges,
> purposely granted, attached the Turkish Aghas to the support
> of his authority, and all the inhabitants, Turks and Greeks alike,
> looked upon him as the real Governor, and grew accustomed
> to take no notice of the Muhassil. The supreme power of the
> Archbishops of Nicosia reached its height during the reigns of
> Selim III. and Mustafa IV., the immediate predecessors of Sul-
> tan Mahmud II., and was unshaken until the beginning of the
> nineteenth century, in 1804, saw an insurrectionary movement
> of the Turks, the prelude of the bloody catastrophe which was
> to extinguish it. The Turks settled in Cyprus were deeply hurt
> at seeing themselves fallen under the rule of men whom of old
> they had conquered. The Turkish population of Nicosia and
> the adjoining villages, stirred by a rumour, true or false, of the

66. Cobham, Excerpta Cypria, 447.

67. Senior Turkish officials involved with tax collection.

insufficiency in the food-stuffs necessary for victualling of the island, rose against the ecclesiastical authority, in whose hands all power rested, and for a while was master of the capital.[68]

Lacroix reports that two Pashas arrived in 1804 with troops and finally restored order. Then he adds, "But the intrigues of the chief Turks against the Greek headmen did not sleep, and ended in 1821 in a bloody *coup d'etat*, which put an end to the administration of the *Muhassils*, overturned the authority of the Greek clergy, and restored the government to the Pashas."[69]

Lacroix's description of the downfall of Archbishop Kyprianos is sobering. He connects the ruin of Kyprianos with the rebellion against Ottoman rule in Greece and Moldavia and the fear among Ottoman rulers that something similar would happen in Cyprus.

> Kyprianos was then Archbishop of Cyprus, and the government of the island had been since 1820 in the hands of Kuchuk Mehmed, a man of imperious and dissembling temper, whom the Captan Pasha had chosen purposely to destroy the influence of the Greek Primate. Circumstances soon favoured the execution of his plan. The first insurrectionary movements in Moldavia and Peloponnesus, which had burst a little after the arrival of Kuchuk Mehmed in Cyprus, while they inspired the Ottoman Government with the liveliest fear, sanctioned every measure which its agents could adopt to keep in check their Christian subjects in the provinces which had not risen. Now the Greeks of Cyprus had remained entirely aloof from the national movement which had stirred the other islands and the Greek mainland. "It was not they who were crying out against tyranny, and thought of taking up arms: it was the Turks, who were impatient of the bondage in which the bishops had kept them for fifty years past: it was for them that reaction and liberation were on foot."[70]

Lacroix explains that the Greek Cypriots allowed themselves to be disarmed as a means of showing that they only wanted to live in peace. He adds that Kyprianos swore his submission to the government of the Grand Signor. But Küçük Mehmed, sent to Cyprus in 1820, was

68. Cobham, *Excerpta Cypria*, 463–64.

69. Cobham, *Excerpta Cypria*, 464.

70. Cobham, *Excerpta Cypria*, 464. It is unclear whom Lacroix is quoting at the end of the paragraph.

determined to exterminate the main religious and political leaders of the Greek Cypriots, so he lied to the Sultan and insisted that the Cypriots were planning a revolt. When he finally received permission, on July 9, 1821, he arrested Kyprianos and other Greek notables and executed them. The savagery described by Lacroix is disturbing.

> The gates of the palace were then thrown open, and the bleeding corpses thrown into the square. This was the signal for a general massacre. The Convent of Phaneromene was at once occupied, and the priests strangled. I was told, says M. de Mas Latrie, that before killing them the Turks, with wild refinement of vengeance, saddled the priests as they would their horses, breaking their teeth to force the bits into their mouths, and making them caper under their spurs. The Greek houses were given over to pillage, massacres began again in all the districts of the island, and confiscation followed massacre. For six months universal terror reigned among the Greek population. The peasants fled to the woods, or Caramania: the notables, the priests and Greeks of means, who had escaped the janissaries, took refuge at Larnaca, under the protection of the European Consuls. Most of them crossed over to Italy or France, and there are few Greek families in whom the names of Marseille or Venice do not still, even now that more than twenty years have passed since their return to the island, awake tender feelings of gratitude.[71]

Lacroix clearly did not believe that Kyprianos was part of a Greek independence movement, which contradicts the current view held by most people in Cyprus.

The dominant narrative today depicts Archbishop Kyprianos as a committed nationalist for the cause of Greek independence who in 1818 joined a society of Greeks who were preparing for a war of liberation from the Ottomans.[72] The revolt began on March 25, 1821, and ended in brutal defeat for the Greek rebels. According to the nationalist narrative, many Cypriots had journeyed to Greece to join the fight; and müsellim Mehmed Silâhşor (called Küçük Mehmet or Mehmed) retaliated. According to this belief, on July 9, 1821, he executed 486 prominent Greek Cypriots, including Kyprianos, whom he hanged publicly on a tree in front of the former palace of the Lusignan kings in Nicosia. Kyprianos thus became a martyr for the cause of Greek independence. However,

71. Cobham, *Excerpta Cypria*, 464.

72. See Michael, "Loss of an Ottoman Traditional Order," 9 n3, for a list of Greek authors who promote the nationalist narrative.

recent scholarship reinforces the political-ambition explanation of Lacroix and challenges the Greek nationalist narrative as yet another example of created history.[73]

Michalis Michael demonstrates that Kyprianos was *not* part of the
Greek independence movement but in fact carefully functioned as archbishop *within* the authority structure of the Ottoman Empire.[74] Michael
stresses that Cypriot history wrongly "placed Archbishop Kyprianos in
the pantheon of national martyrs (ethno-martyrs)" who attempted "to
overthrow the Ottoman *status quo*," stating "this historiography essentially embraces the myth-making of nationalist discourses."[75] He shows
that Kyprianos did *not* support the Greek struggle for independence but
rather saw himself as an Orthodox Ottoman official. His support network
within the Sublime Porte may be seen in the fact that Sultan Mahmud II
appointed Kyprianos to the position of archbishop before Chrysanthos,
the old, infirm, ineffective, but still reigning archbishop, died.[76] In so doing, the sultan disregarded the ruling of the Ecumenical Patriarchate and
Orthodox canonical rules. He exiled Chrysanthos and replaced him with
the much younger, better educated, energetic, and talented Kyprianos—
who was ambitious and ready to accept this early appointment by Sultan
Mahmud II in spite of the ruling of the Ecumenical Patriarch.

Michael explains that Kyprianos sought "to differentiate yet not
eliminate the Ottoman character of the high clergy's political power." He

73. Already in 1981, Paul (Benedict) Englezakis published "Τὸ μελανοδοχεῖον τοῦ
ἀρχιεπισκόπου Κυπριανοῦ," *Kypriakai Spoudai* 45 (1981) 143–60 (English translation
"Archbishop Kyprianos's Inkstand"). He explained that Kyprianos was very ambitious
and adept at promoting his power and grandeur, and that his appointment to the position of archbishop by the Ottomans went against Orthodox canons, because Chrysanthos, the elderly and frail archbishop, was still alive (274–277). The Turks favored
having the more progressive and young Kyprianos as archbishop of Cyprus (274).

74. Michael, "Kyprianos, 1810–21." For an earlier study, see Michael, "Βυζαντινά
σύμβολα ὀθωμανικῆς πολιτικῆς ἐξουσίας: ἡ περίπτωση τῶν προνομίων τῶν
Ἀρχιεπισκόπτων Κύπρου," *Τὰ Ἱστορικά* 51 (2009) 315–32, where he argues that the
three imperial privileges of the Cyprus archbishops did not emerge until Ottoman
occupation of the island, when the archbishops of Cyprus began to unite legendary
symbols of a Byzantine past with their present, Ottoman reality. He believes that the
archbishop's imperial privileges did not exist until the seventeenth century. See also
Michael's 2013 article, "Loss of an Ottoman Traditional Order," where he further de-
velops his case.

75. Michael, "Kyprianos, 1810–21," 41. For an analysis of the myths created by the
Church of Cyprus pertaining to the Ottoman period, see Michael, "Myth and Nationalism" 149–59.

76. Michael, "Kyprianos, 1810–21," 48–49.

appropriated the symbols of power attributed to Emperor Zeno's legendary grant of imperial privileges, but he linked his political power to the Ottoman hierarchy. In effect, he converted the mythical Byzantine privileges into symbols of Ottoman political power.[77] Michael argues that, when Kyprianos told William Turner that he was independent of the other patriarchs because of his imperial privileges, it was because of his self-identification as the one who possessed Ottoman political power in Cyprus. When he appealed to the imperial privileges supposedly granted by a Byzantine emperor, he did so to maintain his position as *ethnarch* of Cyprus within the Ottoman state. Kyprianos did *not* support the Greek independence movement—the *Filiki Eteria*—but rather condemned it because its members were Free Masons, whom he judged to be heretics who acted against Orthodox faith and against the Sultan's orders. In an 1815 circular, "Kyprianos condemned any act that threatened the Ottoman status quo or questioned the Sultan's orders."[78] His position made him a target for other elites in Cyprus who jealously renounced his power and policies.

Michael contends that, when William Turner spoke of Kyprianos's enemies in Constantinople accusing him of tyranny and rapacity, he was describing a move by Cypriot adversaries to have Kyprianos removed. The bribes paid to the delegates sent by the Sublime Porte perhaps were not so much a sign of corruption but of his political skills in deflecting attacks by his rivals.[79] Apparently, Kyprianos became so powerful that "Küçük Mehmed was sent as governor of the island with the purpose of undermining the political power of the Archbishop of Cyprus."[80] Mehmed, described by those who witnessed his attacks as a ferocious and cruel man who hated both Greeks and Europeans, set about manipulating the Porte into allowing him to execute Cypriot officials and thereby restore island power to the Turks.[81]

77. Michael, "Kyprianos, 1810–21," 50. Michael cites Englezakis's article about Kyprianos's inkstand and agrees with him that the earliest written record of the archbishop's imperial privileges appeared in 1676 in a document regarding the ordination of the Bishop of Paphos, Nektarios (K. Delikanis, "The Official Church Documents Kept in the Codex of the Patriarchate Archive, Constantinople," 1904, p. 633).

78. Michael, "Kyprianos, 1810–21," 54.

79. Michael, "Kyprianos, 1810–21," 55.

80. Michael, "Kyprianos, 1810–21," 56.

81. See details in Michael's "Loss of an Ottoman Traditional Order," 20n46.

Michael explains that Küçük Mehmed coerced an Orthodox man, Demetrios from Agios Ioannis of Malounta, to give false witness that plans were being made in Cyprus to revolt; and he then used this pretext as an excuse to ask for permission to execute leading Orthodox men on the island.[82] At first the Sublime Porte declined the execution request, but Mehmed kept manipulating the situation until he finally got permission from the sultan to execute influential people and to confiscate their property. He hanged Kyprianos and beheaded three high-ranking Orthodox priests. He executed wealthy Cypriots—although the often-quoted number 486 is likely inflated—confiscated and sold their fortunes, and then kept much of their wealth for himself.[83] "At the same time, he ordered the demolition of the upper levels of the houses of non-Muslims, thus demonstrating that one of his goals was to destroy the rich Orthodox class living in Nicosia."[84] Evidently, Archbishop Kyprianos was eliminated not because of any lack of loyalty to the Ottoman Empire but because of the jealousy and animosity of his rivals.

Quests for power, prestige, and wealth can end with devastating results when rivals seek these same things—especially when rivals resort to violence to achieve dominance. From the perspective of rich Turkish residents in the 1800s, the archbishops had gone too far in their efforts to control affairs on the island. Turks despised the way Orthodox archbishops exercised power over them. After all, the Ottomans had conquered and subjugated Cyprus. Greek Cypriot control over most affairs on the island became so distasteful to the Turks that they reasserted their dominance—for slightly over half a century.

But the Ottoman Empire was in decline. In 1878, the Sultan rented Cyprus to the British. Greek Cypriot clergy initially rejoiced, thinking they would regain control of the island. The British, however, did not

---

82. Michael, "Loss of an Ottoman Traditional Order," 20–21.

83. On pages 30–31 of "New Interpretation of the 1821 events in Cyprus," Michael demonstrates that the number commonly specified in Greek histories of 486 people being executed by Küçük Mehmed is probably inflated. "In 1888, Georgios Kipiades reports that he collected evidence from eyewitnesses and records 68 executed and 19 people who had escaped." The Ottoman catalogue found in "the Archive of the National Library of Sofia, records 74 names of executed persons and 22 names of people who escaped execution." However, an Ottoman document dated July 16, 1821 reports 16 executed infidels. Another document, dated August 28, 1821, based on information sent to the Porte by Küçük Mehmed, says that he executed Kyprianos, three bishops and about 50 others.

84. Michael, "Kyprianos, 1810–21," 62.

restore supremacy to the archbishop. They brought to Cyprus a different form of government based on the Western concept of separation of church and state. Cypriot Orthodox leaders deeply resented their continuing loss of political power and privilege, and the removal of their role as tax collectors resulted in a major loss of revenue. Once again the stage was set for violence, as nationalistic Greek Cypriots sought to reestablish Greek dominance—and the church led the resistance.

Prior to the violence, however, the Cypriot clergy carefully explained to their new foreign overlords how St. Barnabas ensured autocephaly in the fifth century and gained imperial privileges for his legitimate heirs, the archbishops. Oddly, the British accepted the story of Anthemios without exploring its historicity. British historians hardly questioned what they heard about Barnabas, Anthemios, and Zeno.

British Historians Perpetuate the Legend

Sir Harry Luke (1884–1969) was secretary to the High Commissioner of Cyprus from 1911–1912 and Commissioner of Famagusta from 1918–1920. He claimed to have found a cache of 10,000 documents written in seven languages, which he used as the basis of his research into the history of the island under the Turks.[85] In spite of extensive research, however, he accepted the story of the archbishop's imperial privileges without question.

> . . . the Cypriote Church is the senior of the autocephalous Churches, owing this position to its Apostolic foundation by S. Paul and S. Barnabas, and to the confirmation of its independence by the Emperor Zeno in the year 478. On this occasion Zeno conferred upon the Cypriote Primate certain privileges enjoyed by no other ecclesiastic, privileges which have been jealously retained to the present day. They include the right of signing in red ink, a prerogative shared only with the Emperor himself, of wearing a cape of imperial purple, and of carrying an imperial sceptre in place of the pastoral staff; whence it will be seen that the Archbishop of Cyprus, though his Church was small, enjoyed an exceptional position in the Orthodox world.[86]

85. Luke, *Cyprus under the Turks*, 4.

86. Luke, *Cyprus under the Turks*, 16–17. Luke adds that the Cyprus archbishops in the seventeenth and eighteenth centuries gained "the supreme power and authority over the island, and at one time wielded influence greater than that of the Turkish

George Francis Hill, who in 1940 published a four-volume history of Cyprus, also describes the imperial privileges as if they were granted in the fifth century. After recounting the story of Anthemios and Zeno that traces back to *Laudatio Barnabae apostoli*, he states,

> In addition to securing its autocephaly, the See of Constantia received further extraordinary privileges: to this day the Archbishops sign with red ink (a distinction which none but the Emperor enjoyed), wear a purple cloak at Church festivals, and carry an imperial sceptre instead of a pastoral staff. These privileges, expressing recognition of temporal authority, seem somewhat excessive, and have had frequent repercussions down to the present day.[87]

Hill observes that political problems arose due to the archbishop's political powers, and he questions such temporal authority. But he does not question the tradition itself.

Hill could not have read all of *Laudatio Barnabae apostoli*, or he would have noticed that this long speech never mentions imperial privileges. To be fair, he also would have needed to examine references to Barnabas from the sixth through the seventeenth centuries to notice that no one ever mentioned the three privileges until the Ottoman occupation of Cyprus. Given the time required to track down these matters, I understand this gap in Hill's historical investigations. However, his judgments on the matter of Barnabas are inconsistent.

Pasha himself" (17). Luke provides quotations of de Vezin (English consul in Cyprus) that claim that some of the archbishops fleeced the Cypriots as badly as did the Turks. Drummond, also a consul, reported that "These stipends (i.e., those of the Archbishop and Bishops) are very considerable in a country where living is so cheap, and so many fasts observed; yet all the bishops have other expedients for making sums of money; they move from place to place as traders, without bestowing the least attention upon their charge; and frequently the archbishop raises general contributions under the deceitful veil of employing them in pious uses, or paying some extraordinary *avanie*, or special assessment of the Turks" (p81). He goes on to explain how the Turkish and Greek officials worked together to fleece the people and get rich. A few pages later, he quotes William Turner: "Cyprus, though nominally under the authority of a Bey appointed by the Qapudan Pasha, is in fact governed by the Greek Archbishop and his subordinate clergy. The effects of this are seen everywhere throughout the island, for a Greek, as he seldom possesses power, becomes immediately intoxicated by it when given him, and from a contemptible sycophant is changed instantaneously to a rapacious tyrant" (83–84).

87. Hill, *History of Cyprus*, 1:277–78.

In a footnote, Hill labels as legends the stories of Barnabas's martyrdom and the discovery of the relics by Anthemios. However, Hill
does not apply the same historical judgment to the tradition of the archbishop's privileges. He judges the discovery of Barnabas's relics to be a
clever move fabricated by Anthemios. He also says the Acts of Barnabas
is obviously a late fifth-century text written in Mark's name to address
the problems with the patriarch of Antioch. Yet Hill accepts the story
of Zeno's gift of imperial privileges as a historical event. Indeed, many
scholarly works uncritically state as fact the origin of the privileges in
the late fifth century.[88] Given the significant political implications of this
tradition for modern Cyprus, it is unfortunate that the few historians in
the twentieth century who actually studied the history of Cyprus did not
delve further into the matter.

In 1958, Glanville Downey, when commenting on the "Monophysite[89] Patriarch of Antioch Peter the Fuller" attempting to gain control of
Cyprus, describes *Laudatio Barnabae apostoli* by Alexander the Monk
as highly biased and written in the middle or late sixth century, several
generations after the events. Bluntly, he asserts, "Alexander's encomium
. . . is obviously a tendentious document to support Cyprus' claim to
autocephaly."[90] But Downey does not explore the origins of the legendary
imperial privileges.

In a somewhat challenging lecture delivered in 2000, G. W. Bow-
ersock argued that, far from being duped by the Cypriot Archbishop
Anthemios, Zeno was complicit in the discovery of Barnabas's relics and
the Gospel of Matthew—for the important political reason of keeping the
Monophysites from gaining too much power in the Byzantine Empire.[91]
Although   Bowersock   provided   an   interesting—if   not   overly

---

88. See, for example, Stylianou, *Painted Churches of Cyprus,* 16, 499; Sophocleous,
editor, *Cyprus, the Holy Island,* 109; Tofallis, *History of Cyprus,* 44, and della Dora,
"Windows on Heaven (and earth)," 93.

89. Monophysites believed Jesus had only one nature (from the Greek words *mono*
= one, and *physis* = nature). Emperor Zeno espoused the position articulated by the
Fourth Ecumenical Council of Chalcedon in 451 that Jesus had two natures, both
divine and human. Peter the Fuller and the other Monophysites (some scholars prefer
the word Miaphysite) believed that in Jesus of Nazareth the divine and human natures
were totally merged into one.

90. Downey, "Claim of Antioch to Ecclesiastical Jurisdiction over Cyprus," 226.

91. Bowersock, "International Role of Late Antique Cyprus," 18. See ch. 4, "Early
Creation of History about Barnabas," for a full quotation of Bowersock's words on the
matter.

convincing—theory about Zeno staging the discovery of Barnabas's relics, he did not take the next step of questioning whether Zeno actually granted imperial privileges to Anthemios.

In 2009, D. Michael Metcalf echoed Bowersock's skepticism, if not his theory about Zeno, stating that the discovery of the Gospel of Matthew on the chest of Barnabas was a deliberate, politically motivated deception.[92] And the hoax worked quite well. Within a few years, Severus, patriarch of Antioch, mentioned seeing in Constantinople "the magnificently written copy of the gospel of St Matthew."[93] Regarding Anthemios going to Constantinople with the Gospel and Zeno calling an assembly to decide on Antioch's claim that it should rule over Cyprus, Metcalf observes, "All this was high politics."[94] However, Metcalf does not speculate on the origin of the imperial privileges.

My Own Temptation Just to Leave Things Buried

Honestly, toward the end of my stay in Cyprus in 2011, as I pondered the religious and political implications of the late date of the archbishop's imperial privileges, I wondered if I should ever have started my investigation.

I began my research on Barnabas out of profound respect for this significant leader of the early Jesus movement—and a sincere desire to see what I could discover about the saint and his legacy. What I uncovered surprised me and placed me in the uncomfortable position of reporting that my investigation did not confirm what most Greek Cypriots believe about Barnabas. Indeed, a gap of more than a millennium existed between the time when Zeno supposedly granted imperial privileges to Anthemios and the first indications of them in artwork and in written documents.

Of course, many ancient texts did not survive, and the possibility exists that the tradition of the imperial privileges predates what existing sources indicate. However, the witness of remaining manuscripts and artwork indicates that no tradition of the privileges existed until nearly 1,200 years after the time of Anthemios. Had the story been circulated earlier,

---

92. Metcalf, *Byzantine Cyprus*, 308. See also 309 n24. Michael Metcalf was one of the most delightful scholars I met in Cyprus. We had many stimulating conversations about Barnabas and lead seals. He is a true British gentleman.

93. Assemani, *Bibl. Or.* II, 81–82.

94. Metcalf, *Byzantine Cyprus*, 308.

someone would have mentioned it in the texts that describe Anthemios and Zeno. Alexander the Monk would certainly have described such a momentous event in *Laudatio Barnabae apostoli*. If the grant had actually happened, Alexander would have known about it and used it in his description of events at Constantinople when Anthemios triumphantly took the codex of the Gospel of Matthew to Zeno. Alexander's account of Anthemios appearing before Zeno is a glorified version of an actual event. But the claim that Zeno gave imperial privileges to Anthemios is completely legendary.

Prior to Florio Bustron (1560) no writers mentioned the Cypriot archbishops having special privileges. Bustron probably heard from someone else his version of the archbishop's scepter, so the rudimentary beginning of the legend of the privileges most likely predates Bustron. We simply do not know. Existing evidence indicates that the legend of the imperial privileges evolved during Ottoman occupation of Cyprus as a result of political maneuvering. Around the time the Turkish government granted Archbishop Nikephoros the title of *ethnarch* in 1660, members of the Orthodox elite apparently developed the legend of the archbishop's special privileges as a means of increasing the political power of the archbishop within the Ottoman hierarchy. During this era, the story of Zeno granting imperial privileges to Archbishop Anthemios reinforced the standing of Archbishop Nikephoros with the Ottoman rulers and also enhanced his stature among Greek Cypriots. By the end of the eighteenth century, the modern version of the privileges had fully developed.

For modern scholars at the Archbishopric to explore history to see if the imperial privileges are legitimate might seem to be a blasphemous thought—although in 1981 Paul Englezakis certainly questioned the antiquity of the story of the privileges, and he was a well-respected church historian. I doubt that clergy at the archbishopric are deliberately suppressing details of the research conducted by Englezakis and Michalis Michael, but a lot is at stake.

> *I once asked a Cypriot why I saw more Greek flags than Cypriot flags in Cyprus. He responded that he did not like the Cypriot flag because it was created to represent both Greek and Turkish Cypriots. Flying a Greek flag did not mean he wanted to be part of Greece; it symbolized his ethnic and religious identity: "I am a Greek—not one of those damn Turks."*

The fact that I, an outsider, was reluctant to publish the results of my research confirms the emotional weight attached to the Anthemios narrative. As I ponder the religious and political implications of my investigation with regard to the ongoing, disastrous rift between Greek and Turkish Cypriots, however, I contemplate a statement by Christopher Schabel regarding another often-repeated but historically unfounded story: "Myths are born easily, become established as facts with the passing of time, and die with difficulty. Often this is because they serve a purpose or fit in with the preconceptions of those who believe them."[95]

For many generations the imperial privileges have advanced the power base of Cypriot archbishops. Relinquishing these distinctions would obviously be difficult and cause consternation and resentment. Accepting the fact that part of the national narrative of Cyprus is based on politically motivated deceptions would not be easy.

I repeatedly ponder what Cypriot readers will do with this knowledge. But I also wonder how non-Cypriot readers will respond when reading this book. All of us unknowingly propagate national or regional (or family) myths that are based only on long-held traditions—created histories. When historians probe the past and uncover evidence that some of our own beliefs are fabricated, how will we respond? Will we carefully weigh the evidence or will we dismissively sweep it aside? Are we brave enough to rethink our own cherished beliefs—whatever they may be? Sometimes truth is a hard pill to swallow.

95. Schabel, "Myth of Queen Alice," 257.

CHAPTER SEVEN

Reversing the Created History of Barnabas

As I watched five Muslim men descend the stone steps to the tomb of apostle Barnabas, I thought, "Oh, NO!!!" I saw simmering rage on the face of the gracious Greek Cypriot woman who had driven us to the site. She stood by the tomb of her beloved saint, looking like a mother bear ready to defend her cubs. I sensed a nasty confrontation approaching. Were these men coming to mock a Christian holy site? Did they intend to proclaim the superiority of Islam at the tomb of Barnabas? How would our Greek Cypriot guide respond? How would the other Orthodox woman who was tenderly cleaning the tomb area respond? I took a deep breath and prepared for the worst.

The lead man asked quietly and politely, "Do you mind if we say the prayers?" The two women looked at each other and reluctantly moved aside, allowing the five men to step close to the tomb. What followed amazed me. With great reverence they began chanting their prayers. I sensed no disrespect whatsoever. I stepped backwards and lifted my camera. As I took several photos and recorded a video, I hoped the men would not object. But they were so focused on their prayers they seemed unaware of my activities.

My curiosity skyrocketed. I waited until they finished praying and then approached the imam to ask about their actions. He shook his head and said, "Not here. This is a holy place. We will talk outside." Then he pointed up the stairs. So, we left the darkness of the crypt and ascended the stone steps to the light.

FIGURE 32

**Sufi men praying
at the tomb of Barnabas.**

Once outside the small chapel built over the tomb, we spoke freely. The imam proved to be open and friendly. He explained that they were Sufis and had come to the grave of the holy Barnabas to pay their respect and to pray. The men were all on a pilgrimage and had come from South America, England, and Poland. Here, at the tomb of Barnabas, these Sufis, members of a mystical sect of Islam, venerated a Jewish Christian apostle.

"Would not other Muslims be furious if they knew you were here praying to a Christian saint?" I asked. "Oh," the imam replied, "they are always mad about something, so we do not pay any attention to them." I laughed out loud at his words. Never, ever, had I heard a Muslim talk like this man.[1]

Shortly thereafter, the conversation moved toward the topic of acceptance of people who are different. The imam said he had recently attended an interfaith conference in Washington, DC, where participants sought ways of living harmoniously with each other in spite of their different beliefs. He did not want to convert, destroy, or dominate Christians and Jews so much as to learn to live in peace with them.

Standing there near the tomb of Barnabas, I reflected on the significance of our encounter with these Sufis. What were the odds of having

1. With obvious faith and sincerity, the imam said Barnabas's perfectly preserved body lay in the tomb below. Pinching up some skin on his arm as an illustration, the Sufi said, "The skin of Barnabas's body down there in the tomb is more supple than yours or mine. When Jesus returns to earth, saints like Barnabas will rise from their tombs and take part in the end-time events that will happen then. We think Jesus will return sometime in 2012." I was eager to hear more about his beliefs, but our Orthodox guide inserted herself into the conversation and began quoting verses from Revelation about the end times.

such a peaceful and respectful conversation with men whose beliefs differ so much from my own? The talkative imam was far more interested in explaining what he believed than in asking what I believed, but his reverence for Barnabas provided a marvelous opportunity for dialogue. I could not help but think that Barnabas, a peacemaker in the early church, would be pleased; but the political-deliverer Barnabas of modern Cyprus might think I was fraternizing with the enemy.

FIGURE 33

Chapel over the traditional tomb of Barnabas, at the Monastery of Apostle Barnabas in Turkish occupied northern Cyprus. The chapel was so packed for a special liturgy that no one else could fit inside.

Barnabas and the Impasse in Cyprus

From our first arrival until our departure we repeatedly encountered the reality that Cyprus smolders with animosity between Greek Cypriots and Turks. Hatred, fear, and resentment are so intense that a resolution to the conflict seems impossible. During our ride from the airport to Nicosia on our first day in Cyprus, we had heard our middle-aged cab driver say that at some point both sides are going to have to let go of the past and learn to live together. His viewpoint seems uncommon for people his age. We seldom heard anyone except younger people echo our cabdriver's philosophy.

For younger Cypriots, 1974 happened before they were born. They did not experience the invasion and are not scarred by the loss and devastation resulting from it. For them, it is history, and some express a desire to put the past behind and to make peace with the Turks. However, few who were alive in 1974 expressed similar sentiments when discussing the matter with us. Justice and vengeance are more on their minds. For many of the Orthodox with whom we spoke, Barnabas is their champion who will drive out the Turks and restore the island to the Greek Cypriots. He is their warrior saint who will purge Cyprus of the barbarians occupying the northern third of Cyprus. Mediation seems out of the question for them, and overall the Orthodox Church does not dimish the hatred. The Church of Cyprus website regularly posts nationalistic commentaries that remind readers of Turkish atrocities.

As guests from the outside, my wife and I frequently felt the pain of our Greek Cypriot hosts as we listened to the bitterness and hostility they expressed toward the Turks. As outsiders, we offered no advice on how to fix the problem. We had no agenda to foist on them. The Cyprus problem is far too complex to reduce to a few platitudes. It stymies conflict-resolution experts—who know far more about resolving such matters than we do. For the most part, we just listened to the sad stories.

However, we also experienced events that revealed a glimmer of hope. In 2017, we attended a gathering of Greek Cypriots and Turkish Cypriots at Kakomallis, a campground established by Father Solomon Panagides many years ago. We observed genuine affection expressed by the Greek and Turkish participants toward each other. In a speech, Dafnis Panagides, the patriarch of the group, said that peace could only be accomplished "from the ground up." He explained that the top-down approach had been a total failure. Peace initiatives coming from politicians have not worked. True peace must begin with everyday people meeting each other as human beings and embracing their common humanity. It was inspiring to witness Dafnis, who participated in the armed rebellion against the British in the 1950s, denounce violence and promote love as the only viable answer to resolving conflict. As we watched this multi-ethnic group laugh and sing and talk and eat together, we wondered what Barnabas, the peacemaker, would say about their celebration. They were a great example of people who are not driven by large egos accomplishing harmony by setting aside propaganda and stereotypes and getting to know each other as human beings.

Barnabas Betrayed

My research caused me to formulate with increasing confidence a thesis regarding the transformation of Barnabas from bridge-builder to bridge-burner—from one who developed compromise solutions to ethnic conflicts to one who serves as champion for Greek Cypriots. Centuries ago, Orthodox clergy created a Barnabas who served their religious and political needs, and this Barnabas of convenience slowly became a figure who shares few similarities with the New Testament depiction of the man. In my opinion, the result has been a loss, not a gain.

The evolution of Barnabas took many centuries, but the narrative is now old enough to be part of the cultural heritage of Cyprus and is accepted without question. The tragic loss of Barnabas as a bridge-builder has only added to the contemporary problems on the island. Christians in Cyprus need the negotiating skills of their apostle as they seek to end their long-standing strife with Turks. They do not need a Barnabas transformed into a nationalistic savior figure. The Barnabas of legend has contributed to the demise of the Republic of Cyprus.

I am not so naïve as to believe that, if the Greek Cypriots suddenly began to imitate the model of their apostle Barnabas as he is presented in the New Testament, the incredibly complex and convoluted Cyprus problem would be solved. But I do believe the New Testament Barnabas provides a much better role model than the legendary Barnabas revered today—with his nationalistic overlays.

The Barnabas who won independence and imperial privileges for his people is a hero invented to respond to contemporary circumstances. He was created over many centuries by the accumulation of stories about him, and ultimately the myths were not benign. When Archbishop Makarios became president of the Republic of Cyprus in 1960, his inflexible nationalism helped pave the way for the disastrous Turkish invasion of northern Cyprus. I wonder how the recent history of Cyprus would be different if Makarios had espoused the mediating, compromising approach taken by the Barnabas of the New Testament.

I believe that Greek Cypriots need to reject the Barnabas of legend and to resurrect the model of Barnabas as bridge-builder—a leader who listens sympathetically to both sides of a conflict and helps opponents understand the viewpoints held by their adversaries. For enemies to overcome their hatred and mistrust of each other is monumentally difficult, but it begins with honest dialogue.

In the quest for peace and justice, Christians around the world would do well to consider the leadership example of Barnabas as they ponder the best ways to live as followers of Christ today. I realize, of course, that Barnabas built bridges between ethnic factions *within* the early church. Acts does not claim Barnabas sought reconciliation between Christians and members of other religions. However, nascent Christianity was a largely unknown and relatively powerless group within the larger Greco-Roman world of the first century. Today, Christians exercise immense power across the world.

FIGURE 34

The Most Reverend Neophytos, Metropolitan of Morphou. Neophytos actively promotes peaceful coexistence with Turks and criticizes those who preach fear and insecurity instead of love. Photo by Lynne Cosby.

How might we enhance world peace if we devoted as much time to understanding others as we do to trying to prove why our opponents are wrong? Understanding does not necessarily imply agreeing—nor does it mean ignoring matters of injustice that need to be confronted. After living in Cyprus, I gained a deeper understanding of and appreciation for Eastern Orthodoxy, yet I do not foresee embracing Orthodoxy as my personal faith stance. Too much of it remains foreign to my worldview. But my respect for Orthodox believers has grown, and I feel honored to have been befriended by many of them in Cyprus.

Hermann Göring on manipulating common people to go to war

From the notes of American intelligence officer and psychologist Gustave Gilbert regarding his April 18, 1946 interview of war criminal Hermann Göring, Nazi Reichsmarshall and Commander of the German Luftwaffe in World War 2:

"Why, of course, the people don't want war," Göring shrugged. "Why would some poor slob on a farm want to risk his life in a war when the best that he can get out of it is to come back to his farm in one piece. Naturally, the common people don't want war; neither in Russia nor in England nor in America, nor for that matter in Germany. That is understood. But, after all, it is the leaders of the country who determine the policy and it is always a simple matter to drag the people along, whether it is a democracy or a fascist dictatorship or a Parliament or a Communist dictatorship."

"There is one difference," I pointed out. "In a democracy the people have some say in the matter through their elected representatives, and in the United States only Congress can declare wars."

"Oh, that is all well and good, but, voice or no voice, the people can always be brought to the bidding of the leaders. That is easy. All you have to do is tell them they are being attacked and denounce the pacifists for lack of patriotism and exposing the country to danger. It works the same way in any country."

I can say much the same for friends in Turkey. During my trips to western Turkey, I have found Turks to be hospitable and friendly. Like Christians, most Turks are occupied with making a living and raising families. They do not want war. But, also like Christians, they can be whipped into a frenzy by charismatic, nationalist politicians and stand ready to defend their religion and their land with their lives. Most people are too easily manipulated into accomplishing the self-serving agendas of leaders who seek personal power. We need to develop our critical thinking skills. The ability to evaluate situations in light of regional histories could go a long way toward resolving conflicts.

Today, in the United States, many historians are revisiting local histories and discovering that numerous accounts passed down as facts are, in fact, contrived narratives designed to advance particular political agendas. In other words, all over our nation, people are beginning to hear how their ancestors created histories to make themselves look better. These historians experience considerable pushback from descendents who do not want to hear how their forebearers massacred indigenous peoples or rewrote local histories to present themselves in a better light. Once embedded in the traditions of a community, such created histories become facts for those who grow up hearing them. And it is upsetting to learn that evidence does not at all vindicate local legends. But facing our collective past can go a long way toward resolving old disputes.

I am not a pacifist, yet I believe non-violent conflict resolution is superior to warfare. Conflict situations can be incredibly complex, but hearing the concerns of our adversaries instead of only voicing our own concerns can open avenues of understanding and possibilities of peace. Truly listening can transform situations—if both sides listen.

At the end of my journey with the apostle Barnabas through the history of Cyprus, I emerged convinced that Barnabas's model of leadership as depicted in the Acts of the apostles is important for Christians today. To be bridge-builders instead of bridge-burners is much more effective in achieving positive ends and is also much more in keeping with the teachings of Jesus. Perhaps Dafnis Panagides was correct in saying that true peace only happens from the ground up, when people's views of others are so transformed by love that they are able to reject old animosities and embrace each other as those who are not so different after all.

Appendix A: Timeline of Events

Date	
Date	
47	Barnabas and Paul preach the gospel of Jesus in Cyprus.
49	Barnabas returns to Cyprus accompanied by John Mark. The Acts of the apostles provides no description of this missionary journey.
200s	The Pseudo-Clementine *Homilies*, a fanciful account about Clement, places Barnabas in Rome, preaching the good news about Jesus while Jesus was still alive in Israel. Over time, this fiction becomes a firm belief that Barnabas was the first one to preach the gospel in Rome.
325	Eusebius states that Barnabas was one of the 70 missionaries sent out by Jesus in Luke 10:1, but he does not claim that Barnabas headed the 70.
300s	Athanasius of Alexandria (c. 298–373) uses Acts 13:2 ("the Holy Spirit said, 'Set apart for me Barnabas and Saul for the work to which I have called them'") to argue for the Trinity, and he strongly influenced later writers. Athanasius says the Spirit took divine initiative in choosing Barnabas and Paul. The Spirit did not ask permission from God the Father or Jesus—which shows the Spirit to be co-equal with the Father and the Son.
365–403	Epiphanius, the famous archbishop of Cyprus, showed extremely little interest in Barnabas, but he did assert that Barnabas was first to preach the gospel in Rome. By his time the fictional story in the Pseudo-Clementine *Homilies* had become a created history.
Late 300s	John Chrysostom (c. 349–407) asserts that Barnabas and Paul were childhood friends. On the basis of Acts 14:11–15, Chrysostom says Barnabas's physical appearance made him appear as more esteemed than Paul.
400s	Roman emperors had by this time appropriated for themselves the symbol of the *globus cruciger*, a globe with a cross on it, to signify their divinely given rule over the earth.
431	The Eighth Canon of the Council of Ephesus affirms the independence (autocephaly) of the Cypriot Church.

c. 488	Convenient appearance of the Acts of Barnabas, a text by a Cypriot author that depicts Barnabas as a martyr and the apostolic founder of the Church of Cyprus—thus showing that Cyprus had a legitimate, apostolic originator who established the hierarchy of the Church of Cyprus. In this account, Mark rescues Barnabas's remains and the apostle's copy of the Gospel of Matthew and hides them in a cave west of Salamis.
488	Peter the Fuller, patriarch of Antioch, seeking to rule the Church of Cyprus, takes his case to Emperor Zeno. According to legends later detailed in *Laudatio Barnabae apostoli*, Barnabas, the long-dead saint, saves the day for Cyprus by appearing to Archbishop Anthemios in three dreams in which Barnabas tells him where to find the saint's body and that Anthemios is to take to Zeno the Gospel of Matthew that he will find on Barnabas's chest. Anthemios obeys. Zeno is impressed by the saint's appearance and reaffirms the autocephaly of Cyprus. Zeno also gives to Anthemios a large sum of money and orders him to construct a monastic complex to venerate St. Barnabas. Anthemios complies.
Early 500s	Inscription painted on the wall of an underground cistern in ancient Salamis declares that Barnabas is the apostolic foundation of the Church of Cyprus and Epiphanius is their great governor.
c. 550	Alexander the Monk writes *Laudatio Barnabae apostoli* to glorify Barnabas. He recounts the discovery of the saint's relics by Anthemios and the subsequent reaffirmation of autocephaly by Zeno. This speech in praise of Barnabas presents the entire collection of traditions about Barnabas in existence at the time and adds many details to provide a more complete story. It condemns Peter the Fuller and exalts Anthemios. But Alexander makes no mention of Zeno granting the archbishop imperial privileges. If Zeno had actually done so, Alexander would certainly have included this important detail in his speech. Most modern Orthodox beliefs about Barnabas trace back to this highly embellished speech.
c. 550	Mosaic in the sixth-century apse of the Church of *Panagia Angeloktistis* near Larnaca depicts the archangels Michael and Gabriel each offering to Jesus a *globus cruciger*.
	From 550 to 1191, Michael IV (Byzantine emperor 1034–1041) is the only writer to mention Anthemios, and he does not reference imperial privileges. During this time period, no writer says anything about archbishops wearing imperial regalia or appropriating for themselves any such emblems of imperial power.
645–965	Arabs conduct devastating raids on Cyprus, destroying coastal cities and decimating the complex at the Monastery of Apostle Barnabas.
965	Byzantine emperor Nikephoros II Phokas defeats Arab armies and restores Byzantine rule to Cyprus.

1191	Richard the Lionheart takes over Cyprus to use as a supply base for his crusade to retake the Holy Land.
1192	Guy de Lusignan, a French Crusader, assumes control of Cyprus. The Lusignan dynasty rules Cyprus until 1489. During this entire time there is no mention of the archbishop having imperial privileges.
1472	The Lusignan leader James II marries Caterina Cornaro, from a Venetian noble family. He dies under suspicious circumstances a few months later—leaving his pregnant wife regent of Cyprus. His son by Caterina, James III, dies mysteriously in 1474, prior to his first birthday, making Caterina the queen of Cyprus.
1489	Caterina abdicates the throne and Venice merchants control Cyprus. Venetians rule Cyprus until 1570.
1560	Florio Bustron mentions an emperor granting to Anthemios the right to possess an imperial scepter with a knob on top (not a *globus cruciger*).
1571	Ottoman Turks conquer Cyprus and settle Turkish soldiers there. Most Catholics flee the island. The Turks recognize Greek Orthodoxy as the official Christian presence in Cyprus, and they work through the Orthodox hierarchy.
1573	Étienne de Lusignan claims that the Cypriot archbishop was allowed to wear red, but he makes no mention of imperial regalia. He reminds his readers that Barnabas was the first to bring the gospel to Italy, and he calls Cyprus part of the Holy Land in a failed attempt to inspire Catholic Christians to save the island through another crusade.
1573–1660	Cypriot Orthodox archbishops increase their power in both political and ecclesiastical realms.
1660	Turkish rulers appoint Archbishop Nikephoros the *ethnarch* over Greek Cypriots and delegate to him the responsibility to collect taxes for the Ottoman Empire. Around this time, Nikephoros donates a reliquary to the Monastery of St. John Lampadistis. One panel of the reliquary shows Nikephoros kneeling, and behind him is a scepter topped by a *globus cruciger*.
1673	Archbishop Nikephoros commissions Leontios to paint an icon of Barnabas showing the saint seated on a throne, wearing a red cape and a bishop's *omiphorion*. Under his feet, symbolizing his heavenly rule over the island, is a map of Cyprus. Two angels offer imperial privileges to Barnabas. Nikephoros affixed this icon to his throne as a means of enhancing his power and stature as the legitimate successor of Barnabas.
1676	The Deed of Election of Nektarios of Paphos specifies that Emperor Zeno honored the archbishop of Cyprus with the privilege of signing his name with red ink—a privilege shared by no other patriarch.

1678	Paul Rycaut, British consul in Smyrna, Turkey, emphasizes the Cyprus archbishop's unique privilege of signing documents with red ink, which shows that Cypriot clergy had effectively communicated their story about Barnabas to their Ottoman overlords.
1691	Archbishop James I commissions an icon showing Barnabas seated on a throne and wearing royal clothing. Two archangels offer to Barnabas a crown (miter) and a scepter topped by a *globus cruciger*.
1734–1759	Archbishop Philotheos commissions artists to cover the walls and ceiling of the rennovated national Cathedral of St. John with frescos. A four-panel fresco depicts the story of Barnabas appearing in a vision to Archbishop Anthemios, of Anthemios uncovering the tomb of Barnabas, of Anthemios presenting the Gospel of Matthew to Emperor Zeno, and Emperor Zeno granting to Anthemios the imperial privileges. By this time, the legend of the imperial privileges is complete.
1788	Archimandrite Kyprianos writes his history of Cyprus and describes the archbishop's imperial privileges. He also proclaims Barnabas to be the ideal model of a saint fighting for faith and fatherland.
1806	Don Domingo Badia-y-Leyblich tours the Middle East under the false identity of Ali Bey el Abbassi. The book describing his experiences was published in English in 1816 under the title *The Travels of Ali Bey*. He wrote that greedy Orthodox priests fleeced their Greek Cypriot flock. He described Archbishop Chrysanthos as having considerable power in both religious and political realms.
1814	In 1818, British captain John Macdonald Kinneir publishes an account of his travels in Cyprus in 1814. He describes a very large, archbishopric complex and says that Archbishop Kyprianos had considerable power and prestige and was running most of the political affairs of the island.
1815	British traveler William Turner mentions Archbishop Kyprianos having the privileges of wearing a red cloak, signing his name with red ink, and having the arms of the Greek Church affixed to his throne.
1821	Küçük Mehmet executes Archbishop Kyprianos and other prominent Cypriots on a contrived accusation that they wanted to overthrow Turkish control. Greek Cypriot nationalists later proclaim Kyprianos to be an *ethnomartyr*—a hero for the cause of Greek independence.
1853	Louis Lacroix, a history professor in France, describes the sweeping political power of the archbishop and the deep resentment it caused wealthy Turkish Cypriots. He also explains how, in 1821, the Turkish Cypriots conducted a bloody purge and restored power to the pashas.

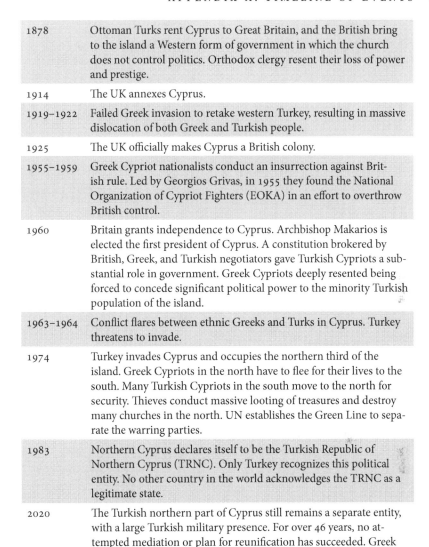

1878	Ottoman Turks rent Cyprus to Great Britain, and the British bring to the island a Western form of government in which the church does not control politics. Orthodox clergy resent their loss of power and prestige.
1914	The UK annexes Cyprus.
1919–1922	Failed Greek invasion to retake western Turkey, resulting in massive dislocation of both Greek and Turkish people.
1925	The UK officially makes Cyprus a British colony.
1955–1959	Greek Cypriot nationalists conduct an insurrection against British rule. Led by Georgios Grivas, in 1955 they found the National Organization of Cypriot Fighters (EOKA) in an effort to overthrow British control.
1960	Britain grants independence to Cyprus. Archbishop Makarios is elected the first president of Cyprus. A constitution brokered by British, Greek, and Turkish negotiators gave Turkish Cypriots a substantial role in government. Greek Cypriots deeply resented being forced to concede significant political power to the minority Turkish population of the island.
1963–1964	Conflict flares between ethnic Greeks and Turks in Cyprus. Turkey threatens to invade.
1974	Turkey invades Cyprus and occupies the northern third of the island. Greek Cypriots in the north have to flee for their lives to the south. Many Turkish Cypriots in the south move to the north for security. Thieves conduct massive looting of treasures and destroy many churches in the north. UN establishes the Green Line to separate the warring parties.
1983	Northern Cyprus declares itself to be the Turkish Republic of Northern Cyprus (TRNC). Only Turkey recognizes this political entity. No other country in the world acknowledges the TRNC as a legitimate state.
2020	The Turkish northern part of Cyprus still remains a separate entity, with a large Turkish military presence. For over 46 years, no attempted mediation or plan for reunification has succeeded. Greek Cypriots in the south and Turkish Cypriots in the north deeply resent each other. Both sides blame the other for all the problems.

Appendix B

Laudatio Barnabae apostoli
(Greek: Ἀλεξάνδρου μοναχοῦ ἐγκώμιον εἰς τὸν ἅγιον
Βαρνάβαν τὸν ἀπόστολον)
Translation[1] by Michael Cosby

The encomium of Alexander the Monk to the holy
apostle Barnabas, after being persuaded by the
presbyter and the supervisor[2] of his[3] venerable[4]
shrine, in which also is narrated the manner of the
revelation of his holy remains. (5)

---

1. The following is a literal translation of Alexander's oration in praise of Barnabas, except in instances where a literal rendering makes little or no sense. As with other ancient texts, there are instances where either Alexander wrote (or dictated) nonsensical phrases or a later scribe incorrectly copied the speech. I resisted the strong temptation to correct grammatical issues, rephrase convoluted sentences or alter passive verb constructions. Alexander strives for eloquence, so parts of his speech are syntactically challenging. Where Alexander quotes or appropriates Scripture, the words are italicized and the biblical passage(s) indicated in a footnote. As much as possible, the English translation matches the Greek words in each line of text—which sometimes produces irregular line length due to the different lengths of the English equivalents of Greek terms. At the end of every five lines, I place a number in parenthesis to designate the line number in the Greek text of the speech.

2. κλειδοῦχος key-holder.

3. I.e., Barnabas's shrine, namely the building that enshrined his body.

4. Or revered (σεβάσμιος).

Your[5] ancestral love of learning set before us most poor
ones the grandest subject of discourse, O noblest of ancestors
and most esteemed father of monks. For he set before us
the most notable *son of encouragement*[6] unto divinely sweet
praise, the greatly honored Barnabas, as truly thrice blessed (10)
even among apostles and (the) illuminator of the inhabited world.

But I, while my own lack of education worked against
this extraordinary proposal, refrained from obedience for a
long time, shrinking from the undertaking; for what sort of
description is able to attain apostolic perfection? (15)

For he has set before not only me such an impossible
undertaking, but also difficult to many others. For I reckon
all nature of men to be inadequate to the narration of
the good deeds of the greatest apostle Barnabas.

If anyone endeavors to say anything concerning him, (20)
he will be left far behind by the immensity[7] of the worth of
the events. But if he is exceedingly *wise and prudent,*[8] he might even
achieve exceedingly powerful words, yet he will still be found plunging
headlong into the depth of marvels. Therefore, whereas another has
received a gift of righteous deeds, each from the Holy Spirit, (25)
the apostles together received the treasure of all of the
spiritual gifts; and they exhibited every virtue. How, therefore,
shall I, a wretch, having been plunged under myriad passions,
be able to swim the apostolic sea?

For *I stammer to speak* articulately *and am slow of tongue, and* (30)
I am not eloquent,[9] in order that I might narrate the beyond human
virtues of the divinely sweet apostle Barnabas. For he
successfully accomplished all the virtues exactly, as
no one of the others had ever done. Because of this, I long

5. The use of the plural ὑμῶν seems odd. The singular σου makes more sense in context, referring to head monk, the elder/presbyter of the shrine of Barnabas.

6. Acts 4:36.

7. Literally "measure" (τοῦ μέτρου).

8. Jas 3:13.

9. Exod 4:10, LXX.

delayed obedience, knowing that my own unworthy (35)
narrative is insufficient for the most famous perfections
of the man.

But lately I was reminded of the God-inspired Scripture,[10]
which says that now the *ignorant son* will be *in destruction*, but the
obedient one will be outside of this (destruction).[11] So reluctantly, with
   (40)
much fear, I roused myself to complete your command,
considering (it) better to be greatly accused for a
defect than to be condemned for a complete lack of
understanding. Only (please), *you all contend with me in prayers*[12]
that the All Holy Spirit will be my advocate[13] in this project. (45)
For he will satisfy, as I suppose, also what is said
to the One being praised by us worthless ones, as when
the poor widow's offering of the two copper coins pleased
the same Master.[14] For it is not the quantity of the things given
to God that is acceptable, but the pure intention of the good gift (50)
being brought, whether small or large.

And while praising Barnabas, I will praise the holy
priesthood of all the apostles together. For their calling and
their glory are one and the same, and their order and rank are
one and the same, and their struggles are equal and their crowns (55)
do not change, and their citizenship is common, and their awards
are equal. Come, therefore, if it seems good, let us focus
our conversation on the divinely sweet Barnabas,[15] determining
what sort of songs of praise we might compose about him. For I am
also the most ardent admirer of the man, and I know and am (60)
persuaded that also among you the apostle is openly named as
the sweetest. Therefore, let us honor him with all our might.

---

10. τῆς θεοπνεύστου Γραφῆς.

11. Cf. Prov 13:1.

12. Cf. Rom 15:30.

13. Or "helper," "defender" or "aid" (ἀρωγός).

14. Mark 12:42–44; Luke 21:2–4.

15. Literally, "after drawing the divinely sweet Barnabas into the middle through the word" (ἑλκύσαντες εἰς μέσον διὰ τοῦ λόγου τὸν θεσπέσιον Βαρνάβαν).

According to our ability, let us speak a generous exposition.[16]
According to our worthiness to speak, let us agree to include every
word to memorialize our champion. (65)

Therefore, let Barnabas, the great one among the apostles,
be commemorated by us insignificant ones. Let the *Son of
Encouragement*[17] be praised by all those who believe in Christ.
Let him be praised by all creation, the one honored by the
Father and called by the Son and perfected by the[18] (70)
Holy Spirit. Barnabas, the great orator of the
church, the trumpet of the gospel proclamation, the
voice of the Only Begotten, the lute of the Spirit, the
instrument of grace. Barnabas, the powerful soldier of the
wars of Christ, the one who, in the body, put to flight (75)
the incorporeal tyrant with all his fellow
apostate army, the godly instructor
of good lessons, the steady guide of the
flock of Christ, the intellectual paradise of God, the one
who has possessed in himself the fruitful blossoms of every virtue, (80)
the blooming offshoot of faith, the fragrant rose
of love, the unfading fragrance of hope,
the sweetest smelling flower of grace, the prolific
branch of a life-giving vine, the honey-sweet grape
of immortality, the unmovable fortress of perseverance, the (85)
cross-bearing soldier of self-control, the fearless
commander against the killers of Christ, the exalted branch of
the crucified Christ, Barnabas, *the son of encouragement*,[19]
the teacher of devotion, the pillar and roof
of faith, the unshakable tower, the unbroken foundation, (90)
the indestructible groundwork, the unmovable rock,
the peaceful refuge of the distressed, the comfort

---

16. The construction is difficult to translate: τὸ γὰρ κατὰ δύναμιν εἰπεῖν εὐγνωμοσύνης ἀπόδειξις. The opening neuter article seems to go with the aorist active infinitive εἰπεῖν. I have chosen to continue the hortatory subjunctive construction of line 62, making a series of exhortations to praise Barnabas.

17. Acts 4:36.

18. The *TLG* Greek text mistakenly has a redundant article at the end of line 70: τοῦ τοῦ ἁγίου Πνεύματος.

19. Acts 4:36.

of all the afflicted, the faithful and wise steward,[20]
the noblest of master builders, the one who accomplished the ethereal
voyage and angelic life upon the earth, the defender of the (95)
churches, the protector of the poor, the provider and
nourisher of day laborers, the consolation of widows and
the most protective father of orphans. Barnabas, the treasury
of the mysteries of Christ, the steward of the orthodox
creeds of the holy church of God, the sincere (100)
physician of the sick, the faultless cheer
of the healthy, the watchful guard
of the flock of Christ, the one who walks upon earth but has
citizenship in the heavens,[21] the one who commands on earth the godly
creeds and receives in heaven an eternal wreath (or garland). The (105)
God-bearing guide of the Gentiles and the God-blessed preacher
of the churches, the meadow of the *sweet smell of Christ*,[22] the rose bed
of heavenly virtues, the productive field of the
gifts of Christ, the one who, upon the earth, approaches the
incorruptible citizenship, living better upon the earth than (110)
the incorporeal angels in the heavens, the one eminent in
training and the advanced in contemplations, and magnified
in marvels, the *highly revered pearl*[23] of virginity,
the chosen gem of chastity, the pure gem
of self control, the one having Christ speaking in himself, (115)
the *vessel* of the *elect*[24] of God, the one who left behind
the world and *considers all things in it to be shit*,[25]
in order that he might gain Christ alone, *the king of the ages*,[26]
the one who undisputedly took up his cross and
who eagerly followed Christ as a true disciple, (120)

20. Luke 12:42.

21. Phil 3:20.

22. 2 Cor 2:15.

23. Matt 13:46.

24. Acts 9:15.

25. Paul uses the same word, σκύβαλον, in Phil 3:8, the text that Alexander uses here in his speech. The primary meaning of the term is dung, excrement, or manure, but Bible translations shy away from assigning this more graphic meaning. The NRSV translates it as rubbish. I believe that "shit" (or at least "crap") more accurately captures the modern sense of the meaning of the word—which was not meant to be delicate.

26. 1 Tim 1:17.

the banisher of demons and inflictor of wounds on the devil,
the one marching the four quarters of the inhabited earth with
untiring gait as a good servant and lover of his master, and
bringing all the Gentiles through the gospel to
faith in Christ, the one who prepared himself to be a dwelling (125)
of the consubstantial Trinity and who became a temple of God
over all. Barnabas, the revered ornament of the Cypriots
and the unconquerable champion of the inhabited world,
the one who loves Christ superabundantly and for him
gives up his life each day and with (130)
him rules for ever and ever.

The word toiled, desiring to exalt the divinely sweet and
thrice longed for Barnabas the apostle with encomiums,
but did not even achieve an introduction; for in the praises it experiences
the unapproachable marvel. Therefore, after giving up as unattainable
    (135)
an adequate presentation of encomiums, I will present to us
a few of the aspects of his life and achievement from
the *Stromata* and from other ancient writings
to your holiness, and thus we will place a limit
on the narration, yielding to the God-breathed (140)
Scripture to crown the magnificent head with song.
For it says, *"And* Barnabas *was a good man and
full of the Holy Spirit and of faith."*[27] Who might
be his equal or ever come near him?
Therefore, the thrice blessed was urged on, he from the (145)
blessed tribe of Levi,[28] from which came Moses and
Aaron, the great prophets of God and first of the
inhabitants of Kaath, descending by kinship from the race
of Samuel the prophet. And the ancestors of this one, after seizing
through battles the land surrounding the Cypriots, (150)
were living peacefully in it. And they were *reverent according
to the law*[29] and were exceedingly rich, whence also among Jerusalemites
they had sufficient property and a beautiful field

27. Acts 11:24.
28. See Acts 4:36.
29. See Acts 22:12, which uses these words to describe Ananias.

near the city, not only adorned with all sorts of natural
fruits, but also in greatness the most conspicuous of surrounding colonies. (155)
For they heard from Isaiah the prophet, who said,
"*Blessed is the one having descendants in Zion and families
in Jerusalem.*"[30] So the children of the Hebrews, who physically
received the prophecy, each of them who prospered hastened
to obtain property in Jerusalem. (160)

Now concerning this righteous man born in Cyprus, when
his parents saw him being refined to God,[31] immediately
they named him Joseph, honoring the child with the
name of the patriarch. And this noble man ran to
live up to the dignity of his name. For (165)
Joseph is interpreted "provision of God"; for the righteous one
received additional grace from God that he might come first
in apostolic perfection; and again, Joseph is interpreted
"glory of God," for he has become through the noblest citizenship "glory
of God." But let no one consider the word to be superior, (170)
but let him understand that it is of the divine Scripture. Paul
at least says, "*A man is not obligated to cover his
head, being the image and glory of God.*"[32] If, therefore, he called
the common man the image and glory of God, the vessel
of election, what would he say concerning the most perfect (175)
man of God?

And after Barnabas grew as a child, his parents
took him up to Jerusalem[33] and they delivered him to learn
the law and the prophets accurately *at the feet of
Gamaliel.*[34] And he had Paul as a schoolmate, who was named (180)
Saul for a while. And day-by-day Barnabas advanced in
learning and in every virtue; not yet, to be sure, was he appointed into
the priestly division of the Levites because of his small

---

30. Isa 31:9 LXX: Τάδε λέγει κύριος Μακάριος ὃς ἔχει ἐν Σιων σπέρμα καὶ οἰκείους ἐν Ιερουσαλημ.

31. Resembles the description of the baby Moses in Exod 2:2.

32. 1 Cor 11:7

33. Cf. the description of the child Jesus in Luke 2:40–41.

34. Mimics Paul's statement about himself in Acts 22:3.

stature, for he was still an adolescent. *But he did not separate himself from the temple, ministering night and day by fasts and prayers.*[35] (185)
Thus, he recited the law and the other writings,
so he did not have to be reminded by the written letters (i.e, he memo-
    rized them).
And thus he had beloved silence, as a mother of
self control. And fleeing the harm of loathsome sexual
intercourse, he became pure, unmixed, and undefiled (190)
honor. And he was glorious to all because of virtue.

And about that time he joined the Lord
to be near [him] in Jerusalem when [Jesus] healed the paralyzed man
at the sheep gate, and worked many other signs and wonders
in the temple.[36] The blessed one, after seeing these things, (195)
was amazed and, after immediately approaching, he fell at
Jesus' feet and asked to be blessed by him. And while
Christ was entering his heart,[37] after approving of his faith,
he kindly admitted him, and he gave [to him] a share of his
divine relationship. And Barnabas greatly burned with love (200)
for the Lord. And after quickly entering *the house
of Mary, the mother of John who is called Mark,*[38]
who was known to be his aunt[39]—therefore they also
called him *Mark the cousin of Barnabas*[40]—he said to her,
"Come, O woman, behold what our fathers (205)
longed to see.[41] For behold, *Jesus, a prophet from
Nazareth of Galilee,*[42] is in the temple, a magnificent
miracle worker, and as he seems to many, he is
the coming Messiah." And after hearing these things, the
wonderful woman also, leaving behind the things in her hand, (210)

35. Here Alexander employs the description of the elderly widow, Anna, in Luke 2:37.

36. John 5:1 ff.

37. Literally "hearts" (Ὁ δὲ τὰς καρδίας ἐμβατεύων Χριστός), which does not make sense in context.

38. Acts 12:12.

39. θεία.

40. Quoting Col 4:10, using the term ἀνεψιός, which normally means cousin.

41. Cf. Jesus' words in Matt 13:17.

42. Matt 21:11.

entered the temple of God; and beholding the Lord and master
of the temple, she fell at his feet, begging and
saying, "Lord, *if I have found favor before you*, come
into the house of your servant and *bless at* your *entry*[43]
your household servants." And the Lord granted her (215)
request. When he drew near, she joyfully welcomed him into
the upper part of her house. Therefore, from that day that
the Lord entered Jerusalem, he rested there with
his disciples; there he celebrated the Passover with
his disciples; there he initiated his disciples through (220)
participation in the secret mysteries. For word
came down to us from the elders that the one who carried
the jar of water, whom the Lord commanded
the disciples to follow,[44] was Mark, the son of this
blessed Mary.[45] And the Lord said "unto such a one" (225)
a household manager, as the Fathers say, interpreting this
passage, teaching us through the riddle that to every one
who readies himself, the Lord abides with him.
Accordingly, the Lord prepared the Passover in the upper room,
in which he appeared to those around Thomas, after he was raised (230)
from the dead.[46] There, after the ascension, the disciples returned,
coming from the Mt. of Olives with the rest of the
brothers, the number being 120,[47] among whom
were Barnabas and Mark. There the Holy Spirit descended
in fiery tongues upon the disciples on the Day of (235)
Pentecost.[48] There now is established the great and
most holy Zion, the mother of all the churches.

Then Barnabas followed the Lord, returning
from Jerusalem unto Galilee. And many from every quarter
were coming to the Lord and believing in him. (240)

43. Cf. the words of Laban in Gen 30:27 LXX.

44. Mark 14:13; Luke 22:10.

45. Acts 12:12.

46. See Matt 26:17–34; Mark 14:12–21; Luke 22:7–38 for Jesus' Passover meal with his disciples. For Jesus' post-resurrection appearance to the apostles and then again when Thomas was present, see John 20:19–29.

47. See Acts 1:12–15.

48. Acts 2:1–6.

Then he said to his disciples, *"The harvest
is great, but the workers are few."*[49] Then he commissioned the
seventy disciples,[50] of whom the first and leader and
head happened to be the great Barnabas. But let no one
who hears that the apostles placed upon him this (245)
title foolishly suppose that he received this title apart from
divine inspiration. For Peter placed upon him
this name through a revelation of the Holy
Spirit. And he through a revelation from the Father received
the divine word of the Son. And as *James and* (250)
John the sons of thunder[51] were called because of virtue, thus
also was Barnabas called the *son of encouragement*[52] because of virtue,
being an encourager of all through his surpassing holiness.

And after hearing the Lord teaching and saying,
"Sell your possessions and give alms. (255)
*Make for yourselves purses that do not grow old, unfailing
treasure in the heavens,"*[53] he wasted no time but immediately
left behind his remaining property, costly property from
his parents—for they were retired from life—
after selling all, he distributed to those having need, (260)
keeping for himself only that field for his own
support. And after the passion and the resurrection and
the ascension of the Lord and the manifestation of the Holy
Spirit, the divine Barnabas was burning greatly
with love for the Lord. And he returned to that same field and (265)
sold it for a sufficient amount of money, he took the whole amount
and *he placed it at the feet of the apostles,*[54] keeping nothing
of it from them for himself. And by his own
example he aroused all of the disciples unto similar
virtue. (270)

49. Matt 9:37–38; Luke 10:2.
50. Luke 10:1, 17.
51. Mark 3:17.
52. Acts 4:36.
53. Luke 12:33.
54. Acts 4:37.

And he was speaking and disputing with Saul,[55] desiring
to lead him to faith in the Lord. But Saul, relying
on strict (obedience) to the law for citizenship,
was mocking Barnabas as being deceived; and he
was blaspheming the Lord, calling him *the son of a carpenter*[56] (275)
and an ignoramus and a country bumpkin and a criminal. But as he saw
  the
great wonders happening through the miracles of the
apostles and the multitude of people every day
being brought to the word of faith, it was stinging
(his) soul. And after encountering, along with *the freedmen and (280)
Cyrenians and Alexandrians*,[57] the great orator of the church,
Stephen, and not being able to match his wisdom and
the spirit with which he was speaking,[58] Saul became crazy. And being
full of rage, he raised up against Stephen the lawless of the people;
and swaying their emotions,[59] he aroused *great persecution against (285)
the church in Jerusalem*.[60] But while he was lawlessly
going to Damascus to do evil to those of the faith,
the Lord humbled him, throwing him upon his face.[61] And after
falling to the ground, he recognized who pursued (him). And *after his eyes
were blinded, he looked up steadfastly to the height of heaven.*[62] (290)
And after returning to Jerusalem, he was seeking *to be united with*

55. The first words in this sentence (ἐλάλει τε καὶ συνεζήτει πρὸς) repeat the beginning words of Acts 9:29, which describe Paul's arguing with the Hellenistic Jews in
Jerusalem: ἐλάλει τε καὶ συνεζήτει πρὸς τοὺς Ἑλληνιστάς.

56. Matt 13:55.

57. These words repeat Acts 6:9 (Λιβερτίνων καὶ Κυρηναίων καὶ Ἀλεξανδρέων),
but the story in Acts describes Stephen arguing with these people.

58. Alexander quotes part of Acts 6:8–10, attributing to Paul a description of
people in the synagogue of the Freedmen: "Stephen, full of grace and power, did
great wonders and signs among the people. Then some of those who belonged to the
synagogue of the Freedmen (as it was called), Cyrenians, Alexandrians, and others of
those from Cilicia and Asia, stood up and argued with Stephen. But they could not
withstand the wisdom and the Spirit with which he spoke."

59. Literally, "and carrying this away" (καὶ τοῦτον ἀνελών).

60. Acts 8:1.

61. See Acts 9:1–6; 22:4–11; 26:12–18.

62. Sometimes, Alexander's jumbled use of pronouns makes it difficult to keep the
subject in mind. Rather than cleaning up the narration, I have provided a rather literal
translation.

the disciples, but they all were fleeing from him,[63] fearing his
great cruelty. But the great Barnabas, after meeting
with him, said, "How long, Saul, will you keep behaving thus?[64] Why
do you so eagerly persecute the benefactor? Stop ravaging (295)
the awe inspiring mystery proclaimed by the ancient
prophets and in our own time revealed unto
our salvation." Saul, after hearing these things, fell at
the feet of Barnabas, with many tears crying and
saying, "Forgive me, guide of the light and teacher (300)
of the truth, for I know the truth in the experience of
your words. For whom I blasphemed, calling the son
of a carpenter,[65] I now confess him to be the only begotten *Son
of the living God*,[66] consubstantial and like minded and sharing the same
throne, co-eternal and without beginning. *Who, being the radiance (305)
of the glory and the image of the substance*[67] of the invisible
God, *in these last days, because of us and because of
our salvation, he humbled himself, taking the form of a
servant*,[68] that is to say a perfect man from the holy virgin
and Godbearer,[69] Mary, unmixed, unchanging, indivisible, (310)
inseparable.[70] *And being found in form as a man, he
humbled himself, becoming obedient unto death, even
death on a cross.*[71] Who also rose from the dead on the third
day and was seen by you,[72] his apostles, and
*he was taken up into the heavens and sat at the right hand (315)
of the Father*[73] *and again comes with glory to judge the living
and the dead,*[74] and *of his kingdom there will be no end.*"[75]

---

63. Acts 9:26.

64. Idiomatic. The Greek reads Ἕως πότε, Σαῦλε, Σαοὺλ τυγχάνεις.

65. Matt 13:55.

66. Matt 16:16; John 16:69.

67. Heb 1:3.

68. Cf. the Christ hymn in Phil 2:6–11.

69. θεοτόκος.

70. These statements of fully developed Trinitarian belief are obviously from a time much later than Paul.

71. Phil 2:7–8.

72. Plural, ὑμῖν.

73. Mark 16:9; Acts 2:33; 7:55–56; Rom 8:34; 1 Peter 3:22; Heb 10:12.

74. 2 Tim 4:1; 1 Peter 4:5.

75. Luke 1:33. Cf. the Nicene Creed.

After hearing these things from the *blasphemer and persecutor*,[76]
the divinely sweet Barnabas was amazed and from joy
his face became as a flower in the morning. (320)
And after embracing him and kissing him, he said,
"Saul, who taught you such divinely breathed words
to proclaim so clearly? Who persuaded you to confess Jesus the Nazarene
the Son of God? Where did you learn of these heavenly doctrines
so accurately?" And Saul, bowing his head in shame and crying with
  (325)
much contrition, said, "The Lord Jesus himself,
who many times was blasphemed and pursued by me the
sinner, he taught me all these things. For *as if
to one untimely born he was revealed also to me*,[77] and I still have
dwelling in my ears his divine and sweet voice. For even after (330)
I transgressed every goodness, he granted mercy to me,
defending rather than *condemning* me. And he said to me, 'Saul,
Saul, why do you persecute me?' And I with trembling and fear
answered, 'Who are you, Lord?' And the Lord with much
fairness and compassion said to me, 'I am Jesus (335)
the Nazarene, whom you persecute.' And I was astounded at
his ineffable patience, and I was bound to him, saying, 'What
shall I do, Lord?'*[78] And forthwith he instructed me in all these things
and even more of them."

Then the great *Barnabas, after taking his hand*, (340)
brought him to the apostles,[79] saying, "Why do you flee from the
shepherd, considering him to be a wolf? Why do you drive away
the pilot as a brigand? Why do you loathe the chief
as a traitor? Why do you dismiss the leader of the bride as
a robber of the bridal chamber? For the church is the (345)
spiritual bridal chamber, of which the Lord himself appointed
(Paul as) shepherd and pilot and defender." Then Paul *narrated
to them* what all happened to him along *the way*, and
that *he saw the Lord and that he spoke to him, and how*

---

76. 1 Tim 1:13.
77. 1 Cor 15:8.
78. Acts 22:7–8.
79. Acts 9:27.

in Damascus he boldly spoke in the name of the Lord.[80] (350)
And he was teaching with them the word of the Lord in
Jerusalem. And he became a huge problem for the Jews, because
yesterday he was persecuting Jesus, but today he proclaimed him
to be Son of God. And *they resolved to kill him.*[81] But after the
apostles learned (about it), they sent him to preach in his (355)
own country.[82]

And *after they were scattered because of the affliction of Stephen,
and came into Antioch and preached the good news of the Lord
Jesus, news of them was heard in*[83] Jerusalem. Then the
apostles sent there the blessed Barnabas, the great (360)
and powerful, to shepherd the flock of Christ
in the holy church. *When he joined (them), he
contributed greatly to those who had faith,*[84] and his
inspired teaching produced a people befitting to the Lord.[85]
Thereafter, under the guiding of the Holy Spirit, he left and (365)
went through all the cities and regions *preaching good news
until he came to*[86] the greatest city, Rome.[87] For he
before any other of the disciples of the Lord
proclaimed in Rome the gospel of Christ. And after many
believed and gave surpassing honor to him, (370)
he cast aside the glory of men. Secretly fleeing,
he left Rome, for again this blessed man also
more than all the men of that time coveted
humility, and he acquired it with supreme success.

80. Acts 9:27.

81. Acts 9:23, 29.

82. Acts 9:30.

83. See Acts 11:19–24.

84. Acts 18:27.

85. Here I have modified slightly the passive construction, καὶ διὰ τῆς ἐνθέου αὐτοῦ διδασκαλίας προσετέθη λαὸς ἱκανὸς τῷ κυρίῳ.

86. Cf. Acts 8:40.

87. Here Alexander repeats the legend contrived in the third century by the author of the Pseudo-Clementine *Homilies* (see *Hom.* 1.9–13).

And he ordained this clearly to all by his own example.[88] (375)
For in the God-breathed Scripture, which everywhere names
him first, he was yielding the first places to those around him.
He joyfully received second place in rank, accurately
imitating the Lord who said, *"Learn from me that
I am meek and humble in heart."*[89] (380)

And Barnabas reached Alexandria, which is in
Egypt, and after speaking there the word of God, he departed,
passing through in order *all the cities until he came
to*[90] Jerusalem. From there, he again departed and arrived
in Antioch. *And when he beheld the grace of God* and the (385)
growing church, *he rejoiced*[91] exceedingly. Then *he went away
to Tarsus, seeking Paul, and after finding him, he led him
to Antioch.*[92] And he worked there *an entire year* and
taught the people competently. And there they *first called the
disciples Christians.* [93] And after receiving the offering from the (390)
church for distribution to the poor, they went up again to
Jerusalem fourteen years after experiencing salvation,
as Paul writes, saying, *"After fourteen years
I went up to Jerusalem with Barnabas."* [94] And after they fulfilled
the ministry and received the *right hand* from the (395)
apostles, *in order that* they might preach *to the Gentiles* and
Peter *to the circumcision,*[95] they went down to
Antioch, taking with them Mark as a servant. *And after being
sent out from Antioch by the Holy Spirit,
they came to Cyprus.*[96] And after traveling through *the whole island* (400)
from Salamis *to Paphos,*[97] preaching the gospel and
performing miracles, they also blinded Elymas

88. Literally "from his own history" (ἐκ τῆς κατ' αὐτὸν ἱστορίας).
89. Matt 11:29.
90. Cf. Acts 8:40.
91. Cf. Acts 11:23.
92. Acts 12:25–26.
93. Acts 12:26.
94. Gal 2:1.
95. See Gal 2:7–10.
96. Acts 13:4.
97. Acts 13:6.

and enlightened the proconsul. And *after teaching many*,
those with Barnabas sailed by sea from Cyprus,
and *they came to Pamphylia*.⁹⁸ And Mark beheld the apostles (405)
going forward together to face dangers on behalf of the gospel,
and that they were about to receive honor as
they went out to war against unbelievers. (Mark) cowered
before the dangers, being only a lad, cowardly and immature
regarding disdain of death. He abandoned the (410)
apostles and *returned to Jerusalem* to his own
mother.⁹⁹

But when the apostles *Barnabas and* Paul completed
the work unto which they were called,¹⁰⁰ after bearing countless
struggles on behalf of Christ, they went to Antioch, where by (415)
the grace of God they had been sent out to the Gentiles. And it happened
that there was again a need for them to go up to Jerusalem unto
the apostles with Peter, because of false apostles
who were teaching that the disciples had to be circumcised and
keep the law. And when Mark beheld them being (420)
honored by all, and that after so many sufferings and dangers
they remained strong and perfect, and observing his own
cowardess, *he wept bitterly*.¹⁰¹ And he was ashamed
to come to Paul, so he went to Barnabas with
tears and fell at his feet, begging (425)
to receive forgiveness for transgressing his vow,
promising assurances of future things, and saying
that "*I am ready* to endure every form of death *on behalf
of the name of our Lord Jesus Christ*.¹⁰²
And being bent over by many tears, this great and virtuous (430)
Barnabas implored him to cease the weeping,
saying, "*Let the will of the Lord be done*.¹⁰³ Only
you better be prepared to fulfill your promises." And after receiving

98. Acts 13:13.

99. Acts 13:13. Alexander's description of Mark differs substantially from the one
presented in the Acts of Barnabas 3–8, which defends and exonerates Mark.

100. Cf. Acts 13:2.

101. Cf. Matt 26:75; Luke 22:62.

102. Cf. Acts 21:13.

103. Acts 21:14.

the written decrees from the apostles in
Jerusalem, they went down to Antioch where they (435)
rejoiced exceedingly with the brothers. And Mark was following
Barnabas, not with boldness.

And after these things it seemed good to Barnabas and Paul
to go through all the cities and to examine the brothers.[104]
Then Barnabas approached Paul and entreated him (440)
to allow Mark, who was now prepared to struggle unto death on
behalf of faith in Christ, to be their traveling companion.
But Paul did not want to take this one with them
to be an assistant. His decision provided the motive for them
to be separated from each other,[105] but it was overseen (445)
by the Lord to be beneficial; for God preordained
to exhibit Mark as shepherd and teacher of people
and nations. But let no one ignorantly receive unto his own
suffering what is said in the sacred history of Acts
concerning Mark that *there was a sharp disagreement.*[106] For the (450)
apostles of Christ were not carried away into passion of anger
and rage. For how could those who *crucified the*
flesh with its passions and desires?[107] They cry
in a great voice unto all those who believe in Christ
and say, "*Let all bitterness and anger and rage and* (455)
screaming and blasphemy be removed from you with all malice."[108]
For we have known from the divine Scripture about exasperations
due to disagreements, for it says, "*And let us contemplate how to provoke*
one another unto love and good works."[109] Therefore, provoking
happened to the apostles, that is to say their zeal for God. For (460)
Paul was seeking precision, conspicuous apostolic
Perfection; but Barnabas was honoring benevolence.

---

104. Acts 15:36–37.

105. Acts 15:39.

106. Acts 15:39.

107. Rom 6:6; Gal 5:24; cf. Gal 2:19.

108. Eph 4:31. Alexander seems here to warn Christians against believing that Acts describes Paul as being exasperated with Mark. If a statement ascribes motives less than what his overly spiritualized view of the apostles allows, he rejects it.

109. Heb 10:24.

Therefore taking Mark, he sailed to Cyprus,[110] and after going
through all (the land) and discipling many people, he came to
Salamis. And there he remained, performing miracles and *preaching*
  (465)
the Kingdom of God; and many people were added to
the Lord.[111] *And he conversed with the Jews in the synagogue*
on every Sabbath, pointing out from the Scriptures that Jesus
is the Christ.[112] And all honored him because
of the divine favor that shown from his face.[113] For (470)
his form was angelic and his appearance austere.
And his eyebrows knit together,[114] his eyes full of joy, not
appearing grim, but inclining reverently downward. His mouth
was noble and his lips handsome, with the sweetness of distilled honey
—for he never spoke excessively but controlled (himself)—; (475)
his walk was restrained and without conceit, and in general
the apostle Barnabas was always a pure pillar of Christ,
illuminating every virtue.

And while he was staying in the city of Salamis and
teaching the word of God, *Jews* from Syria confronted him (480)
and were *contradicting what he was saying and blaspheming.*[115]
They stirred up a crowd against him, saying that
he speaks nothing truthful; and also this Jesus, about whom he speaks,
was a deceiver and against God, rejecting the law and the
prophets and the Sabbath. And they were seeking an opportunity (485)
to destroy him. But the holy apostle of Christ, Barnabas,
after gathering all the brothers, *said to them,*
"You (pl) understand how I was with you (pl) the entire
time, admonishing and encouraging each one to remain

110. Acts 15:39; cf. 4:37 regarding benevolence.

111. Acts 11:24.

112. See Acts 17:1–3, 17; 18:4, both of which describe Paul's activities.

113. Literally, "because of the divine grace/favor having been poured around his face" (διὰ τὴν περικεχυμένην τῷ προσώπῳ αὐτοῦ θείαν χάριν).

114. These words seem to echo part the imaginary description of Paul in the second century Acts of Paul: "with eyebrows joining, . . . full of grace: for sometimes he appeared like a man, and sometimes he had the face of an angel" (Acts of Paul 2:3).

115. These words match Acts 13:45, which states that they were contradicting what *Paul* said.

in the grace and *in the faith* of our Lord Jesus Christ, (490)
and *to keep his commands and to do them* and
to be separated from every evil deed.[116] *For it is necessary*
for all of us to stand before the judgment seat of Christ, in order that
each might give account for the things done through the body, unto which
things he practiced, whether good or evil. For the form of this (495)
world is passing away, and the Lord *is about to come from heaven*
to judge the living and the dead.[117] Therefore, do not be careless,
knowing *that in an hour you do not expect,* our Lord
comes.[118] Therefore, *bear hardship patiently* and in hope *establish*
your hearts, because the coming of the Lord is near.[119] (500)
Remember everything I have spoken to you, saying that the
things of the present life are short-lived, whether good or sorrowful;
and all things will quickly pass away. By contrast, in the coming age
all things are eternal and everlasting. For the kingdom
of heaven will never pass away, neither does the judgment (505)
have an end; but it always remains, undying and unceasingly
chastising the sinners. Therefore *make haste that you might be*
found blameless and *without blemish in that day,*[120] in order that
you might not fall into that never ending death and destruction of
Gehenna. Remember all the signs and wonders (510)
that God did among you through me, his servant, and
pray for me. *For I am already being poured out as a libation*
and my time of departure is imminent, as our Lord
Jesus Christ revealed to me.[121] *I have fought the*
good fight. I have finished the race. I have kept the faith. (515)
Now the crown of righteousness is laid up for me,
and not only for me, but also to all the ones[122] who struggle
because of his name."

116. Most of this sentence is a quotation of Paul's speech to the Ephesian elders in Acts 20:17–38.

117. These words are a conflation of 2 Cor 5:10 (Rom 14:10); 1 Cor 7:31; and 2 Tim 4:1. None of these passages has any connection with Barnabas in the NT. Alexander also freely appropriates other NT passages to construct the rest of Barnabas's speech to the Christians at Salamis.

118. Cf. Paul's words in 1 Thess 5:1–11.

119. Jas 5:7–8.

120. Cf. Eph 5:27; Phil 2:15; 2 Pet 3:14.

121. 2 Tim 4:6; cf. Phil 2:17.

122. 2 Tim 4:7–8.

And after saying these things, he prayed with all of them. And all appropriately wept,[123] because the apostle had said (520) that *"The time of my departure has come."*[124] And Barnabas, after taking bread and a cup, and after doing every proper procedure, partook with the brothers of the mysteries of the Eucharist. And after these things, taking Mark and withdrawing in private, he said to him, "In (525) this day it is necessary for me to be perfected at the hands of disobedient Jews. But you must go outside the city toward the west, and you will find my body. And after burying it, leave Cyprus and go unto Paul and stay with him until the Lord will order events concerning (530) you. For your name is about to be magnified in the whole inhabited world."[125]

After these things, Barnabas entered the synagogue and taught the Jews, *persuading them concerning the* Lord *Jesus, that he is the Christ, the Son of the living (535) God.*[126] And the Jews from Syria, being filled with rage, rose up and grabbed him with their hands and placed him in a dark room in the synagogue until late evening. And after leading him out and interrogating him closely, they led him during the night outside of the city and there (540) the lawless ones stoned him to death. And they kindled a great fire and threw the blessed one into so that no remains of his body would be found.[127] But, in the providence of God, the body of the apostle remained unharmed and the fire damaged nothing of it.[128] And Mark, in obedience to the arrangements given to him, (545)

123. See Acts 20:36–38.

124. 2 Tim 4:6.

125. Seems to echo the words spoken by an angel to John Mark in Acts of Barnabas 3.

126. From Acts 17:2–4 and 18:5, which describe Paul, not Barnabas.

127. See Acts of Barnabas 23 for a different description of the martyrdom of Barnabas.

128. In Alexander's version of the story, God prevents the great fire from burning the body. In Acts of Barnabas 23–24, Mark collects the remains of Barnabas, which are merely dust, and hides them in a cave.

went outside the city to the west with certain brothers
in secret, where they collected the remains of St. Barnabas. And
after burying the remains in a cave about five stadia from the city,
they withdrew, *after making great lamentation over him.*[129]

And in that time great persecution came upon (550)
the church in Salamis, *and all were scattered* [130]
in different directions. And the location of the tomb of the holy
apostle Barnabas remained unknown. And after Mark sailed
away from the land of Cyprus, he came to Paul in Ephesus
and he announced to him concerning the perfection of Barnabas. (555)
And after hearing [the story], Paul[131] wept with great lamentation over
him, and he detained Mark to stay with him. And after these things,
Peter went away to Rome in response to a revelation from God,
and he took Mark with him—in a manner giving birth
to him. There Mark put together the Gospel story.[132] (560)
Peter, after reading the Gospel, was satisfied that
it was inspired by God. And after laying his hands on Mark,
he sent him away as exceedingly competent to Alexandria
in Egypt and to Libya and Pentapolis. While there *he*
preached the gospel of Christ Jesus to them. (565)
And *a great number who believed turned to the*
Lord.[133] And after teaching the word of God among
them for nine years, Mark's witness was finished and he died
in Alexandria.

And after a long time of Christianity growing widely (570)
and of Christian kings of Rome ruling with sovereignty,
God did not fail to perform miracles in the place

129. From Acts 8:2, which describes events following the martyrdom of Stephen. This phrase is also used in 1 Macc 2:70; 4:39; 9:20; 13:26.

130. From Acts 8:1, which describes the persecution of the Jerusalem church after the death of Stephen.

131. Greek "he."

132. See Eusebius, *Hist. Eccl.* II. 15.1–2, for a description of Mark being with Peter and writing the Gospel of Mark.

133. From Acts 11:20–21, which describes the evangelistic work of Christians from Cyprus and Cyrene. Their success set events into motion that brought Barnabas to Antioch.

where the remains of the holy apostle and noble
martyr, Barnabas, lay neglected. *For many of the ones having
unclean spirits, when present at the place, were crying out* (575)
*in a load voice, (as the demons) were coming out. And many who
    were weak*
and lame and had *various diseases and were tormented with
pain*, when they came to lie down at the place, were all
being healed.[134] And there was great joy in the city
of Salamis, because a certain divine power was (580)
working in that place, they knew; but they did not know
the reason for so bountiful a gift. And the
inhabitants of that region called it the place of health.

But when the blessed Marcian[135] ceased the rule,
the lion of divine appointment received the kingdom.[136] He had a (585)
son-in-law, Zeno by name, Isaurian by race,

134. Acts 8:3: πολλοὶ γὰρ τῶν ἐχόντων πνεύματα ἀκάθαρτα βοῶντα φωνῇ μεγάλῃ ἐξήρχοντο, πολλοὶ δὲ παραλελυμένοι καὶ χωλοὶ ἐθεραπεύθησαν. This passage describes Philip's ministry in Samaria.

135. *Flavius Marcianus Augustus* (392–457), the Byzantine ruler from 450–457, reinvigorated the Eastern Empire. When the previous ruler, Theodosius II, died in 450, his sister Pulcheria became the first woman to succeed to the throne of the Empire. Almost immediately, she arranged a politically expedient marriage with Marcian, an influential widower. Marcian stopped paying the tribute that Theodosius II paid to Attila the Hun. His tax reforms, moderate economic policies and strengthening of the military revitalized the Byzantine Empire. He avoided overextending his army, did little to help the Western Empire when Attila attacked; and he did not aid Rome when the city was sacked in 455 by the Vandals under king Genseric. Marcian convened the Council of Chalcedon (451) to consider Christological controversies and address the Monophysite debate. Eastern Orthodox Christians consider him to be a saint, celebrating his feast day on February 17.

136. *Flavius Valerius Leo Augustus* (401–474), known as Leo I the Thracian, served in the Roman army, achieved the rank of *comes*, and became emperor in 457 following the death of Marcian. The patriarch of Constantinople participated in Leo's coronation (a first), and Leo was the first Byzantine Emperor to legislate in Greek rather than Latin. An ambitious military leader, he provided aid to the Western Empire. As part of an alliance with the Isaurians, Leo married his daughter Ariadne to the Isaurian commander Tarasis (son of Kodisa), who changed his name to Zeno to be more accepted by the Greek speakers of Constantinople. Ariadne and Zeno's son, Leo II, became emperor following the death of Leo I. Ariadne and her mother convinced the seven-year-old Leo II that, because of his youth, he should have his father, Zeno, as co-ruler. Less than a year later, Leo II died, leaving Zeno as sole emperor in 474.

who also ruled with him.[137] And during that time
was found in the most holy monastery of the *Akoimeton* (sleepless ones)[138]
a solitary devil, as Judas among the apostles,
named Peter, by business a fuller.[139] And he repudiated (590)
the holy synod in Chalcedon, fighting for the beliefs of
the Eutychianists.[140] The (members) of that
holy monastery expelled Peter from the monastery,
as a corrupter and seducer and enemy of the apostolic doctrines.[141]
But he, while in Constantinople, envied (595)

137. Many in Constantinople disliked Zeno (*Flavius Zeno Augustus*), partly because of his barbarian background. In 475 a revolt in Constantinople forced Zeno to
flee to his native Isauria. He took with him the money from the royal treasury. The mob
murdered almost all the Isaurians remaining in the city. Basiliscus, brother of Verina,
the wife of Leo I, seized power and became emperor (*Flavius Basiliscus Augustus*).
However, he alienated many in Constantinople because he espoused Miaphysite beliefs instead of Chalcedonian Christology. Also, Basiliscus started his rule in financial
stress because Zeno took the treasury. Basiliscus raised taxes, extorted money from the
church and made enemies by appointing his backers to high positions. In 476, Zeno
met little resistance when he moved to regain his kingdom, using his wealth to make
well-placed bribes. The Senate opened the city doors to him. Basilicus took refuge in
Hagia Sophia with his family, but the patriarch betrayed him after extracting a promise
from Zeno not to shed blood. So Zeno sent Basilicus to Cappadocia, where he had the
man and his family shut up in a dry cistern and left to die with no shedding of blood.
Zeno ruled until he died in 491.

138. The identity of these monks is uncertain. Apparently, they resided in a monastery in or near Constantinople. Perhaps they were the group that was well known for
holding continuous liturgy throughout the day.

139. For a detailed article on this man, see Rafał Kosiński, "Peter the Fuller, Patriarch of Antioch (471–488)," in *Byzantinoslavica—Revue international des Etudes
Byzantines* 68 (2010) 49–73. Kosiński provides a wealth of information from ancient
source documents.

140. Eutyches of Constantinople believed that the divine nature of Christ over-
came the human nature of Jesus. Christ was therefore of one nature with God, but not
one nature with humanity. Their opponents called the Eutychianists Monophysites.
Church representatives at the Fourth Ecumenical Council at Calcedon in 451 rejected
Monophysite belief.

141. Alexander clearly claims that Peter was a monastic at the Monastery of the
Sleepless Monks, but he was expelled for heresy. According to Θεόδωρος Αναγνώστης
(Theodorus Lector, reader at Hagia Sophia in the early sixth century), however, Peter came to Antioch with Zeno from the Church of the Martyr Bassa in Chalcedon
(*Epitome* 390; see also *John Malalas* XV. 1). Perhaps he was the leader of this monastery. Nothing is known about the early years of Peter. Alexander claims in line 590
that Peter got his name from his profession as a fuller. *Chonicon ad annum Domini 846
pertinens* 165 states that he got the name because his parents were fullers.

the life of the flatters; and he went about from house to
house, eating gluttonously. And after finding some of those
who belonged to his disgusting heresy, he became part of them;
and through them he became known to the son-in-law of the king,[142]
who was a patrician at the time and a *comes*[143] of the imperial guard.
(600)
And after feigning piety,[144] he was with him
continually, not daring to make known publicly his own impiety.
And departing with Zeno toward the regions of the east,[145]
the Fuller gathered (support) as far as Antioch. And finding there
many of the Apollinarians,[146] he wantonly spoke against (605)
the patriarch,[147] arousing against him the disorderly
of the people. Peter reviled the synod of Chalcedon and
voiced (the beliefs of) Nestorius[148] the patriarch. And when much
confusion and uproar existed in Antioch,
the Fuller went with treachery to the *comes*, saying, (610)
"If the bishop is not appointed in this city,
the land cannot be at rest."[149] At the same time, he arranged

142. Zeno, son-in-law of Leo I.

143. Greek κόμης. The Latin *comes* designated the title of a state office and means a companion (here a companion of the king).

144. Literally "placing on a face of reverence" (περιθέμενος εὐλαβείας πρόσωπον).

145. About 468, Zeno became aware of a plot against him by Aspar, an influential opponent of Leo I. Instead of returning to Constantinople, Zeno went east and spent two years in Antioch. He took with him the monk, Peter the Fuller. At this stage, Zeno appears to have been sympathetic to Monophysite beliefs. Peter, with violent backing from monks who moved into Antioch, challenged Martyrius, Patriarch of Antioch, who went to Constantinople to ask support from Leo I. Leo exiled Peter to Egypt and ordered Zeno to forbid monks from leaving their monasteries to foment rebellion. See *Codex Iustinianus* I. 3. 29.

146. Apollinarius of Laodicea taught that Jesus had a human body but only a divine mind. He rejected Arianism and emphasized the deity of Christ. Opponents of Apollinarians considered them to be Monophysites. See Theodorus Lector, *Epitome* 390, regarding Apollinarians and Peter.

147. Martyrius, Patriarch of Antioch.

148. Nestorius was the patriarch of Constantinople from 428–431. He did not believe that Christians should call Mary the God-bearer (*Theotokos*), because he believed that such veneration of Mary was improper and made her a goddess. Members of the First Council of Ephesus in 431 condemned him of heresy, and he lost his position as patriarch.

149. Apparently, Peter convinced Zeno to back his efforts to oust Martyrius. He was installed as bishop of Antioch while Martyrius was away in Constantinople. Peter's tenure was brief.

a great quantity of gold for him, even though he gained
it by demanding.[150] For he revealed to him the secrets of his
well concealed goal. Then the Fuller persuaded the ones who (615)
were sick like himself and certain insincere and evil men
of the partisans, and he brought (them) to the king (i.e., Leo I),
lying terribly against the bishop. But his cleverness
benefitted him nothing when the king defended the
apostolic decrees. (620)

And after he [King Leo] left this place and passed over[151]
into the ageless kingdom [i.e., died], Zeno became successor of the
kingdom. And immediately, the aforementioned[152] Antiochenes
brought supplication to the king, begging for the Fuller bishop.[153]
And in fact it happened when gold persuaded all those (625)
of the royal courtyard to come to his defense.
Immediately, therefore, he at once condemned by public vote
the holy Synod of Chalcedon. And he desired to please the
Apollinarians, those suffering the Theopaschite heresy.[154] He contrived
the evil innovation to say at the end of the Thrice-Holy hymn: (630)
"The one who was crucified because of us."[155] When our holy bishops
and fathers learned of these things, they were nobly aroused
against his heresy. And first they endeavored[156]
through hortatory letters to summon him from
the pit of impiety. But as they saw him contradicting (635)
and speaking all the more boldly against the orthodox

---

150. The meaning of this statement is unclear.

151. εἰς τὴν ἀγήρω βασιλείαν μετατεθέντος seems to be a euphemism for "he died," suggesting the translation "passed over."

152. οἱ προειρημένοι. In this context this verb construction seems to mean "the ones spoken of before," referring to the Antiochenes mentioned previously.

153. Apparently, they were demanding that (or begging for) Peter the Fuller to be reinstated.

154. The Theopaschite heresy taught that the Godhead suffered in Christ.

155. "To the words, "Holy God, Holy Mighty, Holy Immortal have mercy upon us,' Peter had added, after the word Immortal', the words 'who was crucified for us.' He had done so in all probability precisely to reinforce the christological interpretation of the hymn by stressing that the Logos had truly incarnated and suffered" (Kosiński, "Peter the Fuller, Patriarch of Antioch [471–88]," 70).

156. Although ἐπειράθησαν is an aorist passive construction, translating it as a passive renders the sentence unintelligible.

faith, then they denounced him; and all the bishops
of the inhabited world anathematized him.

And when the word comes, I hope that I will speak with pleasure
against this strange departure from our uncontestable, (640)
received (teachings), with sincere reason and not with bad
judgment. Of what benefit is it, my brothers, to leave behind
the heritage of the orthodox teaching of the fathers and
accept as true the novel inventions of the
heretics? One ought to understand that *they did not follow cleverly (645)
constructed myths.*[157] The saints, our fathers, delivered
this hymn to us to sing. This divine revelation was
not revealed to one or two only, and not to
someone in private, but in midday, to everyone
who loves Christ in the kingdom of the people of Constantinople, on
   (650)
behalf of our holy, thrice-blessed father and bishop Proclus,
who is esteemed among teachers. And God gave the revelation
of every divine grace, so that we lack nothing but have
all that is necessary for a perfect salvation that is not bound
by the addition of human syllogisms, or by removing (655)
what is said in the divinely inspired Scripture. "*The
word, which I command to you today, to keep* exactly
in order *to do* it, *you will not add to it, neither will you
take away from it.*"[158] For the one who takes away or adds anything
to the divine oracles is misleading and dangerous. For we are not (660)
correctors of God but those who obey. And he has many things
to say to us concerning this matter and to show that
it is complete idiocy to receive the invention
of the heretic, even if one does not understand the (ideas) of the heretic.[159]

Consequently, Peter the Fuller was anathematized, (665)
as it is said, by all of the bishops and by Zeno,
who fled his kingdom because of the insurrection

157. 2 Pet 1:16.
158. See Deut 4:1–2; 8:1; 12:28, 31.
159. The intended meaning of this final clause is unclear.

of the petty king,[160] departing as a fugitive to unknown places. But
when Zeno returned to his kingdom, after investigating
Peter the Fuller, he restored the bishop to the (670)
Antiochians, with not even one of the anathemas against him
being abolished. And he banished the blessed Patriarch Calandion
into the Libyan desert.[161] After the Fuller took the throne
by force, seeing that[162] he had renounced the rest and had
no hope, more and more confidently he attacked (675)
in tyranny, killing, confiscating and banishing all
those refusing to join in his ungodliness. But
I will pass over these things, which are many and bound with
personal history, and I will proceed to the important matter, explaining
to all the immeasurable grace of the holy apostle Barnabas and (680)
how great a concern and guardianship he has for his
fatherland. Therefore, the Fuller, not being satisfied
with the countless evils which he did against the East,
also set out to control the jurisdictions that he did
not personally establish. For after buying with gold the (685)
tolerance of the king and of the ones surrounding him, he also
despised the law of his God—and he was
then disposed to mistreat the God-loving and
faith-loving and Orthodox Cypriots of all kinds, since they
guarded the ancestral godliness, not desiring to share in his impiety—(690)
and he endeavored to seize for himself the most sacred, apostolic

160. Greek διὰ τὴν ἐπανάστασιν Βασιλίσκου. βασιλίσκος seems to be the diminutive of βασιλεύς, which could mean princelet, chieftain or petty king. It can also designate a kind of snake, a basilisk.

161. Greek Ὄασις, which designates cities in the Libyan desert. E.g., Herodotus, *Historiae*.

(26.) Ὁ μὲν ἐπ᾽ Αἰθίοπας στόλος οὕτω ἔπρηξε..., ἀπι-
κόμενοι μὲν φανεροί εἰσι ἐς Ὄασιν πόλιν, τὴν ἔχουσι μὲν
Σάμιοι τῆς Αἰσχριωνίης φυλῆς λεγόμενοι εἶναι, ἀπέχουσι (5)
δὲ ἑπτὰ ἡμερέων ὁδὸν ἀπὸ Θηβέων διὰ ψάμμου, ὀνομά-
ζεται δὲ ὁ χῶρος οὗτος κατὰ Ἑλλήνων γλῶσσαν Μακάρων
νῆσος.

162. This phrase is odd. Grammatically, Peter the Fuller is the one doing the action in the two participles (ἄτε ἀπεγνωσμένος λοιπὸν καὶ μηδεμίαν ἐλπίδα ἔχων), but it is unclear why he would be without hope. In the sentence, he seems to be the one in the position of power. I am tempted to make the accusatives into the subject and translate "seeing that the rest were despairing and had not a single hope"—especially in light of Peter's subsequent rampage. "Despairing" is a common translation for ἀπεγνωσμένος and would go nicely with the second participle.

throne of Cyprus, which from the beginning and from above was
  independent,
and to place it under himself. And he makes a report to
the ruler (Zeno), full of lies, because he says *the Word*
of God comes from Antioch *to Cyprus;*[163] and it is necessary (695)
for the Church of Cyprus to be under the throne of Antioch,
because it happens to be the apostolic and patriarchal throne.
But the apostate heretic was not able to escape notice when he falsified[164]
the things ordained in Ephesus by the Holy Synod, according to
Cyril. But Barnabas, the herald of godliness, the (700)
most holy among apostles, refuted his foolishness, and in the nick of
time became the protector of the fatherland. For when
the bishop of Salamis was urged to seize the
rule and to condemn the universal rule of the patriarch
of Antioch, he was stupefied with fear, suspecting (705)
the intrigues of the Fuller. Anthemios was an
admirable man, the most orthodox of all, one who distinguished
himself with a splendid, undefiled life. But he had few arguments
against the opponents. While perplexed, therefore, and
distressed concerning the journey abroad,[165] someone appeared to him
  (710)
at night, while he was sleeping in his private place, having a radiant
face and gleaming light flashing forth (from him), a robe
of light venerably cast over the shoulder. And he says to
Anthemios, "Why have you thus been grieving, bishop? And why this
sluggishness concerning you? And why is your face downcast? (715)
You will suffer nothing terrible from the adversaries." And after saying
these things, he withdrew from Anthemios. And awaking from sleep,
the bishop was terrified. He fell upon his face with many
tears and entreated God, saying, "Lord Jesus
Christ, Son of the living God, if you spare this your (720)
church—and I know that you will spare—and if this vision
has come from you, deem me worthy to show the vision
to me a second and third time, in order that I might be fully assured

163. See Acts 13:4–5.

164. The verb παραχαράσσω means to re-stamp (i.e., re-value a currency); or to
counterfeit. In this context the verb "falsified" seems to be appropriate, because Peter
changed the synod's decree.

165. He had been summoned to appear before Zeno in Constantinople.

that you are with me." Then most earnestly he submitted himself to
prayer, meeting with no one. And in the remaining night (725)
again the same man appeared to him in the same form
and in the same appearance, saying to him, "I said
to you already that nothing of the threats against you will happen.
Therefore, depart eagerly unto the kingdom, viewing nothing
suspiciously." And after saying these things, he departed. And the bishop,
    (730)
after arising, again thanked the Lord, saying nothing
to anyone. And he received also the third vision. When
night came the same man appeared to him, dignified,
saying to him, "How long will you not believe
my words, which will be fulfilled in these (735)
days? Proceed eagerly unto the royal city and with
glory return to your throne. You will suffer nothing
terrible from the enemies, with God protecting you
through me, his servant." The bishop answered, his
mouth being opened: "Who are you, my lord, (740)
who speaks these things to me?" And he said, "It is I,[166]
Barnabas, the disciple of our Lord Jesus Christ,
the one who was set apart by the Holy Spirit as an apostle
to the Gentiles with the apostle Paul, the *chosen
vessel*.[167] And *this is the sign to you*:[168] Go," he said, (745)
"outside of the city to the west about five stadia to
the place which is called the place of healing—for through me
God performs miracles in that place—and
dig at the carob tree and you will find a cave and
a coffin in it. There my entire body is buried (750)
and a Gospel written by my hand, which I received from Matthew,
the holy apostle and evangelist. And since your
adversaries plead their case persuasively, saying
that the throne of Antioch is apostolic, you make a counter
claim before them that 'My throne is also (755)
apostolic and has an apostle in my fatherland'
(or country)."

166. Here is a good example of the idiom that shows up periodically in John's Gospel and which some people view as Jesus claiming divine stature by saying, Ἐγώ εἰμι.

167. Acts 9:15.

168. Cf. Luke 2:12.

After saying these things, he went away. And the bishop arose
and, after praying to the Lord, he gathered all the sanctuary
clergy and the Christ-loving people, and after much preparation, (760)
he went out with shovels to the place that was
shown to him. And after making a prayer, he urged them to dig
up the place. And after a short time digging, they found a cave
sealed off with stones. And after removing these, they found
the coffin. And after uncovering the coffin, they found the honorable
  (765)
remains of the holy and honorable apostle Barnabas,
sending forth a sweet smell of spiritual grace. And they also found
the Gospel resting upon his chest. And after sealing
the casket in lead and making a vow and
praying, they withdrew. The bishop arranged to have (770)
pious men at the place who would glorify God with hymns
in the evenings and in the mornings.

And taking the distinguished of the bishops, Anthemios
hastened to the palace and was ushered into the bishop's
residence. And his coming was announced to the king, who (775)
entrusted to the patriarch [of Constantinople] to hear the case with the
    resident
assembly in order to decide between the proposals presented in
their midst. And when the council was convened and the
proposed action set in motion, the opponents began assailing, for
they considered themselves to be righteous. They were saying (780)
that the throne of Antioch is the patriarchal and apostolic one, and it is
    necessary
for the other districts to be under it. And they seemed to those present
to speak reasonably. But the blessed Anthemios, after a brief pause,
replied, saying, "But, my throne also, O most excellent
friends, is from the beginning apostolic and from above, having (785)
been honored with freedom. And I have a complete apostle in my
homeland, the thrice blessed Barnabas of sacred reputation."
After this was spoken, there was no longer a place for dispute,
with the bishops confirming the word in silence. And the
opponents stood speechless with shame, being amazed at (790)
the good sense of the answer.

The king, after learning these things, hastily summoned
the bishop of Cyprus. He inquired concerning the revelation
of the holy apostle Barnabas. And Anthemios[169] concealed nothing
of the truth; he explained in order all these things to the king. (795)
And after the king heard, he was exceedingly glad, marveling at
the wealth of God's grace; because in the times of his
reign, God did such a great wonder. Then he dismissed from
himself the bishop of Antioch, ordering the rest
absolutely not to annoy the bishop of Cyprus (800)
on account of this matter. Then he summoned the
blessed bishop Anthemios, saying, "Since our
Lord Jesus Christ in the times of your
holy episcopate was pleased to reveal his holy
apostle Barnabas, you must order the Gospel (805)
that was found to be quickly delivered here to me, showing favor
to me, your child, an extremely great favor.
For from now on you will have me providing generous
patronage to you."

And the bishop, after nodding assent, sent one of (810)
the bishops with him, along with a most faithful man of the
king. And after they received the Gospel, which had a folding cover
made of citron wood, they brought it up to Constantinople. And the
king, after receiving and kissing and adorning
it in gold, stowed it away in the palace where it is (815)
guarded to this day. For during the great fifth (day) of
Passover each year, they read the Gospel
in the chapel of the palace. And the great king,
after honoring the bishop, sent him back to
Cyprus with much money and an order, commanding (820)
him to build a temple to the holy apostle Barnabas
in the place where he found his honorable remains.
And many of the great men also gave money
to him for building the temple. And after receiving the (gift)
from Cypriots and gathering a crowd of artisans and workers, (825)
he did not delay the construction, but he raised an immense
sanctuary to the apostle, radiant with subtle contrivances,

169. Greek "he."

a glistening light with complex ornamentation, with porticos
outside closely encircling (the sanctuary). And along the southwest
side of the sanctuary, he made a great courtyard, having (830)
four stoas. And then small rooms (or chambers) and from there
he built the courtyard. He ordered the monks to live in them (and)
to celebrate the divine liturgies in the sanctuary.
And he built a long aqueduct that caused (water)
to gush forth abundantly in the midst of the courtyard, a beautifully (835)
built reservoir, in order that the ones who dwelled in that
place and the foreign visitors might have the bountiful pleasure
of the flowing water. And he built many other guest chambers in
the place for the refreshment of the foreign guests. And
the complex was beautiful to behold, resembling (840)
a very small and exceedingly pleasant city. And he placed
the holy tomb of the apostle at the right of the altar,
adorning the place with abundant silver and marble.
And those who gathered together and celebrated the spiritual
service decided that there should be a yearly anniversary, (845)
a special day to honor the memory of the thrice blessed
apostle and noble martyr Barnabas. The (anniversary) according to
Roman reckoning was on the third day before the *ides* of June. According
   to the
reckoning of the Cyprian Constantians, it was in the month of *Mesore*
   from the tenth to the
eleventh. According to Asiatic reckoning, truly according to the Paphians,
   (850)
(it was) in the month of *Plethupato* from the ninth to the nineteenth,
   unto the
glory of the Father and the Son and the Holy Spirit, because to him belong
glory for ever and ever. Amen.

Therefore, the revelation of the remains of the holy
apostle Barnabas designated this place. And the wonders (855)
pouring forth from his holy tomb, in my opinion, if anyone
wishes to write about each one, he would not be able
to find sufficient papyrus. And we, while remembering
previous events, should celebrate in song this pentathlete
of godliness, this combatant and victor. Let us (860)
congratulate, let us honor. For he, *as a fruitful olive tree*

planted in the house of God,[170] bears sweet smelling
fruits, each to God. He is the glory of kings,
the cheerfulness of priests, the joy of the people. He is the consolation
of the afflicted, the supporter of the oppressed, the hope of the (865)
despairing, the helper of the hopeless, the consoler of foreigners, the healer
of the sick, the protector of the healthy, the strength of spiritual gifts,
the citadel of the church, the supporter of the Orthodox, the fortress
of the faithful, and the boast of all the inhabited world.

But your praise, O truly happy and thrice blessed (870)
Barnabas, apostle of Christ our God, surpasses
every mind and word of men. But nevertheless,
after receiving the gratitude of our poverty, intercede
on our behalf to the one you love, Christ the
only begotten Son and word of God. Thus he might rescue *us* (875)
from the present evil age[171] and *grant* us to *find*
forgiveness of sins and *mercy* and consolation *in that* fearful
day when *he comes to judge the living and the dead.*[172]
And your most holy managing successor of your
throne, the like-minded of your unswerving faith, the (880)
legitimate interpreter of your orthodoxy, the imitator of
your excellence, our shepherd and father and high priest,
the one present now and making bright your holy memory,
earnestly beseeches God to guard your most holy
throne, in many cycles of years, making healthy and (885)
shepherding his people in peace, in all piety
and righteousness teaching correctly the word of truth.
Give heed to your entire fatherland, as always, and
now in your holy prayers, *guarding* her *from every*
evil and from scandals that produce lawlessness, (890)
in order that we might live peacefully, *temperately and godly*
(lives) *in the present age, receiving the mercy of our Lord*
Jesus Christ unto eternal life, which, may we all
attain, by the *grace and mercy and philanthropy*

---

170. Ps 52:8 in the Hebrew Bible. Ps 51:10 in the Septuagint.
171. Gal 1:4.
172. 2 Tim. 4:1; 1 Peter 4:5.

of our Lord Jesus Christ, *with whom* be glory to (895)
the Father *with the Holy Spirit, now and always unto
the ages of the ages (i.e., forever). Amen.*[173]

173. Cf. 1 Tim 2:1–4; Gal 1:3–4; Heb 4:16.

Bibliography

Adler, William, and Paul Tuffin. *The Chronography of George Synkellos: A Byzantine Chronicle of Universal History from the Creation.* Oxford: Oxford University Press, 2002.

Alexander the Monk. "Encomium of Barnabas (*Sancti Barnabae laudatio*)." In *Hagiographica Cypria: Corpus Christianorum,* edited by P. Van Deun. 83–122. Series Graeca 26. Leuven: Leuven University Press, 1993.

Althoff, Gerd. *Family, Friends and Followers: Political and Social Bonds in Early Medieval Europe.* Translated by C. Carroll. Cambridge: Cambridge University Press, 2004.

———. *Heinrich IV.* Darmstadt: Wissenschaftliche Buchgesellschaft, 2006.

Ante-Nicene Fathers: The Writings of the Fathers Down to A.D. 325. 10 vols. Edited by Alexander Roberts and James Donaldson. Edinburgh: T. & T. Clark, 1867–1873.

Arbel, Benjamin. "Cyprus on the Eve of the Ottoman Conquest." In *Ottoman Cyprus: A Collection of Studies on History and Culture,* edited by Michalis Michael et al., 37–48. Near and Middle East Monographs 4. Wiesbaden: Harrassowitz, 2009.

Barrett, C. K. *Acts of the Apostles.* 2 vols. International Critical Commentary. Edinburgh: T. & T. Clark, 1998.

Bars'kyj, Vasyl Hryhorovyč-. *A Pilgrim's Account of Cyprus: Bars'kyj's Travels in Cyprus.* Essay, Translation and Commentaries by Alexander D. Grishin. Sources for the History of Cyprus 3. Altamont, NY: Greece and Cyprus Research Center, 1996.

Bauckham, Richard. "Barnabas in Galatians." *Journal for the Study of the New Testament* 2 (1979) 61–70.

———. "James and the Jerusalem Church." In *The Book of Acts in its Palestinian Setting,* edited by R. Bauckham, 415–80. The Book of Acts in its First Century Setting 4. Grand Rapids: Eerdmans, 1995.

Beck, Hans-Georg. *Kirche und theologische Literatur im byzantinischen Reich.* Handbuch der Altertumswissenschaft, Abteilung 12: Byzantinisches Handbuch Teil 2: Band 1. Munich: Beck, 1959.

Beckwith, John. *Early Christian and Byzantine Art.* The Pelican History of Art. New York: Penguin, 1979.

Bekker-Nielsen, Tønnes. *The Roads of Ancient Cyprus.* Copenhagen, Denmark: Museum Tusculanum, 2004.

Belting, Hans. *Likeness and Presence: a History of the Image before the Era of Art.* Chicago: University of Chicago Press, 1994.

Bolman, Elizabeth, ed. *Monastic Visions: Wall paintings in the Monastery of St. Antony at the Red Sea.* New Haven, CT: Yale University Press, 2002.

Bonnet, Maximilianus, ed. *Acta Philippi et Acta Thomae: accedunt Acta Barnabae.* Leipzig: Mendelssohn, 1903. The Greek text of the Acts of Barnabas is on 292–302.

Bowersock, G. W. "The International Role of Late Antique Cyprus." 14th Annual Lecture on the History and Archaeology of Cyprus. Nicosia, Cyprus: The Bank of Cyprus Cultural Foundation, 2000.

Braunsberger, Otto. *Der Apostel Barnabas: Sein Leben und der ihm beigelegte Brief.* Mainz, 1876.

Brock, Sebastian. "ΒΑΡΝΑΒΑΣ ΥΙΟΣ ΠΑΡΑΚΛΗΣΙΣ." *The Journal of Theological Studies* 25 (1974) 93–98.

Bryant, Rebecca. *Imaging the Modern: The Cultures of Nationalism in Cyprus.* New York: I. B. Taurus, 2004.

Bustron, Florio. *Historia overo Commentarii de Cipro.* Published in René de Ma Latrie, *Coll. de documents inédits* (Paris, 1886). Printed text in *Chronique de l'ile de Chypre par Florio Bustron.* Edited by R. de Mas Latrie. Collection des documents inédits sur l'histoire de France, Mélanges historques 5. Paris: Imprimerienationale 1886; reprinted Florio Bustron, *Historia overo commentarii de Cipro.* Edited by R. de Mas Latrie. Collection des documents inédits sur l'histoire de France. Mélanges historques 5. Nicosia, Cyprus: Kypriologike Bibliotheke, 1998.

Capper, Brian. "The Palestinian Cultural Context of Earliest Christian Community of Goods." In *The Book of Acts in its Palestinian Setting,* edited by Richard J. Bauckham, 323–56. The Book of Acts in its First Century Setting 4. Grand Rapids: Eerdmans, 1995.

Chance, J. Bradley. *Acts.* Smyth & Helwys Bible Commentary 23. Macon, GA: Smyth & Helwys, 2007.

Chatzidakis, Manolis. *Athens Byzantine Museum.* Catalogue, 2009.

Cobham, Claude Delaval. *Excerpta Cypria: Materials for a History of Cyprus.* Cambridge: Cambridge University Press, 1908. https://archive.org/details/excerptacypriama00cobhuoft.

Cohen, Shaye J. D. "Crossing the Boundary and Becoming a Jew." *Harvard Theological Review* 82 (1989) 13–33.

Conzelmann, Hans. *History of Primitive Christianity.* Translated by J. E. Steely. Nashville: Abingdon, 1973.

Cosby, Michael R. *Apostle on the Edge: An Inductive Approach to Paul.* Louisville, KY: Westminster John Knox, 1999.

———. "Galatians: Red Hot Rhetoric." In *Rhetorical Argumentation in Biblical Texts,* edited by Anders Eriksson et al., 296–309. Emory Studies for Early Christianity. Harrisburg, PA: Trinity Press International, 2002.

Daniels, Jon B. "Barnabas." In the *Anchor Bible Dictionary,* edited by David N. Freedman, 1:610. New York: Doubleday, 1992.

Davis, Thomas. "Earthquakes and the Crises of Faith: Social Transformation in late Antique Cyprus." *Buried History* 46 (2010) 9.

della Dora, Veronica. "Windows on Heaven (and earth): the Poetics and Politics of Post-Byzantine 'Cartographic Icons.'" *Journal of Medieval Religious Cultures* 38 (2012) 84–112.

Der Parthog, Gwynneth. *Byzantine and Medieval Cyprus: A Guide to the Monuments.* Interworld, 1994.

DeSmedt, Carolus, et. al., eds. *Analecta Bollandiana, Tomus XXVI.* Bruxellis: Société des Bollandistes, 1907.

Dionysiou, George. "Some Privileges of the Church of Cyprus under Ottoman Rule." *Επετηρίδα Κέντρου Επιστημονικών Ερεύών* 19 (1992) 327–34.

Downey, Glanville. "The Claim of Antioch to Ecclesiastical Jurisdiction over Cyprus." *Proceedings of the American Philosophical Society* 102 (1958) 224–28.

———. *A History of Antioch in Syria: from Seleucus to the Arab Conquest*. Princeton: Princeton University Press, 1961.

Duckworth, Henry Thomas Forbes. *The Church of Cyprus*. Reprint. Boston: Adamant Media Corporation, 2003.

Dunn, James D. G. "The Incident at Antioch (Gal. 2:11–18)." *Journal for the Study of New Testament* 18 (1983) 3–57. Reprinted in *Jesus, Paul and the Law: Studies in Mark and Galatians*. Louisville: Westminster, 1990, 129–182.

du Plat Taylor, Joan. "A water cistern with Byzantine paintings, Salamis, Cyprus." *Journal of Antiquaries* 13 (1933) 97–108.

Ebied, Rifaat, and David Thomas. *Muslim-Christian Polemic During the Crusades: The Letter From the People of Cyprus and Ibn Abi Talib Al-Dimashqi's Response (The History of Christian-Muslim Relations)*. Leiden: Brill Academic, 2005.

Efthimiou, Miltiades. *Greeks and Latins on Cyprus in the Thirteenth Century*. Brookline, MA: Holy Cross, 1987.

Eliades, Ioannis A. *Byzantine Museum Guidebook*. Archbishop Makarios III Foundation. Nicosia, Cyprus: Konos, 2018.

———. *Η ΜΟΝΗ ΤΗΣ ΠΑΝΑΓΙΑΣ ΧΡΥΣΟΚΟΘΡΔΑΛΙΩΤΙΣΣΑΣ ΣΤΟ ΚΟΥΡΔΑΛΙ*. Οδηγοί Βυζαντινών Μωημείων της Κύπρου. ΛΕΥΚΩΣΙΑ, ΠΟΛΙΤΙΣΤΙΚΟ ΤΡΑΠΕΖΗΣ ΚΥΠΡΟΥ, 2012.

Εγγλεζάκης, Παύλος. Ἀρχιμανδρίτης. *ΕΙΚΟΣΙ ΜΕΛΕΤΑΙ ΔΙΑ ΤΗΝ ΕΚΚΛΗΣΙΑΝ ΚΥΠΡΟΥ* (4ος ἕως 20`ος αἰὼν). ΑΘΗΝΑΙ: ΜΟΡΦΩΤΙΚΟΝ ΙΔΡΥΜΑ ΕΘΝΙΚΗΣ ΤΡΑΠΕΖΗΣ, 1996.

Englezakis, Paul (Benedict). "Archbishop Kyprianos's Inkstand." In *Studies on the History of the Church of Cyprus: 4th-20th Centuries*, edited by Silouan Ioannou and Misael Ioannou, 257–78. Brookfield, VT: Ashgate, 1995.

———. "The Church of Cyprus from 1878–1955." In *Studies in the History of the Church of Cyprus, 4th-20th Centuries*, edited by Silouan Ioannou and Misael Ioannou, 421–51. Brookfield, VT: Ashgate, 1995.

———. "The Church of Cyprus in the 18th and 19th Centuries." In *Studies in the History of the Church of Cyprus, 4th-20th Centuries*, edited by Silouan Ioannou and Misael Ioannou, 237–55. Brookfield, VT: Ashgate, 1995.

———. "Epiphanius of Salamis, the Father of the Cypriot Autocephaly." In *Studies on the History of the Church of Cyprus: 4th-20th Centuries*, edited by Silouan Ioannou and Misael Ioannou, 29–39. Brookfield, VT: Ashgate, 1995.

"Epistle of Barnabas, The." Translated by Kirsopp Lake. *Apostolic Fathers*, 1:337–409. Loeb Classical Library. Cambridge: Cambridge University Press, 1912.

Esler, Philip F. "Making and Breaking an Agreement Mediterranean Style: A New Reading of Galatians 2:1–14." *Biblical Interpretation* 3 (1995) 285–314.

Étienne de Lusignan. *Chorograffia et breve historia universale dell'isola de Cipro principiando al tempo di Noè per in fino al 1572*. Bologna: A. Benaccio, 1573. English translation in *Excerpta Cypria: Materials for a History of Cyprus*, translated and edited by Claude Delaval Cobham. Cambridge: Cambridge University Press, 1908.

————. *Description de toute l'isle de Cypre et des rois, princes, et seigneurs, tant payens que Chrestiens, qui ont commandé en icelle.* Reprint. Nicosia, Cyprus: The Bank of Cyprus Cultural Foundation, 2004.

Evans, Harold. "Barnabas the Bridge Builder." *Expository Times* 89 (1977/1978) 248–50.

Excerpta Cypria: Materials for a History of Cyprus. Translated and edited by Claude Delaval Cobham. Reprint. British Library Historical Print Editions, 2011. https://archive.org/details/excerptacypriama00cobhuoft.

Folda, Jaroslav. "Crusader Art in the Kingdom of Cyprus, 1275–1291. Reflections on the State of the Question." In *Cyprus and the Crusades,* edited by Nicholas Coureas, 209–37. Nicosia, Cyprus: Cyprus Research Centre, 1995.

France, Dick. "Barnabas—Son of Encouragement." *Themelios* 4 (1978) 3–6.

Γαβριήλ, Ἀρχιμανδρίτης, ed. *Η ΙΕΡΑ ΒΑΣΙΛΙΚΗ ΚΑΙ ΣΤΟΥΡΟΠΗΓΙΑΚΗ ΜΟΝΗ ΑΠΟΣΤΟΛΟΥ ΒΑΡΝΑΒΑ: Ο ΒΙΟΣ ΤΟΥ ΑΠΟΣΤΟΛΟΥ ΒΑΡΝΑΒΑ—ΟΙ ΠΗΤΕΣ Η ΙΣΤΟΡΙΑ—ΤΗΣ ΜΟΝΗΣ—Η ΑΡΧΙΤΕΚΤΟΝΙΚΗ. ΛΕΥΚΟΣΙΑ, ΚΥΠΡΟΣ: ΜΟΝΗ ΑΠΟΣΤΟΛΟΥ ΒΑΡΝΑΒΑ,* 2009.

Gamble, Harry Y. "Codex." In *Anchor Bible Dictionary,* edited by D. N. Freedman, 5:1067–68. New York: Doubleday, 1992.

Garber, Andre. *Christian Iconography: A Study of its Origins.* Princeton, NJ: Princeton University Press, 1968.

Gelzer, Heinrich, ed. *Georgii Cyprii Descriptio Orbis Romani.* Leipzig: Teubner, 1890.

Georgii Cyprii descripto orbis Romani: accredit Leonis imperatoris Diatyposis genuina adhuc inedita. B. G. Teubneri, 1890.

Gerstel, Sharon E. J. *Thresholds of the Sacred. Architecture, Art Historical, Liturgical, and Theological Perspectives on Religious Screens, East and West.* Washington, DC: Dumbarton Oaks Research Library and Collection, 2006.

Gök, Nejdet. "Introduction of the *Berat* in Ottoman Diplomatics," *Bulgarian Historical Review* 3–4 (2001) 141.

Goodwin, Jack C. *A Historical Toponymy of Cyprus.* 4th ed. Cyprus American Archaeological Research Institute 19. Nicosia, Cyprus: Cyprus, 1984.

The Gospel of Barnabas. Edited and Translated from the Italian manuscript in the Imperial Library in Vienna by Lonsdale and Laura Ragg. Oxford: Clarendon, 1907.

Hackett, John A. *A History of the Orthodox Church of Cyprus from the Coming of the Apostles Paul & Barnabas to the Commencement of the British Occupation.* Research and Source Works Series. Philosophy & Religious History Monographs 103. London: Methuen, 1901.

Hadjichristodoulou, Christodoulos. "A Map of Cyprus in a Post-Byzantine Cypriot Icon." In *Eastern Mediterranean Cartographies. Tetradia Ergasias,* edited by Dimitris Loupis and Giorgos Tolias, 337–46. Institute for Neohellenic Research 25/26. Athens: National Hellenic Research Foundation, 2004.

Hadjianastasis, Marios. "Cyprus in the Ottoman Period: Consolidation of the Cypro-Ottoman Elite, 1650–1750." In *Ottoman Cyprus: A Collection of Studies on History and Culture,* edited by Michalis Michael et al., 63–88. Near and Middle East Monographs 4. Wiesbaden: Harrassowitz, 2009.

Hadjifoti, Litsa. *Saint Paul His Journeys through Greece, Cyprus, Asia Minor and Rome.* Athens: Michalis Toubis, 2006.

Halkin, F., ed. *Bibliotheca hagiographica graeca. 3rd edition.* Subsida hagiographica 8a. Brussels: Société des Bollandistes, 1984.

Hein, Ewald, et al. *Cyprus: Byzantine Churches and Monasteries Mosaics and Frescoes.* Translated by John M. Deasy. Ratingen, Germany: Melina, 1998.

Hengel, Martin, and Anna Maria Schwemer. *Paul Between Damascus and Antioch: The Unknown Years.* London: SCM, 1997.

Hill, Craig G. *Hellenists and Hebrews: Reappraising Division within the Earliest Church.* Minneapolis: Fortress, 1992.

Hill, George Francis. *A History of Cyprus.* 4 vols. Reprint. Cambridge: Cambridge University Press, 2010.

Ιστορία της Κύπρου, εκδιδομένη υπό την διεύθυνσιν Θεοδώρου Παπαδοπούλου, Λευκωσία: Ίδρυμα Αρχιεπισκόπου Μακαρίου Γ΄, Γραφείον Κυπριακής Ιστορίας. [*History of Cyprus.* Issued under the direction of Theodoros Papadopoulos. Nicosia, Cyprus: Foundation of Archbishop Makarios III, Office of Cypriot History.]

vol. Α΄: *Αρχαία Κύπρος. Μέρος Α΄:Φυσιογεωγραφική εισαγωγή.* Προϊστορικοί χρόνοι. Σχέσεις προς ομόρους χώρους, 1977. [*Vol. 1: Ancient Cyprus Part I: Historical Introduction. Prehistoric Times. Contacts with Neighboring Areas,* 1977.]

vol. Β΄: *Αρχαία Κύπρος. Μέρος Β΄:* Αρχαία Βασίλεια – Ελληνιστική Κύπρος, Επαρχία της Ρωμαϊκής Αυτοκρατορίας, Αρχαία Θρησκεία, Αρχαία γραφή, Γραμματεία και Φιλοσοφία, Αρχαία τοπωνύμια, Βιβλιογραφία, Χρονολογικοί πίνακες, 2000. Επιλογή και επιμέλεια Ανδρέας Δημητρίου, 2000. [*Vol. 2: Ancient Cyprus Part II: Archaic Kingdom Hellenistic Cyprus, Province of the Roman Empire, Ancient Religion, Ancient Writing, Scribal Office and Philosophy, Ancient Toponyms, Bibliography, Chronological Tables,* 2000.]

vol. Γ΄: *Βυζαντινή Κύπρος.* Ιστορικογεωγραφική εισαγωγή, Θεμελίωσις της Κυπριακής Εκκλησίας, Πολιτικός θεσμός, Το Θέμα Κύπρου, Αραβικαί επιδρομαί, Η Κύπρος υπό τους Κομνηνούς, Βυζαντινή Αρχιτεκτονική και Τέχνη, 2005, Πίνακες. Επιλογή: Χαράλαμπος Γ. Χοτζάκογλου, 2005. [*Vol. 3: Byzantine Cyprus: Historical Introduction, Foundation of the Cypriot Church, Political Institution, The Topic of Cyprus, Arab Raids, Cyprus under Komnenoi, Byzantine Architecture and Art,* 2005.]

vol. Δ΄: *Μεσαιωνικόν Βασίλειον – Ενετοκρατία. Μέρος Α΄:* Εξωτερική Ιστορία – Πολιτικοί και Κοινωνικοί θεσμοί – Δίκαιον – Οικονομία – Εκκλησία, 1995. Γενεαλογικο Πίνακες [*Vol. 4: Medieval Kingdom – Venetian Rule. Part I: Foreign History – Political and Social Institutions – Justice – Economy – Church,* 1995.]

vol Ε΄: *Μεσαιωνικόν Βασίλειον – Ενετοκρατία. Μέρος Β΄:* Πνευματικός βίος – Παιδεία –Γραμματολογία – Βυζαντινή Τέχνη – Γοτθική Τέχνη – Νομισματοκοπία – Βιβλιογραφία, 1996. [*Vol. 5: Medieval Kingdom – Venetian Rule. Part II: Spiritual life – Education –Literature – Byzantine Art – Gothic Art – Coins – Bibliography,* 1996.]

Hitchens, Christopher. *Hostage to History: Cyprus from the Ottomans to Kissinger.* 3rd ed. London: Verso, 1997.

Huffman, Joseph. "The Donation of Zeno: St. Barnabas and the Modern History of the Cypriot Archbishop's Regalia Privileges." *Church History: Studies in Christianity and Culture* 84 (2015) 713–45.

———. "The Donation of Zeno: St Barnabas and the Origins of the Cypriot Archbishops' Regalia Privileges." *The Journal of Ecclesiastical History* 66 (2015) 235–60.

Jeffreys, Elizabeth, et al., eds. *The Oxford Handbook of Byzantine Studies*. New York: Oxford University Press, 2008.

Kallinikos Stavrouniotis, Monachos (Μοναχου Καλλινικου Σταυροβουνιωτη). *Η Τεχνικη της Αγιοφραφιας*. Λευκοσια: Λατκη Τραπεζα, 1996.

Karageorghis, Vassos. *Cyprus: From the Stone Age to the Romans (Ancient Peoples and Places)*. New York: Thames & Hudson, 1982.

Koch, Dietrich-Alex. "Barnabas, Paulus und die Adressaten des Galaterbriefs." In *Das Urchristentum in seiner literarischen Geschichte*, edited by U. Mell and U. B. Müller, 85–105. *Beihefte zur Zeitschrift für die neutestamentliche Wissenschaft* 100. Berlin: Walter de Gruyter, 1999.

Kollmann, Bernd. *Joseph Barnabas: His Life and Legacy*. Collegeville, MN: Liturgical Press, 2003.

Kosiński, Rafał. "Peter the Fuller, Patriarch of Antioch (471–488)." *Byzantinoslavica – Revue international des Etudes Byzantines* 68 (2010) 49–73.

Koumarianou, Catherine. *Avvisi (1570–1572): The War of Cyprus*. Nicosia, Cyprus: Bank of Cyprus Cultural Foundation, 2004.

Kraling, Carl H. "The Jewish Community at Antioch." *Journal of Biblical Literature* 51 (1932) 130–60.

Κυπρια Μηναια (Ἤτοι Ἀκολουθίαι Ψαλλόμεναι ἐν Κύπρῳ). Τομος Η΄. Μην Ιονηιος. Λευκωσια, Κυπρος: Ἱερὰ Ἀρχιεπισκοπὴ Κυπρου, 2002.

Κυπριανος, Ἀρχιμανδρίτος. *ΙΣΤΟΡΙΑ ΧΡΟΝΟΛΟΓΙΚΗ ΤΗΣ ΝΗΣΟΥ ΚΥΠΡΟΥ*. ΕΚΔΟΣΕΙΣ Κ. Venice, 1778 (3η ἔκδοση, ΛΕΥΚΩΣΙΑ: ΕΚΔΟΣΕΙΣ Κ. ΕΠΙΦΑΝΙΟΥ, 2001). For English translations of sections of Kyprianos's *Chronological History of Cyprus*, see *Excerpta Cypria: Materials for a History of Cyprus*. Edited by Claude Deval Cobham. Reprint. Cambridge: Cambridge University Press, 1908; reprinted in British Library Historical Print Editions, 2011.

Lang, Sir Robert Hamilton. *Cyprus: Its History, its Present Resources, and Future Prospects*. London: MacMillan, 1878.

Lengel, Edward G. *Inventing George Washington: America's Founder, in Myth and Memory*. New York: HarperCollins, 2011.

Lenski, Noel, ed. *The Cambridge Companion to the Age of Constantine*. New York: Cambridge University Press, 2006.

Λευκωμα, Α., ed. *ΤΑ ΒΥΖΑΝΤΙΝΑ ΜΝΗΜΕΙΑ ΤΗΣ ΚΥΠΡΟΥ*. ΑΘΗΝΑΙΣ: Γραφειον Δημοσιευματον Ακαδημιας Αθηνημων, 1935.

Levinskaya, Irina. "God-fearers: The Bosporan Kingdom." In *The Book of Acts in its Diaspora Setting*, 105–16. The Book of Acts in its First Century Setting 5. Grand Rapids: Eerdmans, 1996.

———. "God-fearers: Epigraphic Evidence." In *The Book of Acts in its Diaspora Setting*, 51–82. The Book of Acts in its First Century Setting 5. Grand Rapids: Eerdmans, 1996.

———. "God-fearers and the Cult of the Most High God." In *The Book of Acts in its Diaspora Setting*, 83–103. The Book of Acts in its First Century Setting 5. Grand Rapids: Eerdmans, 1996.

———. "God-fearers: the Literary Evidence." In *The Book of Acts in its Diaspora Setting*, 117–26. The Book of Acts in its First Century Setting 5. Grand Rapids: Eerdmans, 1996.

Liddell, H. G., and R. Scott. *A Greek–English Lexicon*. 9th ed. Oxford: Oxford University Press, 1996.

Limberis, Vasiliki M. *Architects of Piety: The Cappodocian Fathers and the Cult of the Martyrs.* Oxford: Oxford University Press, 2011.

Longenecker, Richard N. "Antioch of Syria." In *Major Cities of the Biblical World,* edited by R. K. Harrison, 8–21. Nashville: Nelson, 1985.

Luke, Sir Harry. *Cyprus Under the Turks, 1571–1878: Record Based on the Archives of the English Consulate in Cyprus under the Levant Company and After.* Reprint. London: C. Hurst, 1969.

MacDonald, William L. *Early Christian and Byzantine Architecture.* New York: George Braziller, 1965.

Maguire, Henry. *The Icons of their Bodies: Saints and their Images in Byzantium.* Princeton: Princeton University Press, 1996.

———. *Other Icons. Art and Power in Byzantine Secular Culture.* Princeton: Princeton University Press, 2007.

Makarios, Hieromonk of Simonos Petra. *The Synaxarion: The Lives of the Saints of the Orthodox Church, vol. 5.* Mount Athos, Greece: Holy Monastery of Simonos Petra, 2005.

Μακαριωτάτου Ἀρχιεπισκόπου Κύπρου. *ἡ ἁγία νῆσος,* ἔκδ. Β΄. Λευκωσία, 1997.

Mango, Cyril. "A Byzantine Hagiographer at Work: Leontios of Neapolis." In *Byzanz und der Westen: Studien zur Kunst des europäischen Mittelalters,* edited by Irmgard Hutter, 25–41. Philosophisch-Historische Klasse Sitzungsberichte 432. Vienna: Österreichischen Akademie der Wissenschaften, 1984.

Markides, Kyriacos C. *Inner River: A Pilgrimage to the Heart of Christian Spirituality.* New York: Image, 2012.

———. *Mountain of Silence: A Search for Orthodox Spirituality.* New York: Doubleday, 2001.

———. *The Rise and Fall of the Cyprus Republic.* New Haven, CT: Yale University Press, 1977.

Martyn. J. Louis. *Galatians: A New Translation with Introduction and Commentary.* Anchor Bible 33A. New York: Doubleday, 1997.

Mastrogiannopoulos, Elias. *Byzantine Churches of Greece and Cyprus.* Brookline, MA: Holy Cross Orthodox, 1984.

Meeks,Wayne, and Robert L. Wilken. *Jews and Christians in Antioch in the first four centuries of the Common Era.* Missoula, MT: Scholars, 1978.

Megaw, A. H. S. "Byzantine Architecture and Decoration in Cyprus: Metropolitan or Provincial?" In *Dumbarton Oaks Papers 28,* 57–88. Washington, DC: Dumbarton Oaks Center for Byzantine Studies, 1974.

———. "The Campanopetra Reconsidered: The Pilgrim Church of the Apostle Barnabas?" In *Byzantine Style, Religion and Civilization: In Honor of Sir Steven Runciman,* edited by Elizabeth M. Jefferies, 394–404. Cambridge: Cambridge University Press, 2006.

Metcalf, D. Michael. *Byzantine Cyprus 491–1191.* Cyprus Research Centre: Texts and Studies in the History of Cyprus 62. Nicosia, Cyprus: Cyprus Research Centre, 2009.

———. *Byzantine Lead Seals from Cyprus.* Cyprus Research Centre Texts and Studies of the History of Cyprus 47. Nicosia, Cyprus: Cyprus Research Centre, 2004.

Michael, Michalis N. "Βυζαντινά σύμβολα ὀθωμανικῆς πολιτικῆς ἐξουσίας: ἡ περίπτωση τῶν προνομίων τῶν Ἀρχιεπισκόπων Κύπρου." *Τα Ιστορικά* 51 (2009) 315–32.

———. "Kyprianos, 1810–21: An Orthodox Cleric 'administering politics' in an Ottoman Island." In *The Archbishops of Cyprus in the Modern Age: The Changing role of the Archbishop-Ethnarch, Their Identities and Politics*, edited by Andrekos Varnava and Michalis Michael, 41–68. Cambridge: Cambridge Scholars, 2013.

———. "Local Authorities and Conflict in an Ottoman Island at the Beginning of the Nineteenth Century." *Turkish Historical Review* 2 (2011) 57–77.

———. "The Loss of an Ottoman Traditional Order and the Reactions to a Changing Ottoman World: A New Interpretation of the 1821 Events in Cyprus." *International Review of Turkish Studies* 3 (2013) 8–37.

———. "Myth and Nationalism: The Retrospective Force of National Roles through Mythical Past." In *Nationalism in the Troubled Triangle: Cyprus, Greece and Turkey*, edited by A. Aktar et al., 149–59. London: Macmillan, 2010.

———. "An Orthodox Institution of Ottoman Political Authority: The Church of Cyprus." In *Ottoman Cyprus: A Collection of Studies on History and Culture*, edited by Michalis Michael et al., 209–30. Near and Middle East Monographs 4. Wiesbaden: Harrassowitz, 2009.

Mitchell, Stephen. "Population and land in Roman Galatia." *Aufstieg und Niedergang der römischen Welt* II 7 (1980) 1053–81.

Mitford, Terence Bruce. *The Inscriptions of Kourion*. Memoirs of the American Philosophical Society 83. Philadelphia: American Philosophical Society, 1971.

———. "New Inscriptions from Early Christian Cyprus." *Byzantion* 20 (1950) 105–75.

———. "Roman Cyprus." In *Aufstieg und Niedergang der römischen Welt: Geschichte und Kultur Roms im Spiegel der Neueren Forschung* II. 7.2, edited by Hildegard Temporini and Wolfgang Hasse, 1285–384. Berlin: Walter de Gruyter, 1980.

Mouriki, Doula. "The Cult of Cypriot Saints in Medieval Cyprus as Attested by Church Decorations and Icon Painting." In *The Sweet Land of Cyprus: Papers Given at the Twenty-Fifth Jubilee Spring Symposium of Byzantine Studies*, edited by A. A. M. Bryer and G. S. Georghallides, 237–77. Nicosia, Cyprus: Cyprus Research Center, 1993.

Muller, Gerhard P., and Klaus Liebe. *Cyprus*. Munich: C. J. Bucher, 1986.

Munro, J. H. "The Medieval Scarlet and the Economics of Sartorial Splendour." In *Cloth and Clothing in Medieval Europe. Essays in Memory of Professor E. M. Carus-Wilson*, edited by N. B. Harte and K. G. Ponting, 13–70. London: Ashgate, 1984.

Nellessen, Ernst. "Die Einsetzung von Presbytern durch Barnabas und Paulus (Apg 14,23)." In *Begegnung mit dem Wort*, edited by J. Zmijewski and E. Nellessen, 175–93. Bonner biblische Beitrage 53. Bonn: Hanstein, 1980.

Neophytos, Metropolitan of Morphou, ed. *Holy Bishopric of Morphou: 2000 Years of Art and Holiness*. Nicosia, Cyprus: Bank of Cyprus Cultural Foundation and the Holy Bishopric of Morphou, 2002.

———. *The Icon Treasury of the Holy Monastery of St John Lampadistes at Kalopanaghiotis*. Peristerona, Cyprus: Theomorphou, 2014.

New Testament Apocrypha, Vol. 2: Writings Relating to the Apostles, Apocalypses and Related Subjects. Edited by W. Schneemelcher and R. M. Wilson. Rev. ed. Louisville, KY: Westminster John Knox, 2003.

Nicolle, David, and Adam Hook. *Crusader Castles in Cyprus, Greece and the Aegean 1191–1571*. Oxford: Osprey, 2007.

Nobbs, Alanna. "Cyprus." In *The Book of Acts in its Graeco-Roman Setting*, edited by David W. J. Gill and Conrad Gempf, 279–89. The Book of Acts in its First Century Setting 2. Grand Rapids: Eerdmans, 1994.

Noy, David. "Where Were the Jews of the Diaspora Buried?" In *Jews in a Graeco-Roman World*, edited by Martin Goodman, 75–89. Oxford: Oxford University Press, 1998.

Öhler, Markus. *Barnabas: Die historische Person und ihre Rezeption in der Apostelgeschichte*. Wissenschaftliche Untersuchungen zum Neuen Testament 156. Tübingen: J. C. B. Mohr, 2003.

Panteli, Stavros. *A History of Cyprus: From Foreign Domination to Troubled Independence*. 2nd ed. London: East-West, 2000.

———. *Place of Refuge: A History of the Jews in Cyprus*. London: Elliott & Thompson, 2004.

Papadakis, Yiannis. *Echoes from the Dead Zone: Across the Cyprus Divide*. London: I. B. Tauris, 2005.

Papageorghiou, Anastasios. *Christian Art in the Turkish-Occupied part of Cyprus*. Nicosia, Cyprus: The Holy Archbishopric of Cyprus, 2010.

———. *E autokephalos Ekklesiates Kyprou: Katalogos tes ektheses*. Nicosia, Cyprus: Byzantine Museum of the Archbishop Makarios III Institute, 1995.

———. *Icons of Cyprus*. Nicosia, Cyprus: The Holy Archbishopric of Cyprus, 1992.

———. *The Monastery of Saint John Lampadistis in Kalopanayiotis*. 2nd ed. Guide to Byzantine Monuments of Cyprus. Nicosia, Cyprus: Bank of Cyprus Cultural Foundation, Holy Bishopric of Morphou, 2012.

Pelosi, O., ed. *Lusignan's Chorography and Brief General History of the Island of Cyprus*. Sources for the History of Cyprus 10. Nicosia, Cyprus: Cyprus Research Center, 2001.

Pentcheva, Bissera V. *The Sensual Icon. Space, Ritual and the Senses in Byzantium*. University Park, PA: The Pennsylvania State University Press, 2010.

Pliny. *Natural History, vol. 2*. Trans. by H. Rackham. Loeb Classical Library. Cambridge, MA: Harvard University Press, 1942.

Radl, Walter. "Das 'Apostelkonzil' und seine Nachgeschichte, dargestellt am Weg des Barnabas." *Theological Quarterly* 162 (1982) 45–61.

Rapp, Claudia. "Epiphanius of Salamis: The Church Father as Saint." In *The Sweet Land of Cyprus: Papers Given at the Twenty–Fifth Jubilee Spring Symposium of Byzantine Studies*, edited by A. A. M. Bryer and G. S. Georghallides, 169–87. Nicosia, Cyprus: Cyprus Research Center, 1993.

———. *Holy Bishops in Late Antiquity: The Nature of Christian Leadership in an Age of Transition*. Berkeley: University of California Press, 2005.

Rehm, Merlin D. "Levites and Priests." In *Anchor Bible Dictionary*, edited by David N. Freedman, 4:297–310. New York: Doubleday, 1992.

Rice, D. Talbot, ed. *The Icons of Cyprus*. Courtauld Institute Publications on Near Eastern Art. London: George Allen & Unwin, 1937.

Robinson, I. S. *Henry IV of Germany, 1056–1106*. Cambridge: Cambridge University Press, 1999.

Roux, Georges. *Salamine de Chypre XV. La Basilique de la Campanopetra*. Paris: De Boccard, 1998.

Rycaut, Paul. *The Present State of the Greek and Armenian Churches, Anno Christi 1678*. London, 1679.

Safran, Linda, ed. *Heaven and Earth: Art and the Church in Byzantium*. University Park, PA: The Pennsylvania State University Press, 1998.

Sanders, E. P. "Jewish Association with Gentiles and Galatians ii. 11–14." In *Studies in Paul and John: In honor of J. L. Martyn*, edited by Robert T. Fortna and Beverly R. Gaventa, 170–88. Nashville: Abingdon, 1990.

Schabel, Christopher D. *Greeks, Latins, and the Church in Early Frankish Cyprus*. Burlington, VT: Ashgate Publishing Company, 2010.

————. "A Knight's Tale: Giovan Francesco Loredano's Fantastic *Historie de' re Lusignani*." In *Cyprus and the Renaissance (1450-1650)* (= *Mediterranean Nexus*, 1), edited by B. Arbel et al., 357-90. Turnhout: Brepols, 2013.

————. "The Myth of Queen Alice and the Subjugation of the Greek Church of Cyprus." In *Identités croiseés en un milieu mevditerraneven: le cas de Chypre (Antiquité - Moyen Age)*, edited by S. Fourier and G. Grivaud, 257–77. Rouen: Publications des Universités de Rouen et du Havre, 2006; reprinted in *Greeks, Latins, and the Church in Early Frankish Cyprus*. Aldershop: Ashgate, 2010.

————, ed. *The Synodicum Nicosiense and other documents of the Latin Church of Cyprus, 1196-1373*. Texts and Studies in the History of Cyprus. Nicosia, Cyprus: Cyprus Research Centre, 2001.

Schürer, Emil. *The History of the Jewish People in the Age of Jesus Christ (175 B.C.-A.D. 135), vol. 1*. Edited and translated by G. Vermes and F. Millar. Edinburgh: T. & T. Clark, 1973.

Senff, Reinhard. "Paphos." In *Der Neue Pauly: Enzyklopädie der Antike IX*, edited by H. Cancik and H. Schneider, 284–87. Stuttgart: Metzler, 1996.

Shaftacolas, Efthymios, ed. *Cyprus: Island of Saints: A Devotional Journey*. Translated by Richard Gill and Efthymia Alphas. Nicosia, Cyprus: Cyprus Tourism Organisation, 2010.

Smith, Sir William Frederick Haynes. *Cyprus, Report for 1900–1901, Presented to Parliament* (April 1902) 59; *Notes and Queries. A Medium of Communication for Literary Men, General Readers, Etc.* Ninth Series 9. London: John C. Francis, 1902.

Soards, Marion L. *The Speeches in Acts: Their Content, Context, and Concerns*. Westminster John Knox, 1994.

Sophocleous, Sophocles. *Cyprus, the Holy Island: Icons through the Centuries 10-20th Century*. A Millennium Celebration of the Orthodox Archdiocese of Thyateira and Great Britain. Nicosia, Cyprus: A. G. Leventis Foundation, 2000.

————. *Icons of Cyprus, 7th–20th Century*. Nicosia, Cyprus: Museum Publications, 1994.

————. *Icons de Chypre: Diocese de Limassol 12e-16e Siecle*. Nicosie: Centre du Ptrimone Culturel, 2006.

Stalley, Roger. *Early Medieval Architecture*. Oxford History of Art. New York: Oxford University Press, 1999.

Starowieyski, Marek. "Św. Barnaba w historii i legendzie." *Analecta Cracoviensia* 23 (1991) 391–413.

Stavrides, Theoharis. "Cyprus 1750-1830." In *Ottoman Cyprus: A Collection of Studies on History and Culture*, edited by Michalis Michael et al., 89–106. Near and Middle East Monographs 4. Wiesbaden: Harrassowitz, 2009.

Stewart, Charles A. "Domes of Heaven: The Domed Basilicas of Cyprus, vols. 1–2." PhD diss, Indiana University, 2008.

Strabo. *The Geography of Strabo, vol. 6.* Translated by Horace L. Jones. Loeb Classical Library. Cambridge, MA: Harvard University Press, 1929.

Stylianou, Andreas, and Judith A. *The History of Cartography of Cyprus.* Nicosia, Cyprus: Cyprus Research Center, 1980.

———. *The Painted Churches of Cyprus: Treasures of Byzantine Art.* London: Trigraph, 1985.

Stylianou, Marios T. *ΑΠΟΣΤΟΛΟΣ ΒΑΡΝΑΒΑΣ Ο ΙΔΡΥΤΗΣ ΚΑΙ ΠΡΟΣΤΑΤΗΣ ΤΗΣ ΕΚΚΛΗΣΙΑΣ ΤΗΣ ΚΥΠΡΟΥ (Apostle Varnavas: the Founder and Protector of the Church of Cyprus).* Nicosia, Cyprus: Stylianou Publishing, 2005.

Swiny, Stuart, et al., eds. *Res Maritimae: Cyprus and the Eastern Mediterranean from Prehistory to Late Antiquity.* Proceedings of the Second International Symposium, "Cities on the Sea," Nicosia, Cyprus, October 18–22, 1994. Cyprus American Archaeological Research Institute Monograph Series 1. Atlanta: Scholars, 1997.

Tannehill, Robert C. *The Narrative Unity of Luke–Acts: A Literary Interpretation.* 2 vols. Philadelphia: Fortress, 1986.

Taylor, Joan du Plat. "A Water Cistern with Byzantine Paintings, Salamis, Cyprus." *Journal of Antiquaries* 13 (1933) 97–108.

Thomson, John. *Through Cyprus with the Camera in the Autumn of 1878: Vols 1 and 2.* London: Trigraph Ltd., 1985.

Tofallis, Kypros. *A History of Cyprus: From the Ancient Times to the Present.* London: The Greek Institute, 2002.

Treadgold, Warren. *A History of the Byzantine State and Society.* Stanford: Stanford University Press, 1997.

Τρίτος, Τόμος. *Μεγάλη Κυπριακή Εγκυκλοπαίδεια, #3.* Λευκωσία, Κύπρος: Φιλόκυπρος, 1985.

Tselikas, Agamemnon. *Antonio Millo Isolario: A Transcription of the Italian Original.* Athens: AdVenture, 2006.

Van Deun, Peter, and Jacques Noret, eds. *Hagiographica Cypria. Sancti Barnabae Laudatio auctore Alexandro Monacho et Sanctorum Bartholomaei et Barnabae Vita e Menologio imperiali deprompta.* Corpus Christianorum, Series Graecae 26. Leuven: Brepols, 1993.

Victor of Tunis. *Chronicon continuans ubi prosper desinit.* Patrologia Latina 68.

Vikan, Gary. *Sacred Images and Sacred Power in Byzantium.* Burlington, VT: Ashgate, 2003.

Von Falkenhausen, Vera. "Bishops and Monks in the Hagiography of Byzantine Cyprus." In *Medieval Cyprus: Studies in Art, Architecture, and History in Memory of Doula Mouriki,* edited by N. Patterson Ševčenko and C. Moss, 21–33. Princeton: Princeton University Press, 1999.

Walter, Christopher. *The Warrior Saints in Byzantine Art and Tradition.* Burlington, VT: Ashgate, 2003.

Wedderburn, Alexander J. M. "Paul and Barnabas: The Anatomy and Chronology of a Parting of the Ways." In *Fair Play: Diversity and Conflicts in Early Christianity: Essays in Honor of Heikki Raisanen,* edited by Ismo Dunderberg et al., 291–310. Supplements to Novum Testamentum 103. Leiden: Brill, 2002.

Weiser, Alfons. *Die Apostelgeschichte, I.* Gütersloh: Gerd Mohn, 1981.

Weitzmann, Kurt. *The Icon: Holy Images Sixth to Fourteenth Century.* London: Chatto and Windus, 1978.

Wharton, Annabel Jane. *Art of Empire: Painting and Architecture of the Byzantine Periphery: A Comparative Study of Four Provinces.* University Park, PA: The Pennsylvania State University Press, 1988.

Whitehouse, Helen. "The Nile Flows Underground to Cyprus: The Painted Water-cistern at Salamis Reconsidered." In *Egypt and Cyprus in Antiquity: Proceedings of the International Conference, Nicosia 2003,* edited by D. Michaelides et al., 252–60. Oxford: Oxbow, 2009.

Wideson, Reno. *Portrait of Cyprus.* The Hague: Deppo Holland, nd.

Wirbelauer, Eckhard. "Clemens." In *New Pauly. Brill's Encyclopedia of the Ancient World,* edited by Hubert Canik and Helmuth Schneider, 3:425–26. Leiden: Brill, 2003.

Witherington, Ben, III. *Grace in Galatia: A Commentary on Paul's Letter to the Galatians.* Grand Rapids: Eerdmans, 1998.

Yilmaz, Nilay. *Icons in Turkey.* Istanbul: TurizmYayinlari, 2007.

Young, Philip H. "The Cypriot Aphrodite Cult: Paphos, Rantidi, and Saint Barnabas." *Journal of Near Eastern Studies* 64 (2005) 23–44.

Zampelas, Michael. *Εκκλησίες και Μοναστήρια της Κύπρου (Churches and Monasteries of Cyprus).* Nicosia, Cyprus: Zampelas Art, 2002.

Zartarian, Giragos. *Photographs: 1935–1950.* Edited by Stavros G. Lazarides. Nicosia, Cyprus: Cultural Centre Marfin Laiki Bank, 2007.

General Index

Author Index

(authors cited other than just in the bibliography)

233

Scripture Index

Romans

1 Corinthians

2 Corinthians

Galatians

Ancient Documents Index